CHILDREN OF THE MANSE

Lewis Richard Luchs

For my sons and my grandchildren,
That they might understand

ISBN: 978-0-578-03523-9

Preface

I HAVE WRITTEN THIS book to honor my adoptive parents, Fred and Evelyn Luchs. This is a true story of how the Luchs in a remarkable act of generosity which some thought foolishness welcomed me and three younger siblings into their home on October 15, 1943. This book is also an account based on case file documents, interviews, and personal memories of the history of neglect the four of us suffered in our biological family and during the 26 months we spent in the Scioto County Children's Home in Wheelersburg, Ohio.

The Luchs held a large and exciting view of the world and its possibilities. They were intellectually alive and socially concerned. They forged a remarkably rich and strong marriage based on complementary needs, similar values, and shared interests. When they differed it was out of our sight and hearing. I do not remember ever hearing their voices raised in anger with each other. They were staunch liberals on social and economic issues but their personal ethics were conservative. Their values were very much in the main stream of traditional middle class Protestant America.

For the four of us these Luchs values meant love, security, nourishing food and good medical care, the opportunity to develop our minds and talents, and the encouragement to become responsible and compassionate adults in our nation and world. What a wonderful environment they provided for four wounded but bright kids delivered from a neglectful biological family and the sterility of a county children's home!

The Luchs were both excellent public speakers and published writers whose articles and sermons appeared in many publications, some of which I have used in telling this story. The membership of First Presbyterian trebled during Dad's fourteen-year ministry in Athens, Ohio. Mom was president of the Ohio Council of Church Women and a member of the National Board of the United Council of Church Women. Unlike our father, who hungered for honors, she tried to avoid them. Even so, she was appointed the first woman trustee of Ohio University in 1949 and later awarded a merit citation by the same university, primarily for her writing and for her work in religious education. She was chosen Mother of the Year in 1951 in New Mexico, where we then lived.

ACKNOWLEDGEMENT

My sister, Janey, worked with me to obtain our Ohio state case files on which much of the first part of this book is based. Janey also located Bob Cunningham, a long-forgotten birth cousin, who arrived at the Scioto County Children's Home with two brothers and a sister months after we left. Bob did more than confirm my memories of the Home. He provided details about daily routines and personalities of some of the adult staff that I had forgotten so many years later. Bob's older brother knew my biological father, Lonnie Boggs, and Grandpa Harry Boggs and shared his memories of both with me. I thank them.

My first reader was Professor James Earl of the English Department of the University of Oregon. Megan Shultz, Executive Director of the CASA program of Lane County, Oregon also read the first version of *Children of the Manse*. Their suggestions and encouragement were most helpful.

Book design by Keith Van Norman

"Looking into the bright eyes of many kids in the (social welfare) system today, with their heart-tugging smiles, their impressive intelligence, and their often amazing resilience, it is difficult to believe they will in turn become their parents, as studies and statistics dolefully predict. Something is very wrong."

Judith Toth, Orphans of the Living, Simon and Schuster, 1997

A manse is "A cleric's house and land, especially the residence of a Presbyterian minister."

American Heritage Dictionary

TABLE OF CONTENTS

PART I

THE SEARCH:
AN INTRODUCTION

THE SEARCH FOR FAMILY

IN 1978 DOCTORS SUSPECTED breast cancer in my sister, Janey, performed biopsies, and concluded they would recommend a radical mastectomy if there was a history of cancer in her family. We are adopted. Janey knew nothing about the medical history of our biological family but she knew how she might obtain it.

In 1974, during an interim pastorate at the Hoge Presbyterian Church in Columbus, Ohio, our parents took a phone call from Nate McNelly, the pastor of a Nazarene church a few miles away. Nate explained he had seen the Luchs name on the church bulletin board and wondered if they were the couple who had adopted his nephews and niece some thirty years before. He was one of their biological mother's older brothers, he explained. Mom and Dad said they had indeed adopted the children and invited Nate and Anna, Nate's wife, to dinner. Nate left a telephone number and address with them should any of us ever wish to contact him. We had not responded to a similar offer from our biological mother a decade earlier and we did not respond to Nate's invitation. Until Janey needed to know our biological family's medical history.

Mom wrote Nate of Janey's need and he set off as quickly as he could to the Portsmouth, Ohio, area to learn what he could about family health history. After Nate had sent Janey what he had discovered — that cancer was rare in our biological family — My sister, Janey, sent him a note of thanks and avoided the mastectomy. They kept in contact and Nate, who turned out to be the unofficial McNelly family historian, began to send Janey documents and photographs. Janey met with Nate and Anna and a few years later called me overseas to say she and our brother Michael were going to meet with our biological mother, Eunice McNelly Vandelier.

I said to Janey without thinking at all, "Don't do it, Janey. Don't open doors you can't close." I was afraid such reunions would hurt the feelings of the Luchs, who had given us so much. I had the parents I needed and had no desire to have anything to do with biological relatives I long ago concluded did not deserve us. Janey was only a baby during the 18 months we were often hungry and terribly cold and sometimes ill and sometimes left by our biological mother and the rest of the McNellys to fend for ourselves for days and — in one case — a week at a time. Janey had no memories of that time at all. I was four and five years old and have never forgotten.

Janey ignored my caution, met with our biological mother — an event I will describe later — and continued to collect and copy and send to me photographs and biographical material Nate had sent her. Despite my general disinterest in reunions with the McNellys, I had my own reason to care about family health history. Some years before, suddenly and without any warning, the oldest of my four sons developed juvenile diabetes.

Erik was not quite four years old and at the time — 1970 — we were living in dry, dusty Bamako, Mali, where I was the American embassy's press and information officer. Our remote location nearly cost Erik's life when a regional State Department doctor was reluctant to authorize a medical evacuation for Erik to the United States. Medical facilities were minimal in Mali and Erik's juvenile diabetes was diagnosed only because a Peace Corps doctor happened to be in Bamako at that time. International flights of any kind left only twice each week and connections to the US were difficult to make. Following a frustrating exchange of cables between my ambassador and the regional medical officer, Erik's evacuation was authorized and after long hours of flying from West Africa to Washington, D. C., Erik arrived at Children's Hospital so deep in the final stages of diabetic acidosis the doctors said they were amazed he was alive.

I had begun to think about writing the story of my childhood years for my sons and grandchildren once there was time to do so in retirement. I began reviewing and organizing the documentation Janey was collecting and passing on to me. Nate later told Janey that he and his wife, Anna, and a biological aunt, Mary McNelly Marshall, would like to meet with me the next time I returned from Malaysia to the United States on home leave. I resisted at first. I had no interest in reviving grim memories of my early childhood or re-establishing relations with biological relatives that had seriously wounded us when we were very young. But I remembered that Aunt Mary, then in her early teens, had taught me to read and the historical family photographs Janey continued to copy and send had aroused my curiosity. I wanted to know more about a Revolutionary War veteran whose name I bear, a Civil War veteran who looked like Moses in federal blue, and closer to my own twig on the family tree, a school-teaching, Bible-reading, whiskey-making grandfather.

I had other questions. Could Nate and Mary fill in the gaps among my memories? Perhaps they could describe the circumstances that led to our abandonment to a county children's home. I wanted to know why I had always felt affection for my biological father, Lonnie Boggs, and none at all for my biological mother, Eunice McNelly. What was the family's history of diabetes? I was curious to see what Nate and Mary looked like and acted like in the flesh. Would similarities to them unmistakably link me and my siblings to the McNelly half of our biological family? I was also intrigued by the accounts of separated identical twins which were found decades later to have independently chosen the same careers or even the same brand of cigarettes. After all these years, was it possible Janey and I would recognize in Nate and Mary personal traits we had inherited?

Finally, published personal accounts of adoption seemed to be mostly about the unhappily adopted who had only been able to find a sense of belonging through reunions with their biological relatives. That did not seem to fit my case at all. But how could I be sure? Perhaps I would also experience a dramatic and fulfilling experience of belonging through a reunion with Nate and Mary. And if that happened, would the identity I had in part accepted and in part forged over the years of living as a Luchs crumble before the flesh and blood reality of a family whose genes I shared? Who would I be then?

In 1986, on home leave from Malaysia, I agreed to meet this Uncle Nate of whom I had no memory. It was bitter cold and overcast as Janey and I left her home in Ann Arbor, Michigan, in early December. An hour later we crossed the Michigan-Ohio border and began the drive across the plains of northern Ohio headed south on Interstate 75 toward Columbus. Snow flurries danced across the highway in the headlights of Janey's black Chevy Blazer. I looked across at my sister as she drove, still a nice-looking woman at midlife, trim and stylishly dressed. Janey's pretty face was marred only by a bump on the bridge of her Roman nose, a trophy she earned during a football game on our grade school playground. I smiled to myself, remembering how Janey then thought God had played a terrible trick making her a girl until she arrived on the other side of adolescence as a honey-haired, blue-eyed beauty. We talked and laughed about our childhood with the Luchs and she told me what she had learned about Nate and Mary and Nate's wife, Anna, as we shifted to state route 23 after Findley, Ohio.

Except for one photograph Janey had sent me I had no idea what Uncle Nate would look like when we met him and Anna for a late breakfast in a pancake house they liked. The restaurant was local, friendly, and relaxed. The paneling and booths were in knotty pine darkened with age, probably unchanged since the 1950s. Nate and Anna seemed to be pleasant people and after a few nervous moments we talked easily together. While we talked I began to search Nate's body for evidence we were kin. His hands were large and thick, his fingers stubby. My hands are of average size, my fingers long and thin. I saw a short, thick man with large bones sitting across from me. I am of average height, medium build, and fine-boned. I searched Nate's face for resemblance. His nose was larger than mine and differently shaped. His ears were small, mine are larger than average. His hair was medium brown and surprisingly curly. My hair is dark brown and only slightly wavy. I was amazed at how little this man Uncle Nate looked like me and began to think Janey and I and my brothers must resemble the Boggs, our biological father's family. There was no sparkle in Nate's conversation, no friendly banter of the kind Janey and I enjoyed when together or when we were with the rest of the Luchs. Nor was the timber of Nate's voice similar to mine. I and one brother had voices so alike people who heard only our voices had trouble telling us apart. Nate and I looked so unlike each other that I thought; if someone had randomly selected an older man off the streets and set him down to breakfast with me, the odds are he would look as much like me as this biological uncle. After breakfast was over Nate asked if I would be willing to go meet Aunt Mary and her family. I hesitated and then agreed to go. I was grateful to Mary because she taught me how to read and in half an hour would remind me how I pestered her to play school with me at every opportunity.

As Janey and I, following Nate's car, drove over to meet with Mary, I felt disappointed. I told Janey I did not see in this

Uncle Nate a single similarity, odd as that may sound, nothing that resembled me. It seemed impossible that I would find nothing that would connect me to an uncle, one of my biological mother's older brothers.

Mary's home was a small brick house in a row of almost identical houses in a working class Columbus suburb built, I imagined, in the 1950s. I had the sense, once I looked around inside at the furniture and the furnishings, of having entered the past. But what most struck me in Mary's house was that nothing was out of order and everything was clinically clean. All magazines and books were squared with the corners of recently polished tables. Janey, a neat housekeeper herself, later said the bathroom was so perfect she was afraid to use it for fear she would disturb the perfect placement of every white towel, the symmetry of a bar of freshly unwrapped soap, or soil the shining gleam of the white basin or toilet. A single drop of water could spoil everything.

As with Nate and Anna, I talked easily with Mary and her husband, Bill, after a few uncomfortable minutes. They introduced us to their son. After five minutes of polite conversation I deliberately moved close to Mary so we could stare deeply into each other's eyes, almost as one peers into the eyes of a lover. It was as if we both were looking for some flicker of connection, some magic spark that would span nearly a half century to unite us. I was suddenly aware that everyone else in the room had stopped talking and was watching the two of us look intently at each other. But whatever we were all expecting or hoping for did not happen. Again uncomfortable, I looked across at Mary's son, my biological cousin. I could see no physical resemblance between him and me or my brothers. I later learned he was a high school music teacher, so he shared our love of music, but that appeared to be all we had in common.

One of the results I was hoping for from the reunion with Uncle Nate and Aunt Mary was more information on us as children, especially the stories that families like to share when they come together. But Nate, who lived in the same city and then later an hour's drive from me and my McNelly grandparents, did not seem to remember anything about our childhood at all and at first Mary was not much more helpful. Perhaps she was nervous, but I had hoped she would be able to answer our questions and tell us anecdotes such as those my own sons liked to hear from me at bedtime, the stories that took place before their own memories were able to take over the role of documenting their personal histories. That Mary could not tell me such stories disappointed me.

During the drive back to Ann Arbor I told Janey about my disappointment. I could understand that they didn't want to talk about the circumstances that led to our abandonment, but I had expected more information. More memories of us as children that would fill in the gaps. More detailed knowledge of family history and personalities.

I continued, "For a few hours I felt I was in a different place, a small world of limited horizons where what they talked about and cared about was so different from the culture we were raised in at the Luchs. Being with Nate and Mary was a little like entering a foreign country. They're nice people, yes. I liked them. But we don't seem to share much. Through the Luchs we were exposed to an adventurous and exciting approach to life. That's not the world Nate and Mary live in." I told Janey I doubted I would ever be able to feel any sense of kinship with this biological aunt and uncle. Our conversations seemed to arrive at a series of dead ends. We didn't seem to have anything in common or much to say to each other. Janey said, "Oh, you're so hard to please!" That's about what I expected my sister to say. "Can you turn the heat up?" I asked. I felt cold after living in the tropical heat of Malaysia.

Beginning to tire of the drive, I looked down at the panel lights on Janey's black Blazer to check the mileage and then out at the frozen landscape, lost in my thoughts. Why did I feel such a sense of freedom when this first reunion with my biological relatives was over? Why was I thinking how grateful I was the Luchs and not the McNellys or the Boggs had raised us? Why did I not even want to think of myself as related to Nate and Mary? Did I have to? I told most of this to Janey. She agreed with much of what I said but her reaction to the visit was different. "After all," she concluded, "They're blood, Lewis."

"Well, there are two issues in that for me," I said. "The first is I believe that human relationships are built on shared experience, especially shared emotional experience, not blood. For most of us this shared experience occurs in the biological family. But not for all of us."

"I think I know why," I continued. "After a lifetime of living as a Luchs, we're different now. The same genetic heritage under different conditions leads to different results. There's a plant — I can't remember its name — but when it grows on land the leaves are like arrowheads, in shallow water they look like lily pads, and in deep water they become ribbons. Or take race horses. Researchers say the performance of race horses owes less than 50% to their genes. Training and the desire to win count for over 50%. What we inherit is not necessarily a good predictor of our future performance. Maybe the truth is our genes determine our limits and our cultures determine our possibilities."

"And one more thing about blood," I said to Janey, "If blood means anything at all, there would have been at least a spark or two of recognition while we were with Nate and Mary. I would have seen some similarity in our facial expressions or body language or something — just some little something — familiar. Like in the separated identical twins

10

studies. There was none of that. They seemed like strangers to me when I met them and they seemed like strangers when we parted. They seemed to be nice strangers, but strangers nonetheless, not kin."

Janey differed. "But you and I are related by blood and we're close."

"Yes, but remember all we went through together as children. Shared experience again, especially shared emotional experience."

I could hear the emotion in my voice. Obviously, this was something I cared about. "In my life," I continued, "I often meet strangers I feel immediately drawn to, that I want to see soon again, men and women who sometimes become friends. I felt none of that with Nate and Mary. Married couples don't normally share any blood, do they? For many of us that is our deepest human connection and maybe the best example of shared emotional experience. Or take the Marines. They form bonds that are closer than those of many blood brothers. Shared dangers and dependence on each other. That's what we went through during our first years together, shared dangers and dependence on each other."

A Missing Link

After I retired almost a decade later, in July 1995, Janey and I drove down through the green hills of southeastern Ohio from Athens — where Janey now lived — to Portsmouth to find the modest white bungalow of our McNelly grandparents and other scenes of our first years, almost 50 years before. We also hoped to begin the process of obtaining records of the years we had lived in the Scioto County Children's Home. After a discouraging day running around the county court house, the children services office, the city newspaper, and the Portsmouth city library, Janey proposed we try to find Gusty Boggs, our paternal biological grandfather's second wife. I was not enthusiastic. The meetings with Uncle Nate and Aunt

Mary and other members of the McNelly and Boggs families since the 1980s, brief get-togethers encouraged and arranged by Janey when I visited her on home leave, had brought me no sense of kinship at all. I was annoyed by the assumption of these biological family members that our blood ties automatically gave us a special bond and relationship. I doubted I would hear anything of value from this 90-year-old woman, who my birth father had sometimes blamed for his problems, if she was clear-headed enough to talk with us at all. Someone in the family had told Janey that we had once lived next door to Gusty and our Grandpa Boggs and that Gusty especially remembered me. I found that curious since I had no memory of her or Grandpa Boggs, while I still had lively memories of my McNelly grandparents, especially Grandma McNelly. So I agreed to help Janey find Gusty, promising myself this was the last time I would let my sentimental sister drag me to yet another encounter with someone she had unearthed in our biological family.

We found Gusty on the 4th floor of a raw concrete block public housing apartment building filled with the elderly and the poor. When we arrived she was sitting outside in a small alcove along the passageway in a pink flower print housecoat, hoping to catch a breeze on a horribly hot, muggy day. When Janey put a bouquet of daisies and other summer flowers into her hands, Gusty smiled and said that, yes, she did remember Janey from her last visit. She looked intently at me when Janey introduced me and nodded her head when Janey asked if she would talk with us about our biological paternal grandfather, school teacher and master whiskey maker, Harry Henderson Boggs.

From the passageway in which Gusty was seated I could look up and down the green Ohio River valley simmering in heat haze, and I thought of how this broad, beautiful river was close by at my birth and how it had flowed through the first decades of my life. Being near the Ohio River brought me an inner peace.

Gusty's gray hair was long and stringy with wisps at the sides of her face. Her deep-set eyes were surrounded by the shadows of those who are not sleeping well and her body seemed mostly sags and wrinkles, but she sat up straight at age 90. She seemed not upset that we had appeared unannounced because she had no telephone, and her body quickened in our presence, either because she was pleased to have company or because she wanted to talk about her second husband, Grandpa Boggs. Gusty told us that Harry was 5'9" tall, wiry and energetic, dark haired, and half bald as an older man. He taught school, grades 1-8, in a small white rural schoolhouse in Caines Creek, eastern Kentucky, for 15 years. When I asked why he quit teaching, Gusty said, "He tired of it. The parents didn't support him. They wanted the children working on their farms and without the parents insisting on it, most of the boys and girls just weren't interested in learning."

Harry decided to leave teaching and eastern Kentucky and settled on a farm near South Webster, Ohio, and a few years later moved a few miles away to Sciotoville and went to work at the Wheeling Steel plant in adjacent New Boston. Gusty told us that from time to time the mill executives tried to get Harry to take a job in the office because he was an educated man but he declined, saying that a man had to earn his living "by the sweat of his brow" in the biblical way. As an older man Harry was diagnosed with black lung disease, probably from his work in the mill. Unlike his co-workers, however, he declined to make a claim, reasoning that Wheeling Steel didn't know his working conditions would cause the disease and therefore bore no responsibility.

Then Gusty paused, folding her hands in her lap and looked up at us. "Harry loved to read," she said. "When he was ailing and bedridden at the end of his life, I would go down to the bookmobile that came by each week and bring back a big stack of books, mostly westerns and histories. His favorite western author was Zane Grey. Harry read every book Zane Grey ever wrote. He loved history books too, oh, how he loved history books, especially American history. He liked to write, too," Gusty continued. "For a time he taught writing for the WPA and he wrote poetry. Some of his poetry was published in the *Portsmouth Daily Times*."

I was listening closely to her now. Reading is among my greatest pleasures and I too am especially fond of good histories. Those are hardly uncommon pleasures but understand that this was the first time in these family reunions I had felt any connection at all with anyone in my biological family. Next Gusty told us that Harry had great interest in the news as long as she had known him, especially politics. "He listened to the radio news several times each day and insisted on silence when the radio news was on."

Gusty talked on, sometimes answering my questions about Harry's personality and habits, his political and religious views, and sometimes volunteering information such as his intolerance of small talk and his tidiness. In some respects I recognized myself in her description of my biological grandfather, to whom she was introducing me. Perhaps, I thought, whatever genes affect our personal characteristics skip a generation or two. On the other hand, Harry had no musical talent and found little pleasure in music, which is important to me. Nor am I as reclusive as this man seemed to have been during most of his life or so little interested in my family and my grandchildren as he was.

I wanted to hear more but Gusty was fading quickly. The strain of talking, the emotional excitement of recalling someone long dead that she had loved, had worn her out. She asked to go inside her apartment to her memories and to "the little things," as she called them, collectable tea cups, tiny china animals, family photographs, greeting cards, memorabilia of a long life, all crammed together on a few shelves in her tiny living room. Janey and I helped her rise and walked her into her apartment and saw that she was made comfortable there and thanked her.

Gusty added something about the four of us as we said good-bye. She said that she would drop by sometimes to see how we were doing and often she would find us playing on the floor alone with no adults in sight. I felt grateful to Gusty as we walked down many floors of concrete stairs to the street. I was moved by her dignity in hard circumstances and hoped I might also accept the final page of my life, old and probably ill, without complaint. Gusty died six months later.

I jotted down some more notes during the drive back to Athens as I reviewed the interview with Gusty. Odd, I thought. I have no memory that Grandfather Boggs, the former school teacher, ever played school with me. He showed no interest in my favorite childhood game or in my development at all, I, who may have been the grandchild most like him. I wondered why.

The Search for Records

When I began to write down the story of our early years I regretted I would have only my own memories as a source for the twenty-six months we spent in the Scioto County Children's Home. Surely, I thought, there must have been some form of official documentation from that time, case records that would confirm that my memories were accurate and the stories I wanted to tell were true. "And you think you'll find those now?" a friend, a social worker, asked. "Do you really believe you're going to find case documentation from 50 years ago?" Probably not, I said, but still it seemed to me worth checking out.

While my sister, Janey, enjoyed establishing links with biological family members that helped me do interviews and collect family history, I found the search for case and institutional records of greater interest because I imagined those could provide a source of documentation for our earliest years. I was particularly interested in the events that led to our being abandoned to a county children's home, the summer I had spent in the home of Probate and Juvenile Court Judge Vernon Smith, our biological family's social history, and any information regarding our health, physical and psychological.

Unlike some who are adopted, I did not think knowledge of my biological family was necessary to the formation of my own identity. Perhaps that was because I had always had living memories of my family, especially of my father, Lonnie Emerson Boggs, and my grandmother, Martha Burton McNelly. However, I did want to write the story of my earliest years for my children and grandchildren, and was most interested in the part I remembered best because I was a little older, our experience in the Scioto County Children's Home.

On the same day we interviewed Gusty, Janey and I visited the towns east of Portsmouth along the Ohio River — New Boston, Sciotoville, Wheelersburg, — in which our biological families had lived and were now buried. We began by locating the house of our McNelly grandparents in Sciotoville and then made a visit to the Scioto County Children Services building in New Boston, formerly New Boston's city hall. The woman in charge was out. Next we talked with a series of receptionists in the gray stone neoclassical Scioto County Courthouse, but were unable, on short notice, to meet with anyone in a position of authority. We then drove to Portsmouth's handsome new city library. We were told a number of times during the day that the records of the county children's home had been burned or lost. In the library we were able to find only one brief article on the children's home, later renamed Hillcrest. That appeared in an unofficial history of Scioto County which reported that the Hillcrest Children's Home had closed in 1970.

During the course of the day I twice heard the name Bob Holsinger and then, mid-afternoon, again in the library, found and read an interview Bob had given to the *Portsmouth Daily Times* on February 5, 1995, only a few months before. I sought Bob out, hoping he would be able to help us. Bob and Floyd Holsinger, who together owned the major tire shop in

Portsmouth, organized annual gatherings for the alumni of the children's home and bought the Hillcrest property shortly after it was closed. "There are no case records, Lew," Bob told me. "I've had hundreds of requests. All those who return want records but there are none. They were destroyed in a fire." Since I had heard two views of the fire during the day — some thought the fire was imaginary — I wanted to hear more about the fire, but Bob was running a busy tire shop and couldn't take out time to talk at length with me. He did suggest we visit the library of Shawnee Community College, which we did. The librarians were helpful but could find nothing.

So, at what seemed to be a dead-end in our search for records, we had managed to find only a recent article in the *Portsmouth Daily Times* based on the memories of Bob Holsinger, and one paragraph about the children's home in a 1986 informal history of Scioto County. In that single paragraph out of a long history of many pages, there was but one sentence given to a description of the lives of the thousands of children who lived in the Scioto County Children's Home from 1924 to 1970. It is:

"The children lived in a good home atmosphere."

Good home atmosphere! That single sentence, fundamentally false, jolted me. I found it an incredibly inaccurate summing up of the lives of the thousands of neglected and abandoned children who lived and struggled there. Time and indifference — and possibly a fire — had apparently destroyed the personal histories of those children as well as the history of the institution. History is falsified for many reasons, sometimes just by our reluctance to preserve the records of unpleasant realities we do not wish to remember. The children's home building had been razed years before. The 17-acre property was now filled with suburban homes and pretty green lawns. Those of us with memories of the place were growing older.

It upset me that "The children lived in a good home atmosphere." would be history's final word. Or that the single paragraph in the unofficial history of Scioto County and the Bob Holsinger interview in the *Portsmouth Daily Times* would be all future generations would ever know of the lives of the children who lived there. I could think of only one way of writing a fuller and more accurate account of what life was like in the Scioto County Children's Home in the 1940s. With official documents. Now I wanted those documents for more than personal reasons.

What also bothered me on that summer day in 1995 was that what we called the Home was family for me and my brothers and sister during those years, all the family we had. I said to Janey, "That's one of the things families do for children, through photographs and letters and memories. They document their lives when they're too young to do so." I somehow felt whatever records existed belonged to us every bit as much as they belonged to Scioto County and the State of Ohio. After all, they were about our lives. "I'm not giving up yet," I said, in part to lift Janey's discouraged mood. "We've only been dealing with people at reception desks today. They may or may not know what they're talking about. It's too soon to give up."

Bob Holsinger was almost sixty years old when he gave his interview about life in the Scioto County Children's Home to the *Portsmouth Daily Times*. He cried as he remembered and talked about those years. Bob was six years old in 1943 when his mother drove her children, Bob, Betty, and Floyd up to the front steps of the big yellow brick building and left them. I was the same age when I and my brothers and sister were abandoned to the Home in 1941. The only difference was I had two younger brothers, not one. Bob told the *Daily Times*, "I was crying that day, too, crying so hard that the officials at the Home couldn't separate us immediately, even though it was the Home policy to do so. Our mother came to visit us the first two weeks but never came to see us again," he recalled. "No one in the family visited us. It was lonely." That was the common pattern. Mothers and fathers and families promised, but did not visit. Once out of sight, many such children were out of mind, finally and completely abandoned by their biological families. Later in the article Bob Holsinger told how he remembered, "Sleeping in dorms with up to 40 or 50 boys in a room...as many as 300 children were cared for, he said, often with only six or seven adults to supervise."

Shortly after that discouraging day in Portsmouth, I retired to Eugene, Oregon, and spent much of the next year settling into my new home and community. When I began the search for records again, I decided to focus on the history and daily life of the Scioto County Children's Home as an institution, since it looked as though I would never be able to obtain our personal case records. Late in 1996, again visiting my sister and sons and grandchildren in the East, I spent two days in the archives of the State Historical Society of Columbus, going through their archives. Little came of that. In early 1997, now happily settled in Eugene, I again wrote the clerk of court, Scioto County Court of Common Pleas, reporting that I had scoured the State Historical Society in Columbus and had only been able to find the name of the superintendent of the children's home in the early 1940s, the redoubtable Inez Norman, whom I had known only as Mrs. Norman. I asked where the records for Hillcrest were being kept and if they were lost or destroyed as I had been told. I wanted to hear that from an official source.

In reply the clerk suggested I write to a Sister S. Deurheren of the Scioto County Children Services Board. I did so on February 14, 1997, and a week later received a letter from Faye Weddington, the Social Program Administrator of the Scioto County Children Services. "We do have some records from Hillcrest, but not all records. It is my understanding that there was a fire at Hillcrest and some information was lost." So there are records! Apparently only some had been burned or lost. Ms. Weddington referred me to Dana D. Lanthorn, supervisor of the Foster-Adoptive Parent Service Unit, if I had additional questions. In the course of our correspondence and telephone conversations, I decided to again raise with Ms. Lanthorn the question of my personal case records. She told me that she had registers for Hillcrest near her desk which recorded admissions and departures of the children. I gave her our dates and asked her to search the registers. She later told me she had searched and could find nothing on us. I asked for an official letter to that effect. On June 6, 1997, she wrote, "It is with deep regret that I must inform you that we have been unable to locate any information regarding your placement at Hillcrest Children's Home." For some reason I doubted a serious effort had been made to find our case records. But again, this seemed to be the end of the road.

I returned to the Portsmouth area when visiting Janey in late 1997 and we made another one-day pilgrimage to the Portsmouth area. The village of South Webster had developed into a mixture of new houses and old unpainted houses set off by a large and handsome, new consolidated high school. We found Grandpa Harry Boggs' grave in the Wheelersburg cemetery. His tombstone had an open Bible carved on it. I observed that two great-grandfathers had died the year I was born. The town of Wheelersburg looked newly prosperous, with bright buildings downtown and newly constructed houses almost everywhere, evidence of economic good times in the 1990s. But we were unable to make any progress in obtaining our case records.

I got more involved in my new life in Eugene, including working as a volunteer for the Children's Advocacy Center and then as a Court Appointed Special Advocate (CASA) for children and let the project drop for most of a year. After another series of letters and telephone calls, I received on March 30, 1998, a letter from the deputy clerk of the Scioto County Court of Common Pleas telling me I must formally petition to release my records because they were sealed. Did this mean my personal records had been found? I sent my petition on April 15. In the meantime a letter to the Ohio Historical Society had produced a brief summary of my biological father's incarceration at the London prison farm in central Ohio.

I was interested in learning more about Judge Vernon Smith, in whose family I had spent the summer of 1942. I had no luck in searching the Internet for a biography of Judge Smith and again wrote to Portsmouth. I was told there was a photo of Judge Smith hanging in the court house and that I might be able to obtain biographical information on him from the Ohio Judicial Association.

I picked up again the thread of my interest in official records of the children's home. Board meetings. Financial records. I thought these might give me some clues in telling our story. I was told the only records for the Home were in the case files and my letter was being passed to the agency's attorney. It was also suggested I should try the offices of the county auditor or the county commissioners. I had already done that. This last suggestion seemed to me another example of being passed from one office to another which, I began to suspect, was what had been going on all along. I heard nothing from the agency's attorney.

In late September 1998, I stopped to spend a few days with Janey, still in Athens, on yet another trip to visit my sons and grandchildren in the East. On October 4 Janey and I drove up to Columbus for a luncheon interview with Aunt Mary, for whom I had more questions. I decided to make one more visit to Scioto County on Monday, October 5, to see if appearing in person would produce access to the historical records I had not been able to obtain through phone calls or the mail.

Breakthrough

I left Athens at 6:15 on Monday morning, October 5, and drove under a full moon through light fog towards Albany and Jackson. In the rear view mirror I could see a red autumn sun rising behind me. I made a stop for breakfast at the Lewis Family Restaurant near Jackson where a friendly waitress drawled, "You want a coffee warm-up, Honey?" Her warm manner reminded me of what I like about southeastern Ohio. Then I made a brief stop at the cemetery in South Webster where my McNelly grandparents and an older sister lie buried under tall, dark green cedars.

Once in Portsmouth, I again walked the hallways of the court house from one office to another, searching for documents, just as I had in 1995. Near the end of my tour of reception desks, a short woman with bright hazel eyes said to me,

"Yes, there are boxes and boxes for Hillcrest. They're stored in the basement."

I stood there staring at her. "Would you repeat what you just said, please?"

"I said there are boxes of records from the old children's home here. They're downstairs."

"Are you sure?"

"Very sure."

It turned out there was much more than just boxes of institutional files in the court house basement. Stored there also were personal case records of the children who had lived in the county orphanage. Towards the end of the day I was promised a new search for my records would be made. As I drove back to Athens I wondered, was there a fire? Were any records actually lost? Or was that a cover story told to those who had spent some or even most of their childhood in the county's children's home? What will they find on us, I wondered? The report of a physical examination? A journal entry or two?

On Thursday, October 7, I received a call informing me that "a few things had been found," and were being copied. I volunteered to pay for any costs involved. I returned to Portsmouth the following morning. What was handed to me when I arrived was a thick folder of papers. The documents included the journals of the social worker at the children's home, Edna Abele, who noted the significant developments in our lives during the years we were there. It included our medical records and medical history. It included the reports of psychologists from the Bureau of Juvenile Research in Columbus, the results of the IQ tests we were given by these same psychologists, and a complete family history written by the social worker who handled our case for the then new Aid to Dependent Children program. It included interviews with members of our biological family and information on the criminal record and prison history of our biological father. There were references to the summer I had spent in the home of juvenile judge Vernon Smith. Many family names had been erased but by then I knew enough about my biological family to fill in most of the blanks. I was invited to scan and take notes from monthly board meetings and financial records during the early 1940s. Once alone, I whooped with excitement! Now I finally had more than just my memories of our time in the Scioto County children's home. Later my sister Janey requested her records and those were provided. I now had a solid record of documentation to fill in, confirm, and complete our story.

Bob Holsinger had told the *Portsmouth Daily Times* he remembered there were about 300 children in the Home in the early 1940s living in a building designed for 100. That turned out to be incorrect, though there were nearly that many children living in the building a decade earlier during the Great Depression. When Bob arrived in 1943, approximately 150 children were living in the Home. But in other respects his memories were accurate. The one hundred fifty children were supervised by six untrained adults, 24 hours a day, and seven days a week. By the time I had obtained my case file Bob had died of a heart attack, still believing all the case files and institutional records had been burned or lost.

There were abundant records still available in 1998. I have used them liberally in this account of my first years. In addition to case files there are documents that would make it possible to research and write about the children's home movement, an important chapter in the history of our nation's neglected and abandoned children that spans nearly a century beginning in the 1880s. In 1998 I suggested the institutional records be sent to the Ohio Historical Society in Columbus for their archives. If that was not done, a resource for future historians may be slowly disintegrating in a basement in Portsmouth, Ohio.

CHAPTER 1

Lonnie

WHEN JANEY SENT ME some old photographs of Lonnie Emerson Boggs in the 1980s, I found some of the images of the biological father I had not seen in over 40 years instantly familiar. Other photographs of Lonnie were images of a man with only some resemblance to my memories of him, memories reshaped over the years by my imagination and dreams. But the heart somehow recalls much the mind has forgotten. Lonnie had been remarkably real in my emotional life, a friendly ghost I had lived with for a long time. During adolescence, in those periods when my life appeared to be going badly, Lonnie was my sympathetic defender, the one who understood me when no one else seemed to. Then he became "First Father," the secret counselor who guided me when I became a young father with four sons of my own. Through the years I had come to picture Lonnie as a handsome wanderer who liked to tease; a loving man strong but tender; a singing man inspired by the beauty in life; a kind man always willing to help out. With only memories from my early childhood to help me sketch a portrait of Lonnie, I had been free to create the ideal father I wanted. I often shared my life with that Lonnie in my imagination and I wanted him, as we do with our fathers, to be proud of me.

I remember a particular moment in France, standing in a grand reception hall under huge crystal chandeliers in the Hotel de Ville in Paris. I was wearing a blue double-breasted pin-stripe suit, the uniform of diplomats. I held a glass of excellent champagne in my right hand, just filled for the second time by a solicitous white-coated waiter, as Mayor Jacques Chirac introduced the poet, President Leopold Senghor, to French cultural elites and the diplomatic corps. I thought to myself, "Lonnie, I wish you could be here, if just for a moment. I'd like to share this moment with you. I'd like you to be proud of me."

Janey's photographs of my biological father were of a man with dark brown wavy hair, a dimpled chin, and clear blue eyes. His ears, like mine, were larger than they needed to be to hear well. There was one photograph in my sister's collection of Lonnie at about age 14 that I especially liked. It was probably taken just before his father quit school teaching and moved the family from Caines Creek in mountainous eastern Kentucky to Sciotoville, Ohio, a scruffy steel mill town along the Ohio River. In the photograph Lonnie is perched on the bench seat of a farm wagon in overalls and a billed woolen cap of the type worn by working class Americans in the 1920s. Next to him on the wagon seat are two wild-looking urchins, boys of four and five years old with downcast eyes, so shy they turn their bodies away from the camera in fear. Lonnie is already long and thin and is looking directly at the camera lens with an expression of open and innocent wonder as he cradles a brown paper sack between his legs. Now that I have learned more about Lonnie's early life I have to suspect the brown paper bag holds a Mason jar of moonshine whiskey.

I like the photograph because I looked much like Lonnie did at age 14, and because he appears to be an unspoiled youth with all of life's wonderful possibilities before him. It's likely this picture was taken shortly before Lonnie's mother, Nola Mae Gambill Boggs, died of measles and quick consumption on April Fools Day, 1923. Nola Mae was a lively, warmly affectionate red-haired beauty, the heart and soul of her family. Lonnie's father, Grandpa Harry Boggs, collapsed in depression when she died, twice tried to commit suicide and became more reclusive, paying ever less attention to his sons.

Still grieving for his mother and not quite 14 years old, Lonnie pulled open the door of a red freight car in Portsmouth, Ohio, hauled himself up onto the rough wood floor, and rode the rails for six months to see America. He liked the clickity-clack of steel wheels on steel tracks and the powerful pull of black steam engines as they chugged up hills and coasted down grades across the rolling countryside of southern Ohio and through the squalid backsides of small towns and big cities beyond. He enjoyed the excitement of a new adventure and the freedom that buoyed up in him when he left his problems behind to see distant places and meet new people. Though barely 14, he walked jauntily, looking older than his age, and went from town to town in the America of the 1920s with a perpetual twinkle in his eyes.

Like Lonnie, I have wandered restlessly most of my life, not just in America but around the world. At age 11 I boarded a dark olive New York Central train for a solo trip from Athens, Ohio, to Elizabeth, New Jersey, but my ticket was fully paid, I had a handful of silver fifty-cent pieces in my pockets to tip African-American porters, and there was a smiling uncle at the end of the journey to meet me and show me the sights of New York City. Even so, over the years I had come to believe my restless yen for travel was something we shared, Lonnie and I, as I had long believed the father of my imagination — a strong but gentle singing man — actually existed.

What I learned from a close reading of the social workers' case file I obtained in 1998, however, called in question any common bonds with my biological father. I found Lonnie's prison history in the files embarrassing and his behavior utterly incomprehensible. I began to wonder what — except for our love of music and teasing and some physical resemblance — we had in common. I had long known that Lonnie had done time because one of my earliest memories is of sheriff's deputies in suits and brown fedoras driving him away in a black 1930s sedan, handcuffs on and his head down. I was not quite four years old at the time.

The full story of my biological father's youth was not at all as I had imagined it. To begin with I learned from the case records that Lonnie's freedom to ride the rails did not last long. On March 4, 1925, at the age of 15, he stood before a white-haired judge in the Scioto County Juvenile Court charged with delinquency. The judge suspended the sentence on that occasion. On July 30, 1925, four months later, Lonnie was again brought to the court and again charged with delinquency. He was sentenced to one year in the Boys Industrial School in Lancaster, Ohio. "Delinquency" in Lonnie's case was almost certainly the theft that would get him in trouble time and again, as it soon would his younger brother Paul and his younger sister Mabel. Lonnie was released to his father the following year on May 22, 1926.

One year later, according to copies of my birth father's prison records, Lonnie joined and quickly deserted the US Army. He was then only 17 and since there is no evidence the army pursued the matter, they may have been happy to be rid of him. The following year he was sent to the Ohio State Reformatory in Mansfield, Ohio, to serve a two-year sentence for burglary. Arthur L. Glattke, the superintendent of the Reformatory, wrote of Lonnie, "While he was here his conduct was not good, having lost 545 days for escape and infractions of our rules. He escaped from the Grafton Honor Camp on July 14, 1929 and was captured and returned to the camp on July 20."

Dr. J.V. Horst, the institution physician, reported that when Lonnie first entered the reformatory, he weighed 164 pounds and was 6' 1" tall. "He denied ever having chancres. On the examination he was found to have Acute Gonorrhea. He was placed in Quarantine on 10-1-28 and released on 10-15-28." On October 7, 1929, Lonnie attempted suicide by trying to hang himself. He was discharged from the prison hospital following that incident on October 9, 1929."

Lonnie was paroled on July 1, 1931, and returned to prison a parole violator on September 15, having managed to stay out of trouble for over two months, in his case an outstanding achievement. He was restored to parole on October 1, 1932, and granted a final release and restored to citizenship on October 27, 1933, now 23 years old. So, while most young men were preparing themselves for a useful life by learning a trade or going to college, my father was behaving so badly he spent five years behind bars serving a sentence that could have been completed in less than two!

When Lonnie was finally freed from prison, the judge stipulated as a condition of his parole that he must attend church every Sunday. He chose a Methodist church in Sciotoville, Ohio, to fulfill that obligation and in the spring of 1933, he spotted a pretty brunette during the first verse of "Onward Christian Soldiers." He couldn't take his eyes off her, which made her blush, and once she caught him winking at her. They began dating. My biological mother, Eunice Elizabeth McNelly, was then not quite 15 years old, eight years younger than Lonnie.

Lonnie managed to get a job with the Wheeling Steel Corporation in the rolling mill for $25 per week, good money at that time. The mill was hellishly hot, the work dirty and hard, but he liked the camaraderie of working with men proud of their naked and sweating upper bodies. The Wheeling Steel plant was the economic heart of Portsmouth in the 1930s and Lonnie was proud to be part of it. But he did not like regular hours and he could not abide being ordered around. Like many other economic immigrants to the Portsmouth area from Kentucky, he lived and worked in the city but his heart and culture were in the hills and hollows to the south.

Despite his good job, Eunice's parents opposed Lonnie's proposal of marriage because of the age difference and his prison record. Thus, on December 14, 1933, Lonnie and Eunice eloped across the Ohio River to Catlettsburg, Kentucky. My mother's family considered trying to obtain an annulment of the marriage but decided against it because their daughter "was already ruined." She was also pregnant.

In the 1930s the soft coal-burning New Boston Wheeling Steel mill belched soot and odorous smoke onto the streets and gardens of Sciotoville. The better homes of the town were small workers bungalows, most with tidy green lawns and white picket fences that sat on flat land near the river. Some had plaster deer in their front yards. The poorer houses in Sciotoville, not much more than shacks and shanties, were sited up along Bonser Creek. Lonnie and Eunice took no honeymoon and found a tiny place to live in, hardly more than a shack, far up Bonser Avenue, a grandly named rutty red dirt road that followed the creek of the same name towards its source in the hills behind Sciotoville. Lonnie's father and his older brothers, Luther and Hubert, lived nearby. As recent migrants from eastern Kentucky, the Boggs clan liked this remote location. It seemed more like home than Sciotoville and New Boston and was less likely to draw federal agents who might uncover and curb Grandpa Boggs' whiskey making. Few of the houses on Bonser Avenue then had electricity. Not many more had indoor plumbing. Only the nicer ones were painted. But I doubt it mattered much to Lonnie and Eunice where they were living at that time. They were in the first flush of love, freer and happier than either had been in years and looking forward to the birth of their first baby.

On July 21, 1934, a girl Lonnie named Nola Mae in honor of his deceased mother, was born in the bedroom of the house on Bonser Avenue and delivered by Dr. W. J. "Bill" Hartledge, who had just finished his medical studies. Before my older sister was a year old Lonnie began to carry her around for company and to hear her beauty praised. He took her everywhere he went except to work. Some people in Sciotoville thought she was the most beautiful baby they had ever seen. The Boggs and the McNellys all agreed on that when they did not agree on much else.

When Nola Mae was fifteen months old, on October 18, 1935, at 6:00 PM, I was born in the same bedroom and also delivered by the young Dr. Bill Hartledge. I weighed eight pounds, had no hair, and bawled at once and loudly when thrust from the comfort of my mother's womb. My parents named me Richard Lewis. Lewis was the first name of a paternal great-grandfather, Lewis Franklin Boggs, and the middle name of my maternal grandfather, Joseph Lewis McNelly. No one is sure why my parents chose Richard as my first name. Possibly because Caines Creek, Kentucky, the Boggs' ancestral home, was named for family patriarch and Revolutionary soldier Richard Caines. The weather forecast in the *Portsmouth Daily Times* the night of my birth was prophetic: "Cloudy, with occasional rain. Turning colder."

In early February of 1936, now 19 months old, Nola Mae, the joy of her father's heart, developed a fever and fussed a lot. After a few days her condition worsened but Lonnie and Eunice were reluctant to take her to Dr. Hartledge because they had not yet paid him the $25 fee for my birth. After two weeks of illness without any medical attention at all, my sister's fever began to soar. Lonnie and Eunice — who had no car — wrapped Nola Mae and me in blankets and carried us to Dr. Hartledge's office. He took one look at Nola Mae and then drove the four of us quickly to Mercy Hospital in Portsmouth. Nola Mae's condition was serious; the diagnosis was acute spinal meningitis. Three weeks after being admitted to Mercy Hospital and five weeks after she first fell ill, on Sunday morning, March 8, Nola May died, probably the first victim of Lonnie and Eunice's parental neglect.

I have carried with me a dim memory of Nola Mae all my life, possibly because she was talked about in the family during the years I was old enough to form memories. But I am quite sure I have a specific memory of my parent's emotional trauma at the time of Nola Mae's death even though I was only five months old. I am looking up at a tiny brown casket on a table, probably in the dining room of our cottage. My father and mother hover over the dead body of their baby girl. No light had yet been turned on as the early spring dusk deepened. I looked at my father and mother and at the tiny casket and then at the dark walls of the room and the faint light drifting through the white lace curtains on the windows. Suddenly my father bellowed in agony and then he and my mother began a moaning duet, clinging to each other, their faces buried in each other's shoulders, sobbing, each trying to assuage the other's grief.

Nola Mae's death crushed Lonnie. He blamed himself for not taking her to the doctor sooner and for giving his daughter his deceased mother's name, as if that had set a curse upon her head. Many years later members of the family told me my father never overcame his grief for Nola Mae. He was never again the same man. When we visited with the family at Grandma McNelly's house during the first year or so after she died, Lonnie would break out in tears for no apparent reason, making everyone uncomfortable, and then silently leave.

When we were in the Portsmouth area trying to interview family members and obtain our case records, Janey and I visited Nola Mae's grave in a pretty green hillside cemetery under towering dark cedars just outside the village of South Webster, Ohio. It was early summer. Water drops from an earlier rain sparkled on the grass blades. We quickly found Nola Mae's grave next to those of our grandparents, Joseph Lewis and Martha Jane Burton McNelly, in the first section nearest the highway. Standing there with Janey, I imagined a ghostly family of grandparents and aunts and uncles and cousins, gathered under their black umbrellas in the rain. I could see the clergyman, the Rev. Selven Percell, lead the sad procession up from the muddied gravel road on which were parked a black 1930s hearse and a line of black and brown cars to which were attached little purple flags with white crosses. I imagined the family gathered around the small open grave. Having almost lost my oldest son, standing beside my sister who had lost her first grandchild, I thought that surviving the death of our children without losing the will to live is one of the most painful tests in this life. But many have passed through that dark night and lived to see another day. I looked up into the dark green cedar boughs as a summer breeze began to move them.

The Golden Age

Parents who lose one child will cling to their second child if they are lucky enough to have one. For almost a year, from the time Nola Mae died in the spring of 1936, I had my father's undivided love and attention and that was the beginning of a golden age in my life. Lonnie had plenty of time to spend with me. In June of 1936 he lost his job at Wheeling Steel during a long and bitter strike at the new Boston plant, a strike that did not end until 1937 when John L. Lewis succeeded in organizing the plant for the CIO.

I do not remember that my happy life with my father changed much when a brother arrived to share him with me. Lonnie Emerson Boggs, Jr., whom I called Brother, arrived on an unusually warm January 2 in 1937 and was also delivered by Dr. Hartledge in Lonnie and Eunice's little bedroom. Lonnie Jr. looked much like me but had blue instead of hazel eyes and short blond fuzz on his handsomely shaped head. He was a sturdy baby, heavier at birth than I, which pleased Lonnie. Unlike me, he was an easy-going baby, which pleased Eunice.

Almost all of my pleasant memories from this period are of my father, not my mother. Perhaps Lonnie's desire to be involved with his children and his capacity to love made him memorably present to me in ways my mother was not. Or perhaps she was just too busy taking care of my younger brother to spend much time with me. The difference in my memories is just as marked among my grandparents. Grandpa Harry Boggs, whom I'll describe later at some length, lived next door to us at this time but had no interest in us at all. I do not have a single memory of him. My mother's parents, the McNellys, lived two miles from us in the center of Sciotoville and my memories of them to this day are rich and detailed, especially of Grandma McNelly, the matriarch of her family, a strong woman with a dominant personality who took considerable interest in me.

It began to rain heavily in the unusually warm days after my younger brother's birth, rain that turned the Ohio and Scioto Rivers into broad, rushing, muddy lakes by the third week of January. The Ohio River crested almost eight inches higher than ever before at Cincinnati, Ohio, and almost seven feet higher than ever before at Louisville, Kentucky. In all, 600,000 families were driven from their homes. Nine hundred drowned or died otherwise as a result of the flood. At one point the Red Cross put the number of homeless at nearly 300,000. In the area where we lived — Portsmouth, the villages of New Boston and Sciotoville — the river missed by an inch rising to the level of the greatest and most destructive of all Ohio Valley floods, the 1913 disaster.

After the 1913 flood Portsmouth built a massive protective flood wall. But during the January 1937 flood Portsmouth's city fathers were compelled to open up six valves to save the flood wall and let the waters rush into the downtown business district. By January 22, all the buildings in downtown Portsmouth were flooded to the level of the second floor. The flood choked and backed up the city's sewer systems. Fifty thousand residents of the Portsmouth area, over 50% of the population, had to be evacuated north to Columbus and other towns between the two cities. Portsmouth darkened as electricity failed. Business stopped. Factories were closed. Food shipments ceased. Farmers watched their livestock float away and even houses and barns rose off their foundations and glided down the raging river.

Disease threatened. The food situation became acute. No trains could run. The city's pumping station was shut down.

Water was rationed to one hour per day and water for drinking had to be boiled. On top of everything else came four inches of snow. Half the telephone lines were out of commission. The only reliable communication was by radio. Many cities along the river declared martial law. Fourteen of us, all members of a McNelly clan that now included my newborn brother, gathered at my grandparents' small bungalow at 5220 Harrison in central Sciotoville, without electricity or running water. How fourteen of us managed to live in a house of 1200 square feet or so with two small bedrooms and one bathroom with no running water I cannot imagine.

The 1937 flood was the kind of crisis that seemed to bring out the best in my father. He gathered buddies and went around helping people move their furniture and other goods to higher levels. Uncle Nate, my mother's older brother, years later told me how Lonnie moved him and his wife up to the second floor of the apartment building they were in.

Nate told me, "You couldn't help but like the guy. He would help anyone. We got word the water was coming up and here he came. I was living at 9364th Street in Portsmouth and your dad showed up without being asked to help move me and brought some other men along as well."

After the flood subsided, some of the bodies recovered were formally dressed. They had been washed out of their soggy graves. Many of those forced out of the city by the flood did not return to the Portsmouth area and the city never fully recovered. Most families who did return were not insured and many lost all they had. Some no longer had the means to take care of their own children. Parents delivered dozens of their children to the Scioto County Children's Home following the 1937 flood and never looked back.

Aunt Mary, one of my mother's three younger sisters, told me my family lived in seven different houses from 1935 to 1941 but I remember only five. The first one I can see in my mind was also on Bonser Avenue, where we probably moved after my younger brother was born. It was painted white and had a pretty red tin roof. The house had four white-washed rooms: a kitchen, a living area, and two small bedrooms. It was the house of my happiness. I think Lonnie and Eunice must have still enjoyed each other. As he grew older, I had a playmate in Lonnie, Jr. whom I continued to call Brother. I can see my daddy walking down across a June field full of daisies towards us. The air is bright and clear in the late afternoon as he returns from work, now with the WPA. My daddy had great long legs. I remember how Brother and I would run out to grab his legs and he would gather us in his arms, both at once and squeeze us up against him. I think I even remember that he said, "How're my little guys?"

It was during that happy time that Lonnie would often put me up on his knee and sing, "You are My Sunshine." As he sang, "You make me happy when skies are gray," I would look up into his face and see his clear blue eyes and his loving smile, while I waited for the lines I liked best. "You'll never know, dear, how much I love you, so please don't take my sunshine away." He always looked right at me with a twinkle in his eyes when he sang those lines, and I have wondered since if he had the sorrow of Nola Mae as well as me on his mind when he sang them, and if the last line was a kind of prayer. My father also loved to sing "Red Sails in the Sunset," the top tune of 1935, and his favorite white gospel song, "Life is Like a Mountain Railroad," part of which goes:

"We must make the run successful from the cradle to the grave. Watch the curves, the fills, the tunnels ...never falter, never fail, Keep your hand upon the throttle and your eye upon the rail!" How I wish my father had followed that song's counsel!

From time to time Lonnie took me to the movies to see Westerns. I loved watching the big MGM lion turn its head and roar as I sat beside my father, feeling happy and secure.

When it snowed in winter, my daddy became a magician, making a delicious snow cream from snow, cocoa, and sugar for me and for Brother.

The only fear I had in that time of sunshine was a childhood fear. Some older boys in the neighborhood told me that garbage men would steal little boys and dump them down storm sewers. Every Wednesday, as soon as I heard the garbage truck approaching, I would run and hide under my parents' bed where no one could find me. Once I heard the truck driving away, I would crawl out from under the bed overjoyed that I would not have to worry about being dropped into a storm sewer for another week. A week seems a long time in the life of a child.

In that same white house with the red tin roof, a second younger brother was born. Charles Wesley Boggs, named for one of my mother's brothers, arrived on May 21, 1938. Every fifteen months, as if that was natural and normal, Lonnie and Eunice produced a new baby. Charlie looked different and was different. He wasn't as well coordinated as Brother and I, and walked awkwardly. He had some undiagnosed problem with one eye. I learned from the case file I obtained in 1998 that because of these differences, Lonnie rejected Charlie and sometimes abused him.

There is another photo of Lonnie in my sister's family collection, one I don't like. Now near 30, his body has filled out across the chest and, normally lanky, he is overweight. He is wearing an open white dress shirt with the sleeves rolled up to his elbows, a pair of stripped slacks, brown and white wing-tipped shoes and a fedora felt hat. He is with his three brothers, Luther, Hubert, and Paul, and looks like what he is, a country boy imitating a city slicker. He is cocky and showing-off. This is the Lonnie I did not see as a child, the Lonnie one member of the family called "a charming scoundrel." All the people who knew him talked about his teasing, his impishness. But his laughter was not easy. Some said he always seemed to have something on his mind, a shadow that followed him around. Aunt Mary said he seemed troubled to her. Most people figured that was because of his grief for his much-loved daughter.

My own memories of my father are almost only of his charm. There are men and women in this life fortunate enough to make others feel good just to be around them. The Lonnie I remember was like that, the warm, loving daddy who made me the center of the world when I was with him. When he was sober he was a caring father. Even Grandma McNelly liked him in spite of herself. Lonnie thought Grandma McNelly was a saint and she liked to hear him sing. On summer evenings they would sit in the white porch swing on Grandma's front porch, side by side, and sing hymns including her favorite, "Abide with Me." Most people found it difficult not to like my father — when he was sober.

But when he was drinking whiskey, Lonnie was full of anger, a disturber of the peace, a fight-picker who could turn on anyone in an instant for no reason: a wife, a relative, a stranger, even one of his own children. Grown men feared him when he was angry. My mother told her sisters Lonnie sometimes beat her and once smashed his fist through a wall with a wild swing that missed her. I remember scenes of physical violence between my parents. I flinch today when anyone's arm comes near me, as if my body has learned to duck before being struck. Later I wanted to doubt that Lonnie struck me or my brothers. How could I have loved him so much if he had abused me physically? Or is it true that children will forgive almost anything of those on whom they must depend?

But it wasn't his alcohol-induced violence that put my father behind bars. It was his bizarre drunken thefts, the masterworks of a buffoon. Once he stole an axe from a hardware store, then shotguns, another time a bicycle. The sheriff found him sleeping off a night of drinking with his arm around the axe along the railroad tracks a few hundred yards from the hardware store. It was as if he wanted to be caught and sent off to jail. On another occasion he walked into the same hardware store drunk, grabbed an armload of shotguns and carried them in broad daylight to his brother's house and hid them under the porch. There were four witnesses who saw him walk out of the hardware store, his arms cradling four brand new shotguns.

I've wondered since I learned the details of his criminal record and prison history in 1998, how to make any sense of my felonious and alcoholic father, unlike me in so many ways. I had to let go of the romantic and sympathetic father figure I had created over the years based on a young boy's remembered love for his daddy. But I could not help wondering how Lonnie managed to get into so much trouble as a young man.

Did the cultural values and realities of isolated and impoverished eastern Kentucky contribute to my father's behavior? Consider his quick desertion from the army, his dislike of orders in the workplace, and his unwillingness to comply with rules in prisons and his many attempts to escape. Fierce defiance of authority and government-hating independence seem to be cultural values in eastern Kentucky.

Was my father's problem isolation? His remote ancestors came from North Carolina to eastern Kentucky around 1800. Their old country origins were northern Scotland and England and some were the offspring of thieves and street orphans, impressed from the streets of large British cities to work on plantations in America. Some died from beatings by their plantation masters. Others escaped to the mountains and spread up along the hidden hollows to become Appalachian mountaineers. Most of Lonnie's forebears remained isolated in one small area of Louisa County, Kentucky. Later some left their homes to fight in the Civil War, most on the side of the Union, but they returned to their small world once the war was over.

It's possible to have an accurate idea of what young Lonnie's life on Caines Creek was like from a memoir by Cratis Williams, a Boggs relative who eventually, in 1929, followed Lonnie's father Harry Boggs as the teacher in the one room school at Caines Creek. In *"I Become a Teacher,"* Cratis tells how he, just like Harry, was only 18 years old when he began teaching at the school. The tiny community of Caines Creek was so isolated that everyone there seems to have been kin to everyone else. Cratis was a relative and had been a pupil of Harry's at the same school. The school in question was called the Boggs School and was on land owned by Jay Boggs, one of Harry's cousins. The teacher that immediately followed Harry was Ulysses Williams, another Boggs cousin, and after Ulysses, Ora Boggs, yet another of Harry's relatives, taught at the school for three years. The school board, which selected the teachers for the school, was full of Boggs relatives. Arb Gambill, the chairman of the school board, was related to Nola Mae Gambill, Harry's wife. Even Harry and Nola Mae, man and wife, were related. They were one-half first cousins, as Harry's parents had been before them.

The chief claim to fame of Caines Creek, according to Cratis Williams, was an abundance of family distilleries whose high quality whiskey was renowned. Harry made some of the area's best bourbon and kept the local sheriff well-supplied with his fine product. Whiskey was absent in few households in eastern Kentucky and the railroads offered a means of developing an export market in other regions of the country, especially in the large cities. The market grew rapidly as prohibition took hold. Harry expected his four sons to help out with what was becoming a lucrative family business and they did. They also began testing out the product at early ages, which recalls the photo of Lonnie sitting on a farm wagon with a paper bag between his legs. Cratis Williams, who tells of playing around his grandfather's distillery as a boy, writes that his brother came up to him a couple of weeks into the school year to report that a seat mate was drunk. The boy was too drunk to walk home until hours later. Cratis cites the incident as an example of how to handle a sensitive situation well. The boy had not misbehaved, Cratis wrote. He was just very drunk and it did not happen again.

The Cratis Williams memoir describes other realities in Caines Creek in the 1920s. One was physical and gun violence. Cratis tells how as a boy he witnessed many family fights and saw bloody encounters on the local church property, a popular killing ground. "I saw bleeding men dying after gun battles. My teacher during the third grade was shot and killed at church one Sunday."

Violence was also part of Boggs family history. Nola Mae, Lonnie's mother, was a child — one of three — of her father Lafayette Gambill's long-term mistress. In his late 40s Lafayette became interested in yet another woman, this one some 25 years younger than he was. A young man courting the same young woman showed up one day with a pistol in his shirt. Lafayette tried to scare him away. When the young man pulled the pistol out of his shirt, Lafayette began to taunt him, moved towards him and, pointing at his own chest, said, "Shoot me! Right here! Come on, shoot me!" and he kept moving toward the young man. When Lafayette was almost on top of him the young man obliged by shooting him at point blank range and Lafayette fell dead, unable to complain that was not exactly what he had in mind.

There are other characteristics associated with the region around Caines Creek: the isolation and poverty and lack of modern medicine; the disinterest in formal education; the suspicion of outsiders; the hatred of governmental authority; and the biblical fundamentalism. These are all present in the Cratis Williams account of his life as a young school teacher at the Boggs School. I think these were influences that contributed to Lonnie's troubles.

But I suspect the major source of Lonnie's difficulties as a youth is the lack of any guidance from his father. Family sources paint Harry Boggs as an uncommunicative man who was distant with his sons and a stranger in the midst of his own family. Even so, one wonders how Harry, a school teacher, could be so little interested in Lonnie's future that he let his son drop out of school in the fourth grade.

Harry became an enigma to everyone in his family. He did not speak easily or freely, not even with family members, and sometimes would not even acknowledge them when they walked by him. There was one exception. Politics. Harry would talk politics with any adult at any time. He was a life-long Republican among neighbors who had mostly shifted to the Democratic Party by the 1930s. After Jesus, Franklin Delano Roosevelt was first among their heroes. But FDR was Satan incarnate to Harry. Also, as he aged and spent more time with his Bible, Harry became less tolerant of small talk. He developed the notion that small talk was sinful and interpreted narrowly the verse from the Sermon on the Mount that reads, "But let your communication be, "Yeah, yeah; nay, nay; for whatsoever is more than this cometh of evil."

Grandsons who saw Harry as an older man found him as mysterious as everyone else and never developed a normal relationship with him. They never called him "grandpa" or "gramps" or even "grandfather." When his grandsons came to the house he nodded his head at them and returned to reading. One said he read books and newspapers and the Bible almost continuously and could talk intelligently about anything, but would only talk about politics.

In the case files I obtained in 1998 social worker Helen Middleton described Harry as, "quiet, well-mannered and bears a good reputation. He has no criminal record and his health is good." But that was not true of his children. Of his six boys and girls, the three youngest — which included Lonnie — were in Ohio state penal institutions in 1939 when Helen Middleton compiled the family history. Paul had been sentenced to the Ohio State Reformatory in Mansfield in 1938, convicted of larceny. Mabel, Lonnie's younger sister, had been sent off to the girls' industrial school in Delaware, Ohio at about the same time, also for theft.

For such a well-mannered, Bible-reading, Roosevelt-hating Republican, Harry Boggs left another strange legacy. Eight of his grandchildren would be abandoned to the Scioto County Children's Home to be supported by state and county tax-payers. While his eight grandchildren were in the children's home, not five miles from where he lived, Harry Boggs did not visit them. Not even one. Not even once.

Lonnie was arrested again in May 1939 following a break-in theft at a local liquor store. He was held in the county jail pend-ing trial and was permitted to leave the jail only once, when my younger sister Janey was born on July 23, 1939, the first of us to be delivered in a hospital. The new baby girl was not given a name until later, my Aunt Mary told me. Eventually, she said, I was the one who named Janey. I named her Mary Jane, combining the first name of my Aunt Mary and the mid-dle name of Grandma Martha Jane Burton McNelly.

I remember the day we were taken to see Janey and our mother at Mercy Hospital in Portsmouth. I can recall standing beside her hospital bed, looking up at our new baby sister. But I best remember the occasion because I got to see my daddy again. He gave me and Brother and Charlie sticks of Wrigley's chewing gum in light green paper wrappers. He was with a sheriff's deputy, to whom he was handcuffed.

When the visit was over we all walked out of the hospital together and I saw the black sheriff's car and two more depu-ties to take Lonnie back to jail. He tried to hug me but couldn't because of the handcuffs. When he looked up at the depu-ty, asking to be freed for a moment to hold me, the deputy shook his head. They opened the car door so my daddy could get in and he sat between two men in suits and fedoras and they sped away. I can't forget seeing him like that, being driv-en away with his head down. My aunt Mary told me I came running into my Grandmother McNelly's house afterwards crying, "Grandma! Grandma! They took my daddy to jail! They took my daddy to jail!" I believed, Aunt Mary said, Grandma McNelly could do something about it. All I knew was the joy of my heart was gone and my Aunt Mary said I cried inconsolably long into the night. Nothing my grandma or Aunt Mary said or did could help me.

My father's trial took place two days later, on July 25. He was convicted and sentenced from 1 to 15 years for breaking and entering. He had been out of prison only long enough to sire five children. A nephew who saw a good deal of Lonnie over the years wrote me recently, "Lonnie's burden was having a personality which enabled him to get his way far too often. He could talk men out of their money, women out of their virtue, and too many times, court officials out of doing their duty." But obviously, not always.

CHAPTER 2

Eunice

W HILE MY MISBEHAVING FATHER was a friendly presence in my life, I rarely thought about Eunice, my biological mother, and as an adult never felt much heart connection to her at all. Nor was she, like Lonnie, in my imagination or dreams. I often wondered why. I assumed she had played the major role in raising me as a young child as most mothers do. That I felt no affection at all for my mother puzzled me. After all, we're supposed to have feelings for our biological mothers. Whatever the reason for my indifference, I wanted to learn more about her personality and her role in the circumstances that led to our abandonment. My interviews of her younger sister and older brother, Aunt Mary and Uncle Nate, and the social workers' reports in the case file I obtained in 1998 contained some clues.

In the case file social worker Helen Middleton described Eunice in 1939 as, "a rather attractive brunette of average size." My Aunt Mary, one of my mother's younger sisters, told me Eunice, "liked to look good. She was small-boned and had beautiful hands." I remember Eunice as having long, dark hair and brown eyes. As I child I thought she was beautiful, as most children think their mothers are beautiful. Aunt Mary also told me, "Eunice walked with her head way up. She thought she was better than her peers, who considered her a snob." Aunt Mary added that Eunice resented the family's working class status and emulated an unmarried and wealthier aunt, Belle Burton, who belonged to the DAR. Eunice wanted to be rich and a member of the best society, Aunt Mary said. She was a good student and especially liked literature. In the case file another social worker, Lois Smith, wrote of my biological mother, "It seems the mother had been so deprived and thwarted herself that she now primarily rejects her children." But Uncle Nate and Uncle Charles, Aunt Mary and Aunt Martha, two older brothers and two younger sisters, saw my mother as the favorite of their father and spoiled. "Dad put Eunice on a pedestal. She was spoiled rotten," Aunt Mary told me. "Grandpa McNelly never disciplined her," Uncle Nate said. Eunice would also tell social workers later that she had, "raised her younger sisters, and did all the house work." That was also untrue according to her brothers and sisters. They told me she was the family complainer and blamed others for her own failings. Everything bad that happened to Eunice was most of the time someone else's fault.

Eunice also told social worker Helen Middleton that her family, especially Grandma McNelly, picked on her and criticized her. But Aunt Mary disagreed. She said the conflict with Grandma McNelly developed, "Only because mom was trying to get Eunice to use good sense." Above all Grandma McNelly was concerned because she thought Eunice was, "aggressive with men." A brother later said of my mother, "Eunice liked to run around and have a good time." Some in the family believed my biological mother married young to escape my grandmother. All her brothers and sisters described Eunice as "stubborn" and "headstrong."

After my father was driven to the state penitentiary in the summer of 1939, my mother, Brother, Charlie and I moved in with our McNelly grandparents. Eunice applied for Aid to Dependent Children and when that was granted, we moved into a tiny brick apartment over a garage on Harding Street. There was plumbing in the apartment but no hot water. We used kerosene for cooking. As far as I was concerned, the best thing about the apartment was its proximity to my McNelly grandparents. Our apartment was a safe and easy walk to their small white bungalow and I went there as often as they would put up with me, sometimes without my mother's permission.

My mother's ancestors, the McNellys and the Burtons, Scotch-Irish people mixed with English and German stock, arrived in southern Ohio from Virginia and Maryland in the 1830s. One patriarch of the clan, William Deavers, served seven years in the Revolutionary War. The McNellys and the Burtons developed prosperous neighboring farms near South Webster, Ohio, and the two families "crisscrossed," that is, they frequently intermarried. One of my mother's grandfathers, John Calvin McNelly, born in Ohio in 1836, eventually owned three farms on which he cultivated corn and wheat, orchards, and tobacco. A photograph of John Calvin depicts a man with a great gray beard and his strong features make him look more like a granite carving than a human being. John Calvin was active in politics all his life and a leader in his United Brethren church. His third son, James Wesley Burton, was ordained into the Methodist ministry by Bishop Wright, the father of Orville and Wilbur. John Calvin enlisted in Company C, the 91st Ohio Volunteer Infantry when the Civil War began, served honorably for three years, was awarded a disability pension for his wounds, and discharged. Then he was mistakenly drafted for a second tour. Ever dutiful, off he went again to war. Seven months later the War Department discovered its mistake and released him. Despite his wounds, John Calvin McNelly lived to be 89.

John Calvin's fourth son, my grandfather, Joseph Lewis McNelly, spent his young manhood working one his father's farms. When he married Martha Jane Burton in 1904, they moved into the house on the farm and their first children, a series of seven sons, were born there. Joseph tired of farm work, moved into Sciotoville and eventually became a boilermaker for the Wheeling Steel plant in neighboring New Boston, Ohio. He bought a modest white bungalow in Sciotoville at 5520 Harrison Avenue. The relocation apparently caused a shift in gender of the McNelly children. After seven sons, my mother was the first of four daughters born at that address and was always her father's favorite daughter.

Though my Grandfather McNelly had left farming as a young man, he never lost his joy in working the soil and watching the growth of what he planted and nurtured. Like so many men in southeastern Ohio, his vegetable garden was his chief recreation. I can still see him in the early spring turning over the rich black earth of his back yard plot, spade cut by spade cut, in almost perfect rectangles. I liked to watch the dozens of pink and red worms wiggle in the upturned soil. Through his garden he followed the natural cycle of the seasons from spring planting to the full harvest of autumn and the deep sleep of winter. He liked feeling connected to nature.

Grandfather McNelly's specialty was strawberries and I loved what I called "scrawberries" best of all fruits. Most people canned at that time. July through September, when they weren't busy canning, it seemed to me women sat for hours on porch swings talking about nothing but canning, how many quarts of tomatoes and green beans they had put up, and what kinds of pickling they had done. In other seasons adult women seemed mostly to talk about their flowers.

I remember Grandfather McNelly's neatly coiffed white hair stood high on his head like a rooster's comb. He was a natty dresser on Sundays and other special occasions and favored dark suits with matching vests for his spare six-foot body. He wore rimless glasses and could have stepped out of a Norman Rockwell illustration as the ideal grandfather of the 1930s. But he was so passive and silent a man that he could be in a room and no one would know it.

Grandmother McNelly, on the other hand, was larger than life, a vibrant and dominant personality who tucked her gray hair back into a tight bun. Grandma was always dressed neatly, as neatly as her pleasant house was kept. Her face was more handsome than beautiful and showed determination and granite-solid strength. But she smelled sweet like lilacs and her own fresh homemade bread. I could feel her presence as well as see her, stout and sturdy, over 200 pounds and barely five feet tall, sitting as if enthroned in the center of the couch in the living room, the rock and anchor of her family.

Grandma always sat beneath her favorite picture, a print in rich dark blues and purples of a stormy Sea of Galilee. Peter is sinking into the waves as he cries out for Jesus to save him. Grandma McNelly devoutly believed we are all sinking in this life and need Jesus to save us. My McNelly grandparents were Methodists but when a newly-ordained minister expressed some doubt that Jesus was truly God, Grandma marched her entire family into the Berean Baptist Church the following Sunday.

I surely remember Grandma McNelly so well because she took great interest in me. I was probably her favorite grandchild, even though she did not get on with my mother. I loved being with Grandma and looked forward to the hours we spent in her home. Aunt Mary later confirmed my memory of spending long periods seated in her white porch swing, side by side talking, just the two of us. Aunt Mary said Grandma talked with me as if I were a little grownup man.

My mother's younger teenaged sisters, pretty Mary and Martha, lived at home and often played the upright piano which sat against the front wall at the entrance of the house. I was Mary's favorite and would sit beside her when she played. Brother was Martha's pet and she and he were often together. Sometimes Brother and I were given books with crayons that we colored which spread out on grandma's living room floor. I carefully chose standard colors, especially red, blue, and yellow, and kept my coloring neatly within the lines. Brother worked with a wildly colorful palate and paid no attention to lines at all. Both aunts babysat us and Mary often took us for long strolls through the neighborhood.

I learned a few years ago that my biological mother had another younger sister, Ruth Ann. I have no memory of her at all because she took no interest in us at all. She and Eunice were then and forever rivals.

At this time my mother received a monthly ADC payment of $50 per month, worth approximately $640 today. She also began to collect $8.40 of welfare from Scioto County, making her total combined state and county welfare payments worth approximately $750 monthly in today's dollars. My McNelly grandparents paid the rent for the apartment so that more of our mother's welfare money could be used for food and clothing for us. This was a happy time in my life, despite missing my father. I had Brother and Charlie as playmates. We were fed regularly and were warm in winter. Best of all, we lived almost next door to my McNelly grandparents where I could enjoy the company of my grandma and of Aunt Mary. But after only six months in the tiny apartment we moved again because of an argument between my mother and Grandma McNelly.

Relations between Eunice and Grandmother became severely strained because my mother's reputation had become the subject of a great deal of neighborhood gossip. Grandmother McNelly and my mother argued about the neighborhood gossip, but what troubled Grandmother McNelly more was our mother was using welfare money to pay for beer and cigarettes for her friends. This so upset Grandma McNelly she rumbled over one day and chased our mother's friends out of our apartment, which so angered our mother she moved us all down to a sordid brown tenement building in the slums of south Portsmouth. The neighborhood was run down to the point that our aunts Mary and Martha were afraid to go there to deliver the brown bags full of groceries Grandma McNelly bought for us.

Of the seven different houses and apartments Aunt Mary told me we lived in, I remember best the unpainted gray house at 6438 Bahner Road, down next to the Norfolk and Western Railroad loading yard in Sciotoville, and a mile or so from our grandparents' house. We moved there after leaving the apartment in south Portsmouth. From the outside the Old Gray House looked abandoned. Some of the windows had cardboard in them where the glass was broken. The front porch sagged. Inside the wallpaper had gone brown with age, was torn in places, and was water soiled. Floor boards were loose. The roof leaked. I recall that the house smelled dirty and dusty, as old, uncared for houses do. To make matters worse, the house was chaotic and unclean.

A black pot-bellied stove stood in the center of the living room. To the right upon entering was the front bedroom in which we four children slept on a single mattress placed on the floor. When it was cold and there was a fire in the pot-bellied stove, we moved the mattress into the living room to be near the stove. The other rooms were my mother's bedroom and the kitchen. I do not remember a bathroom inside the Old Gray House. Probably we had a privy. I do not remember a bathtub or a shower. I do remember a white bathtub with feet and a toilet with a white seat at our grandmother's house.

I have memories of being left alone with my younger brothers and sister in the Old Gray House. Sometimes our mother was gone at night, sometimes overnight. There were rats in the house that came out at night and scampered around the floor. In the dark they seemed fearless. We could hear them in the darkness and sometimes feel the pressure of their tiny paws running on top of the blankets that covered us. Sometimes their whiskers and fur would brush against our cheeks.

A biological cousin who lived with his brothers and sister in a similar house in Scioto County tells a story about rats. The children were given four dime store Easter baby chicks, dyed purple, pink, and blue, as baby chicks were in the 1940s. They placed the chicks in a brown cardboard box with food scraps and water and listened to their pleasant peeping sounds as they feel asleep. When they awoke the children could not hear the chicks peeping. When they looked into the box, only four tiny yellow beaks and eight tiny yellow feet remained.

I began to have nightmares about rats, not gray rats but black rats, and not normal-sized rats, but giant rats as large as bears with yellow eyes and ivory white incisor teeth that clicked together incessantly. My nightmares ended as one of the rats charged me and I awoke screaming. I put my hand up on my face and could still feel the hairy side of the rat that had just brushed against my cheek. I wanted to throw the covers back and flee to my mother but was afraid to leave the warm bodies of my brothers and sister on the mattress beside me. I was afraid the rats would attack me if I left the mattress. I thought I saw one rat stop and turn and face me. I could just make out its bright little eyes peering at me out of the dark, much as in the nightmare. The rat's whiskers were in motion. I was terrified and pushed up against the warm bodies of my brothers for comfort. I tried closing my eyes and could hear more rats scurrying about our bedroom.

Finally, unable to control my fear any longer, I jumped out of bed and dashed into my mother's room. She wasn't there! I began to shout, "Mama, Mama, where are you?" I called for her in the house, "Where are you? Where are you?" I ran outside to the front porch to escape the rats and to scream for her. There was one distant street light shining in the dark. I become even more upset and shouted as loud as I could for her, first in one direction, than in another. I did not give up, shouting for her again and again and again. When my throat was so sore I could not go on, I stopped shouting and only cried. Finally, exhausted, I crumbled to the porch floor, curled up in a ball to keep warm and went to sleep, where my mother found me when she came home the next morning.

Once, Eunice left us alone for an entire week. I first heard that story from Aunt Mary. It most likely occurred in the spring of 1941. I would have been five years old, and my brothers and sister four, almost three, and 18 months old. At first I discounted Mary's story. But then I found a report in the social workers' case files I obtained in 1998 that our mother had indeed left us without any adult care for an entire week!

We suffered in the bitter winter of 1940-41. I can remember how the four of us spent entire days curled up on the mattress, huddled together under blankets, trying to keep warm. In the case file I also found an account of a fire we built on the living room floor in January of 1941. We did not know that our house was a tinder box waiting to ignite in flame, and were so desperately cold we would not have cared. Helen Middleton, the social worker with ADC, reported, "The police were attracted to the Boggs home about 5:00 AM by a bright blaze in the living room. Investigation showed that the youngsters had built a fire of papers on the living room floor to keep warm." The police report also noted that, "The mother was not present, having left after the children were put to bed." When she returned, "The mother appeared remorseful," the police reported," and told us a friend was supposed to have stayed with the children." I have no idea why the police were attracted to our old house in a remote area next to the loading yard of a railroad in Sciotoville, Ohio. Were they summoned by a neighbor? If so, that neighbor and those policemen saved four young lives.

Most mornings I would be the first to rise and would try to build a fire in the black pot-bellied stove with whatever I could find. I remember that coal was rarely available, wood sometimes, and occasionally I could find newspapers in the house. Some mornings there was nothing to burn at all, even though the ADC checks Eunice was getting could have covered the cost of coal. Grandmother McNelly's lectures that our mother should put our needs first had had little effect. Eunice was spending welfare money on alcohol and food for the parties she organized and attended. When weather permitted the four of us would wander along and between the railroad tracks behind our house and up and down Bahner

Avenue picking up scraps of anything that would burn. What we found — twigs, pieces of wood and cardboard, small lumps of coal that had fallen off the coal cars in the yard — we put in our cardboard box and carried back to the house. Janey, only 18 months old at the time and often ill, suffered most from the cold and I could do little to help her. She has no memories from those years except being cold, a cold she thinks she can feel today when we talk about that time in our lives. The body, like the emotions, seems to remember what the mind has forgotten.

At that time my career ambition was to be a telephone lineman. There was a post — or perhaps it was a dead tree trunk — 6 or 7 feet high behind our house. Grandfather McNelly gave me an old belt I put around the post and my waist to climb up and down just at I saw telephone lineman do. At the top of the post I had a better view of the dozens of black train coal cars in the holding yard behind our house. Most of the cars were full of shining bright anthracite coal. I remember wondering why we had to suffer from the freezing temperatures when I could see black train cars loaded with coal from our back yard.

One day a nice-looking, dark-haired man in jeans and a plaid shirt picked up some boxes and a basket and asked me to go with him. We walked out among the coal cars with white letters on them. He told me to follow him closely and not to talk as we walked across one set of tracks and worked our way down between two rows of coal cars. I walked behind him and remember admiring his brown work boots. The sky was gray and the cold and wind began to chill me. When we arrived at a full car of black coal chunks he lifted me to where I could climb the remaining distance up a metal ladder on the side of the car, boost myself on to the pile of coal on top, and look down. From there I could see in the near distance dozens of black cars full of coal and beyond, white smoke plumes from the stacks of factories along the Ohio River and the black limbs of bare trees along the river beyond the tracks.

I could even see across the river to Kentucky. The man — who turned out to be my mom's boyfriend — told me to throw the biggest pieces I could lift onto the ground as he stood to one side. I lifted and rolled large hunks of coal over the side of the coal car as my hands turned oily black. Once the baskets and the boxes were full, we returned to the house, I carrying just one lump of the oily black coal because the boxes and baskets were too heavy for me. That was called "poling" coal in the Portsmouth area. I quickly got over my fear of being caught for doing something wrong because I was so happy to have that coal.

For the next couple of weeks I would rise as soon as I woke up to build a fire in the black pot-bellied stove, crushing the newspapers and arranging kindling wood crossways so that it could hold a few small pieces of coal to get the fire burning well. Then I would jump back into our common bed until I could see the fire began to roar and then rise again to add more coal and begin the day. Those winter days with a good fire burning in the pot-bellied stove were the best days in the Old Gray House.

We were often hungry, so hungry we would eat anything we could get our hands on. When Eunice was gone and they were available, Brother and I ate raw potatoes and fed those and raw onions to Charlie and Janey. We ate uncooked flour. Aunt Mary told Janey that once we ate bread that had been spread with rat poison. We were violently ill, Mary said. On another occasion Charlie managed to find some badly molded biscuits. When we bit into them the taste of the biscuits was so foul we spat them out at once. The memory of that foul taste remained for years among the molars on the right side of my mouth. On another occasion Brother cut his hand badly with a large kitchen knife while trying to peel an orange. His blood splattered all over the floor. I took a sheet from our bed and buried his hand in it and then wrapped the bloody sheet around his hand. I learned how to light the gas range with blue-tipped Ohio kitchen matches and if Eunice was gone and we were hungry, I would try to cook anything I could find. Most of my attempts turned out badly, boiling over and down the sides of the pot to the top of the gas range or even the floor, but once I succeeded in making some good cocoa. My mom returned as we were drinking it and spanked me.

One of my mother's older brothers told a social worker that our house was frequently raided by the police during this period because of noisy parties. He said his sister had done a lot of drinking after Lonnie was taken to jail in 1939. I do not remember any parties at the Old Gray House. By that time I think my mother probably did most of her drinking in the homes of friends or in local bars. What I do remember is my mother being absent, leaving the four of us alone.

I do recall strange men and women in the apartment we lived in briefly in South Portsmouth. I was too young to know what was going on behind closed bedroom doors, but I was loyal to my daddy and saw Eunice's relationships with other men as disloyalty to Lonnie. I loved my father and my mother and wanted them to be together. I didn't know Eunice had divorced Lonnie in November of 1939 and I doubt it would have meant anything to me if I had known. Sometimes I let her know it upset me to see her being affectionate with other men, which she did not appreciate. Likewise, I would stand for no criticism of my father. Aunt Mary told me that if anyone sitting at the McNelly dinner table began to malign Lonnie, I would shout them down with, "No! No! Don't say that! Stop!"

During the spring and summer of 1941, we spent some good days with our McNelly grandparents at their white bungalow on Harrison Street. Small as it was, my grandparents' home was the nicest house we knew as children and was the scene of many of my pleasant early childhood memories. I remember working with Brother and Charlie to help my grandfather in his neatly-kept vegetable garden by toting watering cans to him. I remember an egg and bacon and pancake breakfast, all of us seated happily at the round table in grandma's kitchen. I remember the time, probably July 4th, we were given our first cap guns. We liked to sniff the gunpowder in the discharged red caps. We look mischievous in the only existing photograph of me and my younger brothers taken at that time. We're wearing home-sewn shorts with matching suspenders to hold them up. I manage an impish grin. Brother, who looks ill, is staring vacantly off into the distance and Charlie turns away from the camera in fear. Our six arms are held rigidly and appear to be glued to our bodies. Our six fists are tightly clinched. We are children under stress.

I remember the excitement of the first blackout exercise that summer as Hitler's advance in Europe and rising tensions with Japan pushed America towards a world war. The adults talked about it all day and when evening came they pulled down tan roller blinds over the windows and we all took seats in the living room. After the radio announced it was time to turn off all lights, I could see only the little orange radio dial on Grandpa McNelly's radio. The adults whispered like ghosts in the darkened living room as if enemy bombers could hear noise as well as see the lights of Sciotoville and the Wheeling Steel mill, only two miles or so distant. In mid-summer violent thunderstorms moved up across the Ohio River from Kentucky. Grandpa McNelly liked to sit in his chair on the front porch during thunderstorms and I was with him when a thunderbolt blast cleaved in half the trunk of a great oak that fell across Harrison Street half a block away.

On July 15, 1941, Lonnie was released on parole from the prison farm in London, Ohio. A day later he arrived in Sciotoville and on July 17 told social worker Helen Middleton he had been offered a position to manage a farm halfway between London and Springfield, Ohio. He would have a free house, a $500 salary per month in today's dollars, all the eggs he wanted, and milk from several cows. He said the position would provide adequately for his family, which he wanted to reunite. But when Middleton held a final interview with Eunice and Lonnie a few days later, she noted their relations were strained. Eunice made it clear to Middleton she intended to put the four of us in a children's home and seek employment for herself.

On July 18, after this final interview with Lonnie and Eunice, Helen Middleton referred our case to the Child Welfare Services in New Boston. Lois Smith, the social worker assigned to our case, began to develop a file on us that included what Middleton had been able to learn of our family history and Middleton's case notes. Middleton had written that Eunice's standard of housekeeping had decreased steadily after she began to receive her ADC check. She had moved several times, it was noted, and it was finally necessary to obtain a WPA housekeeper's aide to help her with housework. "She seemed unable to manage the household or to keep the children clean."

On August 15, exactly one month after Lonnie was released from prison, Eunice walked to the Child Welfare Services office in New Boston. "She displayed considerable resentment against her husband," Lois Smith wrote, and said she was worn out from, "the constant strain and worry of caring for four active children." Eunice told Smith she wanted to put us in the Scioto County Children's Home, five miles away in Wheelersburg, Ohio until she could straighten out her confused thinking and find a job. She could return to her parents' home but they would not take the children. "She seemed helpless in making any plans for her children," Smith wrote. Eunice also told Smith all four of us were sick again, this time down with whooping cough. In that case, Smith told her, it would not be possible to put us in the children's home until we were well.

On August 17, a Sunday, Lonnie came to our Old Gray House on Bahner Road hoping to see our mother again. He had spent a month trying to persuade her to re-establish our family and move up to London, Ohio to live on a farm. Probably he was coming to try once more. I had not seen my daddy since I watched him leave, handcuffed, for jail in the back seat of a sheriff's black Ford two years before.

I was alone in the house, denied a Sunday afternoon family visit with my McNelly grandparents because my mother blamed me for nap-time roughhousing with my brothers. I could not believe she would take the others without me. She knew how happy visits to my grandparent's bungalow made me. After they left and I had cried it out, I went to the front porch to await their return and saw a man in the distance walking up Bahner Road towards me. As he came closer, I could see he had a tan jacket slung over his shoulder and was wearing a flat brown cap of the sort commonly used by working class men at that time. All at once I realized I knew that lanky body and that amble. "It's my daddy! It's Lonnie!" I shouted to myself.

He saw me looking at him and cocked his head of dark brown hair to one side and grinned. Then he knelt and held his arms out and I ran off the porch and up the street to him. He pulled me up and swung me around and around. Then he hugged me up against him, and then lifted me above his head, looking into my eyes. It felt so good; I was so hungry to see him and be with him and hear his beautiful voice again. It was just as before in the golden time.

"How's my little man? How've ya been? Then he said, "Where is everybody?"

He put me down and we walked back to the porch hand in hand and I told him the others were at grandmas and why I was alone. We reached the back of the house near the railroad tracks and he gazed at the long rows of black Norfolk and Western coal cars standing silently in the yard. A cloud shut out the sun and a shadow moved across the train yard and covered us. Then we walked back into the house and we visited for some time, time that seemed no more than a minute to me. Then he said.

"Well, I gotta go." He sounded sad.

When we were back in front of the house he reached into his jacket pocket and pulled something out and knelt down and put it into my hands. Then he looked into my eyes and said,

"Remember me by this."

It was a green fountain pen. I turned it around, admiring its marbled green finish, the black of the flat cap, the shining gold pocket clip.

Then he talked for a few minutes to me, softly, almost whispering, about his life and my mom and about me and him and about the green pen. For those few minutes, nothing else existed. Lonnie had a charm like no other human being I have ever known. When he was talking to me in that gentle, sincere way he had — looking into my eyes with love — all of my love hunger for my daddy was fulfilled. He made me feel warm, whole, happy, strong, just like the old times when he sang to me with the two of us in Grandmother McNelly's porch swing, when we went to cowboy movies together, just the two of us, and when he made ice cream of snow. All the happy memories I had of the pretty white cottage with the red roof flooded back and I realized I had been waiting for this moment ever since he was taken to prison two years before. I didn't understand half the words he was saying to me and that didn't matter. It was the tenderness in his voice, the smile on his handsome face, the playful twinkle in his deep blue eyes that were talking to me at a level beyond everyday existence, as if we had died and gone to heaven together. Oh, how I did love my daddy!

Finally, he stood up and readjusted the jacket on his shoulder.

"Gotta go, son."

"Not yet," I begged. I didn't want to be without him. Not again! No! No! Not ever again!

I grabbed his knees. "Don't go!" I said and my eyes began to fill with tears.

"Gotta. Gotta go." He gently pushed me off him.

My throat was tight and my eyes burned as he began to walk away. When he was down the road a piece, I shouted at him,

"Daddy, don't go!"

He turned and looked at me. The sunshine was all over him.

"Hey, you be good, OK?"

He walked away from me again and I shouted again,

"Daddy, don't go! Please don't go!"

He turned again and each time I shouted, "Daddy, don't go!" he turned until he could no longer hear me but I kept shouting anyway, even when I knew he could not hear me anymore.

I kept my father's gift of the green fountain pen for a long time as my dearest treasure and often fondled it as I remembered him. I did not understand what he said when he gave it to me but I chose to believe he gave it to me for a purpose and as a promise that he would return. In the meantime, the green fountain pen sustained me. So did memories of my father and our golden time together — as I entered a darkened world of shadows I thought would never end. But in 1941, I did not know the purpose of the green pen, Father, nor did I know... but that must come later in this story.

CHAPTER 3

1941 The Abandonment

O N A BREEZELESS SATURDAY in late August the silver line of mercury in the thermometer on Grandma McNelly's front porch climbed above 95 degrees. After dinner, apron still on and a fan in her chubby hand, Grandma led me out to the white front porch swing. I saw sweat beads on her brow as she settled her large body slowly into the swing. Her hand gripped one of the chains that supported the swing as she began talking to me softly as we sat swinging, side by side. I looked down at the gray porch floor as Grandma talked about how our mother could no longer take care of us. I turned towards Grandmother and saw Jesus kneeling in the Garden of Gethsemane on the back of her fan.

As I looked away from her at the blue hydrangeas along the porch's border, Grandma quietly announced we would be going away to a children's home. At first I was confused, not knowing what she meant. When my mind began to understand I would be separated from her and from my mother, fearful emotions began to surge through my body. I jumped out of the swing and faced and shouted at my grandmother,

"No! No! I won't go! I won't go!"

The vehemence of my response to her announcement surprised her as it did me. I was now crying. Grandma heaved herself out of the swing and put her arms around me, trying to calm me. After a few minutes my mother pushed the screen door to the porch open and the two of them tried to comfort me. They told me we were going away only for a little while and promised we would all be together again soon. They said they would visit us often. But I continued to sob, stopping only long enough to catch my breath and argue with them, desperately trying to make them change their minds. I thought we were being sent away because we had misbehaved. I said again and again we would all be good. Only five years old, I could imagine nothing worse than being separated from my mother and grandmother. Aunt Mary told me years later I cried long into the night of that day, just as I had when I saw the sheriff's men in their fedoras drive Lonnie off to the state prison right after Janey's birth two years before.

The following morning after breakfast Grandma McNelly took me by the hand again to the front porch. I felt spent and sad after the emotional turmoil of the night before. We did not swing together. She stood on the porch looking down at me. Then Grandma, who looked tired and older, put her hand on my shoulder. "Dick," she said, "Dick, I want you to promise me something"

I waited for her to continue.

"Whatever happens," she said, shaking one finger down at me for emphasis, "Promise me you will not let them separate you. Never! Never!"

My grandmother's charge seems odd to me now, coming from the matriarch of a family that willingly, without any coercion by the state of Ohio, withdrew its care and protection, renounced any responsibility for us based on our connection of blood and kinship, and had us carted off, unorphaned, to an orphanage. But her words were unnecessary. Because of Lonnie's absence and our mother's serious neglect I was already a child-parent to my younger siblings. I was already committed to keeping the four of us together. At times over the next few days I felt angry and defiant, at times I begged and pleaded with my mother and grandmother not to send us away, at times I dissolved in tears. I felt utterly helpless.

On Tuesday, August 26, social worker Lois Smith drove to Grandpa Harry's house to talk with my father who "expressed an interest in the children and their mother, but could offer no plan for their future." Smith then drove to our Old Gray House on Bahner Road. She found our mother laying face down on the floor, "the picture of utter dejection." My mother told Smith she could not pay the rent and had received a three-day ejection notice. In a later court report Smith wrote, "Under pressure, the children were admitted to the Scioto County Children's Home 8-26-41 on a temporary commitment." That same day Juvenile Judge Vernon Smith signed the legal Complaint filed by my mother authorizing our placement because "The mother is unable to give the children financial support and the father is unemployed."

Our family dressed us in new clothes for the occasion of our formal abandonment as if it were Easter, but it was social worker Lois Smith who bundled the four of us into her car the early afternoon of August 26 and delivered us to the county children's home five miles down route 52 in Wheelersburg. No one from our family came with us, Aunt Mary confirmed years later. In a bit of legal housekeeping after the fact, Judge Smith issued a warrant on August 29 to Fanny Cole Anderson, the clerk of court, "to convey and deliver said children to the Scioto County Children's Home."

Edna Abele, the social worker attached to the children's home, began a new section in her journal for us. "The children were brought to the institution," she wrote. "They did not want to get out of the car upon arrival but had to be persuaded to do so." My memory is that Lois Smith's sedan pulled up in front of a large yellow brick building with high steps and white pillars. Three women dressed in white dragged us out of the car and pulled us up the steps through the entrance, all crying, and then took us to the nursery dormitory. Someone recorded our arrival in the Official Registry of Admittance and Indentures. My number was 2822, Brother's 2823, Charlie's 2824, and Janey's 2825.

"All four are attractive children," Edna Abele continued. "Dick has dark brown hair and large dark eyes." Abele noted that I in particular had not wished to enter the children's home. "There was an apparent attachment to both his maternal grandmother and his mother." Her first impression of Brother and Charlie was of "nice looking youngsters with brown hair and regular features." Janey she found lighter in coloring, with "blond hair and blue eyes."

The following morning, to ease the adjustment to the regimen of the institution, the four of us were seated for breakfast at a separate table within the nursery dining area with pretty blue plates and place mats with yellow flowers on them. We were served canned fruit, fried eggs and buttered toast with jam, which we would soon learn was not normal daily fare. From our secure table of four I could look out upon the vast windowless and starkly-lighted basement dining hall. I watched a young woman with close cropped brown hair walk among the tables and chairs to a stairwell to our right. She began ringing a brass bell, swinging it back and forth before her as she walked. Moments later dozens of children of all shapes and sizes began to pour silently into the dining room. A few wore nylon stocking caps on their heads for lice. The children stood quietly behind their wooden chairs until a brief grace was said, boys on one side of the room, girls on the other, at tables of six and eight.

Some of the children turned and stared at us, the newcomers, and seemed to be talking about us. I knew I would soon be sitting among them, a thought that made me anxious. After the grace and the scraping of 150 chairs on the polished concrete floor, I could hear only the din of metal utensils on white plates. The children ate under a rule of silence. I could see that if they needed table service, a leader at the end of each table raised a hand or an empty milk pitcher to ask for more milk. I noticed the adult supervisors were talking at their separate table on the left side of the dining hall.

Older girls provided the table service in the dining hall and, under the supervision of a cook, prepared our food. I would soon learn that the children's home was maintained mostly by the boys and girls who lived there. This included serving food, washing dishes and pots and pans, mopping floors and cleaning interior rooms, raking and burning leaves, cutting the vast lawns of the institution with hand sickles, washing and ironing clothes, and cultivating a large vegetable garden. If a girl or boy of 13 or 14 years of age showed a talent for ironing, for example, he or she could expect to iron 80 shirts in three evenings a week during the school year. In those days shirts had to be sprinkled and rolled and then unrolled and ironed. Originally the plan for the Home called for the raising of pigs and chickens and tending an apple orchard, but those projects had been dropped by the time we arrived in 1941.

There were plenty of children's hands available for work. The Scioto County Children's Home, described in an unofficial history as "a new and spacious home," was opened in 1924 to accommodate 100 children. In the pit of the Great Depression 248 children were crammed into the building. When we arrived in 1941 the census was down to 148.

I observed everything closely during those first weeks and began to put together a picture of our new environment. A row of grand oak trees lined the asphalt drive which curved up the hill on which the children's home was built. The front entrance, rarely used except by official visitors or children at their first admittance, was dominated by four large white columns that supported an arched portico. From this grand facade, which brought to mind a southern mansion, could be seen the distant hills of Kentucky on the other side of the Ohio River. Behind the facade was a functional building with a central core and two plain wings with rows of windows in them that with some internal rearrangements of space could have been a county old people's home or county hospital for the indigent or even a minimum security prison.

Daily deliveries and comings and goings took place at the rear of the building at the rim of a great expanse of cement known as the Concrete. Further back, on a hillside that rose to the east, was an untended orchard that covered three acres or so of the 17-acre institutional property. In the old orchard were swings for the boys. The north border of the orchard was a series of concrete steps up the hillside that had once led to a school building used exclusively by children of the Home. That was gone by 1941. The children walked to the schools in Wheelersburg, a mile or so away along state route 52, also called Gallia Pike. Beyond the concrete ribbon of steps to the north was a dense woods, the favorite escape route of runaways, and for that reason off limits to the children except when accompanied by adults. To the south of the Concrete were playgrounds with swings and teeter-totters for the girls and for pre-school-aged children. Boys, I soon learned, were not allowed in that area. The rule of strict separation of the sexes applied to the playgrounds as it did to the dining hall.

When after two or three weeks I was separated from my brothers and sister and moved into the main dining hall, eggs and toast at breakfast disappeared forever. Instead I was served the normal daily fare: one bowl of watery oatmeal, untoasted white bread, margarine, and milk. No fruit of any kind, fresh or canned, was served and that breakfast diet did not vary. There were no second helpings at any meal but we were allowed to break white bread in pieces and pour milk over it to fill our stomachs. Lunch, when we were not in school, was soup and more white bread and margarine. Supper, served at 5 PM, was mostly pasty carbohydrates, often macaroni or potatoes in some form. Meat was available only on Sundays. There were no salads but we were occasionally served coleslaw. We quickly learned to eat what was put before us and to be grateful for that. The penalty for not eating was hunger and no snacks were available.

I think it was sensitive of the Home's staff to have the four of us eat and sleep together the first few weeks after our arrival, but our special privileges created resentment. So did the nice outfits the McNellys had purchased for our abandonment. Those set us apart from the other children. Also I, younger or smaller than the other boys at my table, was made head of my table within weeks. That move disturbed the natural hierarchy among the boys in which I as a newcomer should have served my time at the bottom of my age group.

Some of the larger or older boys in the dining hall tried to take our food, especially desserts when those were served. Their verbal threats were accompanied by pinches that left purple marks on our upper arms in case we did not get the point. If we refused to surrender our food we could expect physical harassment or a beating during the unmonitored one-mile-walk back and forth to school. Protest seemed useless. There was too much six supervisors did not see, too many opportunities for emotionally-wounded boys to make their own rules and inflict their own punishments.

I was moved into the Little Boys dormitory at the same time I was moved onto the main floor of the dining hall. This was standard practice since I would soon be six and was about to begin the first grade. Nursery children played in a special area apart from the older children, which meant I was rarely with my brothers and sister. Six months after we were admitted to the children's home a report by a team of visiting psychologists noted our extraordinary closeness and urged that we be brought together more often. One result of that report was that Brother, to my great joy, joined me in the Little Boys dorm. He was no longer Brother, however. The supervisors now called him Billy. I am not sure why because Home authorities surely knew his given name was Lonnie Emerson after our father. Perhaps they did not like my name for him and chose Bill or Billy, a real name that sounded something like Brother.

When we arrived, there were about 25 boys in the Little Boys dormitory, ages six to eight. The room was entirely filled

with cots so closely placed there was not a foot of distance between them. The mattresses were lumpy and urine stained,
the sheets clean but frayed. None of that bothered me much
because these new sleeping arrangements were an improve-
ment over what I had known at the Old Gray House. The children's home was also well- heated. What did bother me was
a boy I tried to avoid looking at, who normally had two lines
of greenish-white snot running from his nose to his mouth.
His condition was chronic and did not clear up. There was a
dressing area with hanging pegs and open cubby holes for our
clothing and a single wash basin. Downstairs on the ground
floor — we were on the second floor at the back of the building — were toilets, two shower heads for group showers, and
four or five basins to wash up and brush our teeth.

The 25 of us were supervised by one woman, the gentle
Eva McKenzie, a white haired frumpish woman in her 50s.
She could hardly care for our physical needs and certainly
had no time or energy left to give us the hugs and individual
attention for which we hungered. I remember her sitting near
the front window, using the natural light as she bent over a
piece of boys' clothing, sewing repairs, which says something
about the range of her duties.

Children sense some of their needs and can sometimes
provide for them. In such crowded conditions I felt strongly
the need for privacy and solitude. As winter approached, the
early morning clanging, hissing steam radiators awakened
me and I would rise before the 6 AM wake-up call. I dressed
quickly from my cubby in the alcove, brushed my teeth,
washed my face, and combed my hair. Then I would quietly
make my bed and pull a brown straight chair over in front
of the radiator and a window. From that perch I could gaze
out at the old apple orchard passing through the cycle of the
seasons — late autumn's frosts and winter's bitter winds and
ice and snow. In spring, I watched as day by day the orchard
burst with white blossoms and then clothed itself with tender

green leaves. That was my special time and I hardly noticed the stirring of the other boys as Mrs. McKenzie woke them up with, "Time to get up, boys. Time to make your beds."

Some seasons I was seated and waiting as the first sun rays flashed over the rim of the hill behind the orchard. I especially liked to watch the great shimmering red ball of a winter sun rise out of the orchard hill. Often I felt completely relaxed, warm and whole, the pleasant condition that a child's deep sleep creates. Sometimes in those moments of early morning solitude, something deep within me rose into my consciousness to flood me with joy and fill me with hope, without any effort on my part at all. This experience would end only when Mrs. McKenzie told us it was time to line up in the downstairs hall for breakfast. There we waited for the girl with the clanging brass bell to walk through the dining hall.

I was excited to be going to school for the first time and loved the early morning and afternoon walks to and from school. Though the purple-brick Wheelersburg School for the first and second grades — two classes for each grade — was only a mile away and about a thirty minute walk, it seemed longer to me as time and distance do to young children. There were acorns and hickory nuts to inspect and rustling leaves to run through and soft golden light under the tall oaks and sycamores that towered over the path along the road. There were leaves of all colors and combinations and shades of reds, greens, browns, yellows, and oranges. Each leaf I chose to look at closely was not quite like any other leaf I had ever seen. Dear intoxicating, precious, dying autumn, queen of all seasons!

When I began the first grade in September 1941 we formed a line in the basement dining room each morning to pick up identical brown bags filled with baloney sandwiches with a splash of bright yellow mustard spread across spongy white Wonder Bread. There was one piece of fruit in each bag, always a banana or an apple, and no vegetables. Almost at once school became the happiness center of my life in which I could escape from the dismal routines of the Home. School was an exciting place of bright colors and activities so interesting they took me right out of myself. School was the place I could excel and gain self-confidence. I looked forward to school every day. My Aunt Mary's willingness to play school and read with me had made me a reader before I stepped into the first grade. Sugarcoated as they may seem to some, the Dick and Jane readers contributed much to the pleasure I took in school. My name was Dick and I looked much like the boy in the readers. I even had a blond-haired younger sister named Jane.

School was safe. The Home bullies were constrained and a few of the town children from Wheelersburg befriended us. That's what we called each other, town kids and Home kids. Almost everything about school made me happy. I remember especially the observance of seasons: of autumn when we cut out leaves and patterns in gold and red and brown; of Thanksgiving with turkeys and pumpkins standing at the foot of dried corn stocks; and Christmas, when we made decorative chains of red and green construction paper. How bright and wonderful that was and what joy those teachers brought me!

School activities were stimulating after long hours of dreary humdrum days at the children's home. Rarely were organized activities planned for us at the Home, either after school or during the long summer vacation. No equipment, not even playground sports equipment, was provided so that we could entertain ourselves. We played hopscotch and some of the kids had roller skates and all of us had a few marbles. Some of the children knew how to manipulate white kitchen string in the cat's cradle game or had got their hands on yo-yos and entertained themselves with those.

On October 13, almost two months after our arrival at the children's home, Edna Abele wrote, "All the Boggs children have made a good adjustment, put on weight, and look better nourished." We probably did look better nourished as we recovered from the horrible year in the Old Gray House, but we continued to be underweight and malnourished. The four of us gained only one pound each year during our first two years at the children's home. Normally children our ages would gain 12-14 pounds in that span of time. Also, our pattern of frequent illness continued. We were sickly children.

Edna Abele noted that, "The mother visits at times, usually accompanied by grandmother." No one in the family doubts it was Grandmother McNelly who visited us most often. According to Aunt Mary and Uncle Nate, our mother's visits were infrequent because she left for Columbus almost immediately after we were admitted to the children's home, lived and worked in Columbus, and rarely returned to the Portsmouth area. It's likely that Edna Abele, seeing Aunt Mary with our grandmother, thought Aunt Mary was our mother. To those who did not know the family, Aunt Mary and our mother resembled each other. My sixth birthday, on October 18, passed unobserved as did the birthdays of all children at the Scioto County Children's Home. Home authorities explained there were just too many children to mark the passing of birthdays.

At a December meeting after a discussion of money for Christmas gifts, the Board of Trustees authorized a total of $70.00 ($840 in today's dollars) for gifts and a party for 14 employees and 144 children. Purchase of the children's gifts was organized by telephone operators in Portsmouth who distributed our letters to Santas throughout the community. For months my heart's desire was a red dump truck. That's what I asked for in my letter to the North Pole in which I carefully penciled the two little loops, top and bottom, of the first capital D in Dear Santa. At the Christmas Day party we waited for what seemed like hours for Santa's arrival. Once he arrived I watched him empty three bags of gifts for other children as they marched up one by one to receive them. I stood on my tip toes to stare anxiously as the fourth bag shrank to almost nothing, not distracted by the squeals of joy as other children opened their gifts and showed them around. Had my letter been lost? Santa put his hand deep into the last bag and lifted out a red dump truck and called my name. I ran toward the front of the room beaming with joy. No Christmas gift ever made me happier.

CHAPTER 4

1942 Our Darkest Year

FTER THE JAPANESE ATTACK on Pearl Harbor in December 1941, we were taught to sing "Anchors Aweigh" and "The Caissons Go Rolling Along" as we lined up outside the dining hall waiting for our daily oatmeal breakfast. Those morning marching songs, my first opportunity to sing at the Home or at school, soon became a high point of each day. At school we were divided into two reading teams, both Army Air Force units, the Flying Tigers and the Flying Eagles. The teacher chose me as squadron leader of the Flying Eagles, a role I relished. We pledged allegiance to our flag and took to heart the messages of "A Man without a Country" and other films intended to build patriotism during wartime. I was shocked when Lt. Philip Nolan shouted, "God damn the United States!" for which he was stripped of his rank and forced to sail imprisoned on US naval ship after naval ship, never again permitted to set foot on the soil of his native land. I did well in all subjects in school except for handwriting. Try as I might, I simply could not form the lovely graceful white letters that stood before me in a row on the blackboard. But I found I enjoyed words.

In early February, Persis Simmons of the Juvenile Research Bureau in Columbus came to Wheelersburg to conduct a field clinic. She had earlier administered the Stanford-Benet IQ test and the Vineland Social Maturity Scale to Billy. After that visit she reported Billy was progressing well and that he was poised during the various tests. During her second visit in early 1942, she tested Charlie and Janey. Simmons found Charlie an attractive child but more reticent than Mary Jane. She discovered that Charlie refused tests which required the use of a pencil or crayon. Whenever a test was to begin he would respond by saying no or shaking his head. "He had brought a doll with him," Simmons noted. "When I suggested that the doll might like to see how the test worked, he was quite willing to show his doll how he could use a pencil and thus completed the tests."

Simmons found three-year-old Janey enjoyed being examined. Of Janey's speech she observed, "She pronounces words rather well when she pronounces one word at a time. When she puts several words together, her enunciation is poor." During that same visit I was examined by a second psychologist from the Bureau of Juvenile Research, Mary Catherine Smith. Of me Smith wrote, "Richard seems to be afraid that he will do something wrong. He pondered many of his answers for a long time and needed much encouragement because he did not want to make a mistake." She concluded I needed to be given as much security as possible and have my confidence built up through being "loved and entirely accepted."

There's no doubt Mary Smith was right about my fundamental insecurity at that time, but she may have missed something. Oldest children compelled by circumstances to become parents to their younger siblings are often children who think they must be perfect. I could not admit to myself I was not up to what adults such as Grandma McNelly seemed to expect of me. Mary Smith also noted in her conclusion my special affection for Janey. She recommended that the two of us be kept together.

Over half a century later I still remember Mrs. Norman, superintendent of the Scioto County Children's Home, with a mixture of awe and dread. It's possible she would be surprised to know that her name evoked panic fear among the

Little Boys and she would surely be surprised to learn that we believed she had an electric paddle that she used on runaways and other offenders. Some of the Little Boys had heard it used. They told me so when I arrived in the dorm. The screams of the victims were unforgettable, they said, agony in the middle of the night. I believed in the Great Electric Paddle as sincerely as I then believed in Santa Claus.

Even a six-year-old could see that Inez Norman stood out from everyone else on the Home staff though she was only of average height. Mrs. Norman was austere, patrician in her posture and attitude. Her carriage was erect, her manner businesslike, her speech precise. She wore rimless glasses and no makeup. Her hair was black and gray and pulled away from her face with a severe bob in the back. She seemed to possess a natural gift for authority that could be heard in her voice and felt in her very presence. Had she been a man it would have been easy to imagine her as an infantry colonel. Some of the children found her snooty and some found her menacing.

Mrs. Norman was hired as superintendent in January of 1940 and must often have felt burdened by her responsibility for the care of one hundred and fifty orphaned or abandoned children with inadequate funds and staff. For this responsibility she was paid $85.00 per month, about $1,000 in today's dollars. She was not given a vacation in 1940 or 1941 and the board had to hold a special meeting to grant her a vacation in 1942. Whatever difficulties she had in providing for the needs of the children with the county board of supervisors or the county auditor, who held the purse strings tight, she did not complain. She did what she needed to do, however much she disliked going to local merchants and civic organizations to beg for donations of shoes and clothing for the children. The staff was even more poorly paid than she was. Our Mrs. McKenzie earned $41.80 a month in 1941, or $535 in today's dollars. True, she had a bedroom at the Home and ate there, but she was also on duty 24 hours a day except for her one day off each week.

In the late spring of 1942 Mrs. McKenzie said to me,

"Mrs. Norman wants to see you this evening."

Her announcement so unnerved me I didn't think to ask why Mrs. Norman wanted to see me. I knew at once I was in serious trouble. Mrs. Norman's office was directly across from the Little Boys dorm, separated only by a door and a narrow hall. Only weeks before, still awake one night, I had heard doors opening and closing but could see only the light that leaked under our door from the hall and could hear only the murmur of a late night conversation. Later I heard whacks and howls of pain. The boy in the bunk next to me whispered "yeah" when I asked him if he could hear them too. That night reinforced my belief in the Great Electric Paddle.

Since I had never been called to appear before the Chief Official Electric Paddler and was fearful of Mrs. Norman, I was sure I had graduated into the ranks of the Home's major culprits and would, for some offense I had unknowingly committed, soon meet my doom. The mere thought of the Great Electric Paddle defeated my normal stratagem of controlling fear by thinking pleasant thoughts. The more I tried to shove the Electric Paddle to the back of my mind, it more it pushed its way to the front of my brain, demanding attention.

All day, as if preparing for confession, I consulted my memory again and again, thinking of every act and everything I had said in the past few weeks that could possibly have come under the gaze of the all-seeing eyes and all-hearing ears of Inez Norman. Was there anything I had done that justified the use of the Electric Paddle? I could not think of anything. But I was not relieved.

I was so upset I could not eat supper and there was no danger I would fall asleep as did the other boys after 9 PM on the fateful night of my meeting with Mrs. Norman. I kept my clothes on and waited, washed and combed, as Mrs. McKenzie had asked me to do, waiting to be called by Mrs. Norman.

I waited and waited and waited. Finally I was told to walk across the hall to Mrs. Norman's office. When I arrived she was standing, her back to me, opening boxes. Her office was warm and pleasant.

"Come here, Dickie," she said. "I think you need some new shoes."

She motioned me to come over and sit on a chair and she leaned over, as if she were a clerk in a store, and asked me to place my foot in the first of a series of donated shoes. She found a pair that she thought fit me reasonably well. I liked them. They were medium brown and came up around my ankles like boots. The fresh new leather smelled warm and good. My mood shifted immediately. Not only was I not to be beaten with the Great Electric Paddle. I was to have a handsome new pair of shoes.

Back in the dormitory I placed my new shoes on the floor at the side of my cot and took off my pants and shirt in the dark and climbed into bed. I leaned over the side of my cot and looked down at my beautiful new shoes. I could just make them out in the light that leaked under the door from the hall. I stroked them with my hand a couple of times, pulled the covers over me and fell asleep at once to dream about shoes. The first thing that popped into my consciousness when I awoke in the morning was my new brown shoes. I leaned over my cot to look at them. There they were, as handsome as I remembered them. I lifted one onto the cot and ran my hand against the soft brown leather and then smelled its clean fragrance. I was almost as happy with my new shoes as I had been with the red dump truck.

The foot path to our school ran along the main road on the northern shore of the Ohio River. The path was a zone of freedom for escape from the boredom of the Home but also a wilderness we had to dart through when threatened by the Home's bullies. We had only our alertness and speed to avoid being caught and tormented. Otherwise we dallied along the path, stopping to chase the first garter snake of spring or join a snowball fight in winter or just meandering, reluctant to end our brief sojourn in freedom. Our feet seemed heavier as we trudged back to the Home.

Sometimes the path was a war zone filled with ambushers behind hedges and wide tree trunks. We younger boys tried to enlist champions to protect us. One autumn afternoon a bully caught me alone and beat me because I had refused his demand to surrender my favorite dessert, apple brown betty. He was finishing the job as he grabbed my hair and ground my face into the cinders on the path when, suddenly, he was off me. When I looked around a much older boy I knew only by sight was holding my attacker by the scruff of his neck, shaking him, and telling him to never do that to me again.

The older and bigger boy turned out to be Dutch, who then befriended me and Billy, walking with us to school most days and often giving each of us in turn rides on his shoulders. Dutch had a pug nose and the body of a wrestler. I am not sure why Dutch took a special interest in Billy and me. He was probably 16 or 17 years old at the time, already a young man. Nothing was said but everyone understood that Dutch had become our protector and that anyone who tried to harm us would have to face him. I knew immediately the value of this new connection. I would no longer have to fear bullies, give up food in the dining room, or surrender any of the other meager privileges I had to older or bigger boys. Dutch provided me the kind of protection the supervisors in the children's home could not.

In April 1942, Charlie came down with pneumonia and was taken by ambulance to Mercy Hospital in Portsmouth. Penicillin was not yet available but Charlie survived. Edna Abele wrote in her journal on April 10, 1942 that our mother had married Lloyd Vandelier nine months after abandoning the four of us to the children's home. She and her new husband "recently visited the institution and stated that they hoped to take the children at a later date when they 'got on their feet financially.'" The name or names from Edna Abele's next sentence were among those excised from the case files I obtained in 1998 and one of the few I found impossible to decipher. The sentence reads, "Superintendent suggested that they take only (blank)."

Edna Abele also noted in her journal that our mother had told her Charlie had been rejected by Lonnie. "Mother felt that it wasn't because he wasn't bright, but he did not seem to have the abilities of the other children." Ironically, Charlie was the brightest of us all. His IQ was tested by Persis Simmons at over 140. Charlie was the first of the four of us to go out of the Home on an extended stay with prospective adoptive parents, in this case our mother's brother and Charlie's namesake, Charles Wesley McNelly, and his wife, Elizabeth. Charlie was four years old when he left the Home in the custody of this uncle. When he was returned to the Home after six months Edna Abele noted, "His back showed evidence of a severe whipping, and the boy himself did not want to return." Aunt Mary told me she suspected the severe whippings were administered more than once over six months, which Uncle Charles later more or less confirmed.

In April I began a series of weekends in the summer home of juvenile judge Vernon Smith as a companion to the Smith's only son. Edna Abele noted, "Dick adjusted so nicely the judge said he hoped to be able to have him in his home every weekend." On June 2, I joined Judge Smith and his family for the summer.

The Smiths' son, for whom I was to be a companion, may have been named Robert. I no longer remember. Robert was a year older than I, taller, had dark brown hair like me, and we got on well at first. I remember Mrs. Smith as a tall, nicely dressed and well-spoken woman who made every effort to make me feel at home. We spent most of our time that summer at the Smith's country place where they kept horses. This was my first experience of the culture and affluence of the upper middle class, which I found exciting after the gray tedium of the Home. During those first weekends we were all on our best behavior and worked hard to please each other.

The center of the Smith's country place was a large white 19th century farm house, trimmed in green, with an enclosed porch at the back. Beyond the porch was a spacious yard and beyond the yard a corral and outbuildings. It was by far the nicest house I had ever lived in and, furnished and decorated as it was by Mrs. Smith with casual elegance, by far the most comfortable. I enjoyed especially the back porch, my favorite reading place, which was furnished with lounge chairs and shaded by large trees that kept it cool on hot summer afternoons. With the house came a dear old female collie named Queenie. I had never been around a family pet before. My biological family had not had animals of any kind except the pigs Lonnie once tried to raise, and there were no pets at the children's home. Handsome black and brown horses with shiny backs grazed within sight of the porch. The farm's caretaker and the judge sometimes led the horses into narrow white travel trailers, probably to show or race them. I had never seen horses before except in books and they frightened me.

I had rarely been in an automobile before the summer with Judge Smith's family and especially enjoyed the drives we made at night as we returned to the city from the country place on Sunday evenings. I enjoyed the feeling of the car's great power as we raced along the highway. I liked watching the play of the car's headlights on the dark bluffs above the Ohio River. I felt warm, safe and content in the back seat of the judge's car. Those were moments when I did not have to worry about what I would say next or about doing the right thing. As the car moved through the dark night all anxiety seemed to leave me and I felt a pleasant, half-conscious emptiness within me, a delightful absence of myself.

There were other new experiences at the Smiths. Half a dozen different dry cereals were set out on the breakfast table each morning. Toast was made. Eggs and bacon were available on request. Radio was not entirely new to me but there was no radio at the children's home, as there were no movies at the children's home. At the Smiths, the radio was on most of the day, music and news and serial soaps in the morning sponsored by Oxydol and Rinso White laundry powders for Mrs. Smith, and adventure series in the late afternoon, The Lone Ranger and Tom Mix, for Rob and me. I had my first haircuts in a real barber shop while at the Smiths.

Edna Abele noted early that summer that "Dick went to Judge Smith's to spend the summer. From all reports he is getting along very nicely." But weekends trips and being together day in, day out, are as different as dating and marriage. The first clue to what was likely to go wrong was in Edna Abele's original note that the judge was seeking a companion for his son. That was the primary motivation of the Smiths, though I don't blame them for thinking that everyone's interests would be served by such an arrangement. In some degree they were. But for the Smiths I was a means to fill a perceived need of their son, not wanted for myself. Midway through the summer I think we all realized that Rob and I were not getting on. He was an only child used to having his own way and I, the oldest child of four, liked to claim the same privilege. But there was a bigger problem. While I can no longer recall specific incidents, Rob would take or break something, finger me as the culprit, and when it was a case of my word against his, his version was accepted without question as true. I was probably naive to think that the Smiths would accept my side of the story, a boy whose family history would at the least suggest I had a defective understanding of honesty and perhaps even a proclivity to steal. Moreover I was an outsider, not a son with whom Judge and Mrs. Smith had shared seven or eight years of life. But my child's sense of right and wrong expected the adult world to treat me justly. Probably nothing offends a child's sharp sense of justice more than the perception he is not being treated fairly by adults.

After two or three attempts to set the record straight with what I knew I had not done, and — in two cases — what I had seen Rob do with my own eyes, I withdrew. I realized this was an unequal struggle I could not win. Rob and I had less and less to do with each other. I spent more and more time alone. I longed for Billy. I even began to miss the children's home. I began to doubt that going to live with strangers could ever be any good for me or for my brothers and sister. During the last weeks that summer I kept company with Queenie, the family's aged collie. She had the habit of lying on hot August mornings under shaded shrubs at the back of the house. I would lie down next to her on my stomach and hang an arm over her shoulder. I talked to her, pouring out my heart. I became much attached to Queenie. I learned that summer the deep joy of companionship with an animal and the consolation they offer when our human relationships are not going well. I returned to the Home at the end of August 1942, a week or so before I began the second grade. Edna Abele's journal records that the following summer I was invited back to spend another summer with the Smiths. I told Mrs. McKenzie I did not want to go.

On June 25 Janey was given a physical exam. It was noted that she, as the rest of us, had had whooping cough in 1941, not long before we were placed in the Home. A month later she and Billy were given their first smallpox immunizations and we were all vaccinated for the first time for diphtheria.

On August 8 Edna Abele noted in her journal that Lonnie had again been arrested for theft. While there's no confirmation in Edna Abele's journal, the McNelly family tells the story of Lonnie arriving — for the first time — at the children's home in the late summer of 1942. The McNellys said he came to visit us with a new blond on his arm, which he introduced to Home authorities as his former wife's sister. When they called Grandmother McNelly for verification, she told them, "She can't be one of my daughters. There are no blondes in our family."

The view of the psychologists that we should be kept together was apparently ignored for Janey, now three years old, was sometimes presented to prospective parents for adoption. Infants and toddlers were highly adoptable and went quickly. Three and four-year-olds for whom Home authorities hoped to find parents were sometimes paraded out on the stage of the chapel for the viewing of interested couples seated in the pews below. Janey remembers being paraded in that fashion and as a young adult dreaded to go into an open room during a reception or cocktail party, afraid she would be stared at. Sometimes nursery children not selected for presentation would wander into the halls or even into the chapel, soliciting the interest of visiting adults, trying mutely to persuade someone to take them home. It was our good fortune that Janey, a darling blond when she was well, was not taken, likely because at age three she was often ill and her speech was almost impossible to understand. That would frighten most prospective parents away.

On October 15, 1942, Abbie Hawk, supervisor of Ohio child welfare services in Columbus, sent a hand-written memo to Mrs. Norman. "If these youngsters test up high enough and if you can get a permanent commitment on them," there is a family that will take "all three of them" It is not clear why Abbie Hawk didn't write four instead of three, but presumably because she had earlier been told Charlie was going to be permanently placed with our Uncle Charles and Aunt Elizabeth. There is no more mention of this potential adoption in the case file. In the same handwritten memo Hawk suggested to Mrs. Norman, "If I were you, I would get the permanent commitment just as soon as possible." This is the first reference in our case files to changing our legal status to a permanent commitment, which would make us available for adoption.

I dreaded the end of the school year. Except for a field day organized by the American Legion on July 4th, which included an exciting bus ride to see fireworks, there were no organized summer activities at the children's home. No trips to swimming pools, no camps, no sports. It's now hard to believe that in the early 1940s the Scioto County Children's Home did not even have sports equipment for us to play with. No bats. No baseballs or softballs and certainly no baseball gloves. No basketballs or basketball hoops. No footballs. Not even a kickball, a game we could have played so easily on the Concrete. There was no sports equipment at the Home until the late 1940s when a new superintendent allowed the boys to go into the community to mow lawns and do odd jobs. Since they were not allowed to keep the money they had earned, they asked that what they earned be used to buy communal sports equipment.

Boys above the age of nine dreaded the end of the school year for another reason. When school was out the older boys had to begin mowing with hand sickles, on their hands and knees, three wide terraces on steep banks in front of the children's home building, and the grassy swards that stretched 500 feet to the entry drive. In addition, they mowed the weeds and grass in the old orchard and on the playgrounds and the borders along the driveway down to route 52. Their hands were full of blisters and their backs sunburned the first week or two, but the boys were soon as brown as berries and their palms as tough as cowhide. Stroke by stroke, they swung their sickles, keeping the blade low and parallel to the ground to get a good cut. Every day but Sunday, all day, all summer, they mowed the three terraces and the borders of the entry drive and the orchards with their sickles. They started as soon as breakfast was over and continued until about 4 PM unless the heat became unbearable. They hoped for rainy days when they would not have to sickle grass. But when the rains came the grass grew faster. So then they hoped it wouldn't rain. They were freed of the sweaty drudgery of hand mowing the Home's terraces for another year only when school began.

Those of us under nine worked at creating our own activities and sometimes unusual opportunities arose. In the late summer of 1942 someone dumped a truck load of used lumber in the lower orchard behind the Home. The boards, of various lengths and widths, were all askew and most were weathered gray. Many of the boards had rusty nails. The pile seemed a great mountain of wood to six to eight-year-olds, but was probably not more then five feet high and perhaps 15 feet wide and 25 feet long. This wood pile became the center of interest for the Little Boys for a month or so because it provided exactly the kind of activity that boys of almost any age enjoy. Building!

After a few boards had been pulled from the pile and used in various forms of play, a pair of older boys discovered that by burrowing down into the pile and pushing the boards around, they could eventually arrange them into walls that created small pits or caves just big enough for two boys to sit on the floor in comfort. The rest of us paired off, staked a claim on a section of the wood pile, and set to work. We discovered that our spaces opened up in the pile of boards could be made deep enough that it was possible to put a roof of boards on our small dwellings, as a pot covers a kettle. These roof boards were attached with nails scavenged from the pile and carefully straightened and hammered in with rocks. As a refinement we scrounged some waste cardboard and covered the inside floor and walls and even the ceiling of our dwellings with that, which created a cozy space protected from the winds. Soon the wood pile was pocked with dwellings of various shapes and depths. The most desirable spots in the pile were in the center where it was highest and therefore, the dwelling could be deepest and most spacious. Young boys ceded these to older and stronger boys and chose areas closer to the edges of the wood pile.

In this enjoyable activity we seemed to be following primal human urges older than recorded history as we created warm and comfortable nests against the approaching winter winds. We were also building tiny rooms as substitutes for the homes of our dreams we so longed for and did not have. And once within our little space, which I sometimes occupied alone, we could have two of the rarest experiences of our children's home, privacy and solitude. Building that little cave with another boy whose name I no longer recall was one of my happiest experiences. As long as we played quietly we were allowed to build our dwellings without any adult supervision at all. To our dismay, the following spring a truck came in and hauled the wood pile away.

In October, 1942, Edna Abele noted in her journal she had sent letters to the Boy's Industrial School, the Ohio State Reformatory, and the London prison farm asking about Lonnie's "physical and mental condition, adjustment, etc." She wrote that such information about the father "would help us in an understanding of the children."

In November, Persis Simmons returned once more to the Home for a field clinic. This second round of Stanford-Benet exams produced higher results, especially for Charlie who was seriously ill during the first round and for me, who took the second round of tests with more confidence. Even so, Persis wrote of me, "He made practically no spontaneous comments. He responded only when he felt very sure of himself." The Simmons reports on the four of us again noted the unusual strength of our ties to each other and our mutual dependence. She concluded, "When the children play together there seems to be an unusual spirit of cooperation in the group. Although each is dependent upon the others for emotional security, no one child dominates the group." She found it unusual to see how each one of us would show the others how to do something without actually doing the task for them. Despite Janey's IQ result of 133 Simmons noted, "She has not yet learned to talk correctly. Her speech is similar to baby talk." Simmons concluded Janey would learn to talk if she were placed with a family where she heard correct speech.

On December 9, Edna Abele again wrote the superintendent of the London prison farm, this time asking about Lonnie's whereabouts. She had heard he had violated his parole granted in 1941 and was back in prison. She wrote that because the consensus was that our mother was an "inadequate person," considerable thought was being given to adoption placement for us. Edna wanted Lonnie's views on the matter and asked prison authorities to discuss it with him.

A few days later, on December 13, my Grandmother McNelly died at age fifty-nine of a heart attack. The family decided not to tell me of her death and decided the four of us should not attend the funeral. I remember being told of grandma's death but not by my family. Perhaps Edna Abele or Inez Norman told me. I was much attached to my Grandmother McNelly but I do not remember grieving her, perhaps because a few days later a new development overwhelmed me.

With few exceptions, I have no memories of visits my mother made to the children's home. Aunt Mary years later confirmed such occasions were rare and told me that grandmother McNelly had frequently pressed Eunice to see us more often. But I will never forget my mother's last visit in December of 1942, made while she was in Sciotoville for Grandmother's funeral. She surprised me by arriving accompanied by a new baby, whom she carried wrapped in a fluffy white blanket. As I had not been told by anyone in the family of Grandmother's death, I had not been told my mother had a new baby.

Our meetings with family members took place in the chapel. I remember sitting in a pew on my mother's right side, the only one of Lonnie's four living children present during that interview. I could not see the new baby's face and did not want to. There are moments in life that transform our future that pass almost unnoticed, their significance appearing days or months or even years later. There are other moments

89

whose full significance bursts in on us at once to make us aware our lives will never be the same again. This was such a moment for me. I sat silently as my mother talked. I was still as a cat but my mind was in chaos. I was on fire with jealousy and resentment. Here she was with a new baby, which could only mean she would have even less time and concern for me and Billy and Charlie and Janey. She was with a new husband who did not look anything like me, which had ended my dream that she and Lonnie, the father I still loved, would be together again. Whatever she was saying I did not hear. Whatever she was telling me made no difference. The baby she was holding in the white blanket, the man she was with, said it all. I knew too well what this strange new man and new baby wrapped in the fluffy white blanket meant for me and for my brothers and sister. I could not let this bad news in all at once. I slammed shut the door to my inmost being. I could not face this. Not all at once. Not yet.

Only weeks later did I dare reopen the door, just a crack, to begin to let the bad news soak into the depths of my being. I would guess that's normal during emotional shock. It's as if we have a door within that opens to only as much reality as we can bear at any given moment. Eventually this new reality sank in and the invisible bonds to my mother, already stretched by her neglect and indifference, snapped. The emotional ties frayed by her abandonment of us to a county children's home came loose. I realized I no longer had a mother. I did not lose my mother in an instant, as some children do through accidental death, but I had lost her just the same. Perhaps it was more like children who lose their mothers slowly to cancer and in one sense it was worse, because I had to live with the knowledge that she was still alive but was unavailable.

Mothers and fathers can destroy the natural love and attachment of a child, the love that asks only that mothers and fathers be there and for nothing else. If parents fail often enough, disappoint often enough, hurt often enough, the trusting love of a child given without any questions asked can finally begin to shrivel and die. But I had not given up on Lonnie. He remained, despite all his failings, my father. Why did I continue to feel love for Lonnie and not Eunice? The social work case files I obtained in 1998 held one answer to my question. Once out of prison Lonnie wanted, as I did, to reunite our family. Eunice did not. A second answer to my question was what Aunt Mary told me in an interview a few years ago. Before he went to prison, she said, "He took good care of you kids. He really did."

The death of my grandmother and my mother's last visit were my final memories in 1942. I have no recollection of Christmas that year at all. In the days and weeks that followed, amidst the bleak routines of the Home, I was trying to adjust to the loss of my grandmother and my mother. My mother was no longer present in my thoughts about the future. I began to think I was now old enough to become the protector and nurturer of my younger brothers and sister. Waiting for me around the corner of January 1943, however, was another threat.

Final Trials

Scarlet fever struck three-year-old Janey in February 1943. When her soaring temperature caused her to convulse, an ambulance rushed Janey to Mercy Hospital in downtown Portsmouth. Scarlet fever was followed by pneumonia and then by inflammation of Janey's urinary bladder. Pus accumulated in her lungs. She hovered near death for weeks but eventually began to recover. She was released from the hospital at the end of March, the same month and the same hospital ward in which our older sister, Nola Mae, had died.

In early 1943, Kline Dawson and his wife, Alice, arrived to take charge of the Big Boys and Big Girls dormitories. Kline Dawson also supervised us in the Little Boys dormitory on

Wednesdays when Mrs. McKenzie took her one day off each week. On Wednesday evenings we ran down to Route 52 to wait for Mrs. McKenzie to step off the bus and danced around her joyfully. Her return signaled the end of another miserable day under Kline Dawson. We dreaded Wednesdays.

Dawson, a retired postal worker in his 60s, moved about with a blond wood crutch under his left arm, possibly the result of years of carrying heavy mail bags. Because he disliked sunlight his face was sickly white, as was the bald patch on his crown, an albino island surrounded by gray crew-cut hair. Kline Dawson did not laugh and rarely smiled. He never placed his hand kindly on a boy's shoulder to give a word of encouragement. Sometimes he dropped his blond wood crutch to the ground to grab a boy within reach by the arm. Like a predator Dawson would pull his victim to his left side and strike him across the face with his open right hand, on one finger of which he wore a bulging Masonic ring. We lived in fear of Kline Dawson and came to believe he hated us just because we were Little Boys.

As soon as warmer weather arrived in the early spring of 1943, Dawson began taking us on hikes through the woods on the south side of the Home property. He was assisted by one or two high school students from the Big Boys dormitory. We did what boys love to do: run along paths in the April sunshine, yell to celebrate the arrival of spring, chase butterflies and hunt for tadpoles. Our joy was short-lived when, during the day, one of us would offend some unknown rule of the Dawson code. This included straying off the path or playfully scuffling. Dawson would then order us back to the old apple orchard to set up a switching gauntlet, a disciplinary innovation of his own creation.

While he leaned on his blond wood crutch, Dawson sent his high school assistants to cut long branches and when they returned, he and they positioned themselves across from each other, four or five feet apart, forming a gauntlet through which we had to run. In our fear, time stopped. The orchard hardly existed. In our fear, we could see nothing but Kline Dawson and his lieutenants in two rows waiting for us, swaying their long black switches back and forth low to the ground. Anxious, stamping our bare feet in place, we took turns running as fast as we could the ten yards or so to where our tormentors stood. If we ran fast enough we felt the switch lashes only half a dozen times. Once through the gauntlet we looked back to see pale-faced Kline Dawson, swinging his switch in broad arcs, leering at the other victims as, one by one, they ran the gauntlet. We rubbed the purple welts and our sometimes bleeding legs to ease the sting.

On another occasion, a Wednesday when Kline Dawson was ill, his wife Alice substituted for Mrs. McKenzie. We were all gathered in the first floor bathroom. Alice Dawson was the double of the wife in Grant Wood's American Gothic painting except that Alice had a glare that girls in her dormitory said could whither daffodils and turn boys to stone. She spent part of her days hiding behind curtains and doors to observe us secretly, looking for infractions of the Home's rules or misbehavior she could have her husband punish. We called her "the spy."

On this occasion Alice pointed a long crooked forefinger at a spot on the wall less than a foot in circumference from which plaster had fallen. We all knew the plaster had been falling for weeks, bit by bit, dislodged as we reached up to pull our toothbrushes off little brass hooks with our names above them. We stood silently, eyes cast down or raised to the ceiling, as Alice Dawson harangued us. Our legs began to ache from standing. Alice ranted on with the tenacity of an inquisitor, determined to identify the guilty. Such interrogation eventually leads to doubts. Maybe I was guilty, I thought. Not that I had kicked all the plaster off the wall, but I could well have dislodged a piece as I reached up the wall for my toothbrush. The possibility that I might have had something to do with the fallen plaster was not strong enough to make me admit responsibility, however. I feared admission of any guilt at all would mean punishment by Kline Dawson, for whom Alice lovingly reserved the pleasure of disciplining errant small boys. Then she threatened us with a switching gauntlet. Suddenly, to my utter surprise, my hand rose in the air as if someone else was controlling it and I heard myself saying, "I did it." I immediately felt isolated and embarrassed to become the center of attention. To this day I do not know why my hand suddenly developed an independent will of its own, but it was not to spare the other boys in an act of self-lessness. The greater surprise was that Alice Dawson did not turn me over to her husband-executioner. She made me stand in the hall facing the wall for 30 minutes, the lightest possible sentence in the Home for any offense.

Nine of us in the Little Boys dormitory had infected holes in our tonsils and a morning of surgery was set for late August so that we would have a week or so to heal before school resumed. Our anxiety grew as some of the beds were removed from the dormitory floor to create space for the movement of a gurney and a recovery area. Newer sheets were provided for our beds. A chubby red-haired nurse with freckles and a white hat bounced about and two pretty young women, volunteers from Wheelersburg, moved from bed to bed to reassure us. We were showered and waiting when the chubby red-haired nurse burst into the room to tell us the doctor had been called to an emergency. The operations were rescheduled for the following week.

Again we prepared, were showered, waiting, and anxious. I could feel waves of anxiety surge through my body and worked to control my fear. I was number five or six of a dozen in line for the gurney ride down the hall to meet with Dr. Tunis Nunemaker in the Home's small hospital room. The chubby red-haired nurse pushed the gurney with boy number one out of the dorm and down the hall. After 15 minutes or so he returned, pale and motionless, but still alive, his slicked-down blond hair mostly in place. The second boy disappeared down the hall. He, too, looked more or less normal when he returned. The powerful smell of ether wafted through our dormitory. The third boy returned with a single line of bright red blood that had trickled down from his mouth to his neck. I searched the face of the redheaded nurse. She looked concerned. I felt a new surge of anxiety rise within me. The fourth boy had an even wider line of blood that ran all the way down his neck. I figured he was a goner. My fear rose. Somebody had to stop Dr. Tunis Nunemaker before he mortally wounded any more boys! And I was next!

By this time the first boys to return from the dispensary were emerging from the ether. They moaned. Frightful sounds. Some of them were coughing and spitting up blood into porcelain receptacles held against their cheeks by the pretty young women volunteers. By now the smell of ether was so strong it made me nauseous. The young woman by my bed began to prepare me for transfer to the gurney. My hour had come. The red-haired nurse and the young woman lifted me onto the gurney and wheeled me down the hall. I looked up at the high ceiling, momentarily forgetting my fear as I discovered how different the world looks from a gurney. Then I was in a small room surrounded by Dr. Nunemaker in a white gown and the red-haired nurse, peering down at me and asking how I felt. I lied and said I was fine.

Dr. Nunemaker smiled as he put an apparatus for administering the ether over my mouth and throat. As the ether was poured from a can, he asked me to count backwards from 100. I saw flashing lights and began to hear high pitched sounds. Then I went on a trip in and out of semi-consciousness. My dreams were vivid, about knives and killing. When I awoke later in the dorm all I could feel was the local pain of a sore throat. I was alive! I was still alive! I was so happy to be alive that I smiled despite the raw pain in my throat. When I looked around all the other boys were still alive, even the ones that had had streams of blood oozing out of their mouths. I relaxed and began to enjoy the special care and attention we were getting.

The Decision to Free Us

In June of 1943, Lois Smith, our case worker in the New Boston office, and Edna Abele began a series of family interviews to determine if anyone in our birth families was willing to provide a home for us. Smith interviewed our maternal grandfather in Sciotoville, the uncle my brother Charlie had stayed with in Columbus, and Eunice and her new husband, Lloyd Vandelier, also in Columbus. There are no interviews in the file of the Boggs side of our biological family. It is possible Lonnie's brothers and our grandfather, Harry Boggs, had so little interest in us they turned away requests to discuss our future. Lois Smith later wrote for a court report: "An effort will be made to contact the paternal relatives regarding the adoption question, but there has been little or no interest evidenced in the children from this side of the family." Her statement is easy to verify. With the single exception of Lonnie's aborted attempt in early 1942 to visit us with a new blond on his arm — a story told among the McNellys — there is nothing in family lore or the case files to indicate that any member of the Boggs family ever visited us at the children's home. A few years ago a rediscovered birth cousin wrote me that when he and his brothers and sister were left at the same children's home in 1943, no one on the Boggs side of their family ever visited them.

My Grandfather McNelly, now a widower at age 64, was much as Smith remembered him; tall, thin, nicely dressed, with a full shock of white hair which he kept neatly combed. To begin the interview Smith reminded him she had been in his home once before, the day his four grandchildren were taken to the children's home. My grandfather said he did not remember her or the occasion, which surprised Smith. She asked for his help and counsel in determining what plans should be made for the future of his grandchildren. He remembered they were all fine youngsters. He said he had heard Janey was quite an object of interest during the month she was so ill in Mercy Hospital. But he had not visited her during her illness.

Asked if adoption had been considered for the children, he told Smith the family, "was not favorably disposed." Lois Smith was on the mark when she wrote in her court report a month later that Grandpa McNelly, "had always given the impression of being dominated by his wife," and "would probably oppose the adoption placement if his daughter was opposed."

Later in June Smith found Uncle Charles in a working class neighborhood of small single cottages in Columbus, Ohio. Aunt Elizabeth met Smith at the door and told her if she was going to ask them to take one of us, her visit "was of no use." Elizabeth called Uncle Charles, then 29, to the door. Smith described Uncle Charles as, "a nice-looking man with light brown hair, blue eyes, and even teeth. He was quiet and deliberate in his speech." Lois Smith began the interview by saying that the children should not be made to live in an institution forever. "The question is, whether you and other members of your family and their father's family will take responsibility for them, or if the children should be adopted."

Uncle Charles told Smith he thought both parties, Eunice and Lonnie, were responsible for the failure of their marriage. "Lonnie drank and got into trouble with the law. Eunice was willing to bear a man's children but not to look after them. Lonnie was left to do the housework." Smith said she had some question about Eunice's interest in her children. Uncle Charles agreed. "She had an opportunity to keep them, receiving ADC assistance, but that did not work out. Several funny things happened," he said. "She went away for a week and left the children alone. She said she was going to Columbus but the family checked with me and she wasn't here."

When asked about adoption, Uncles Charles told Smith his sister didn't want her children but didn't want anyone else to have them. "She just wants to know where they are. I talked the situation over with my mother several times," Uncle Charles continued. "She was worried because Eunice did not visit her children and did not show any interest in them."

Smith then asked about the six months my brother Charlie had spent with Uncle Charles and Aunt Elizabeth. "If the boy had not been such a problem, we would have him still. Things went well enough at first. He really liked Elizabeth." Uncle Charles paused and looked down at the floor. "But he didn't like me. He didn't seem to be afraid of me. I figured he was homesick for his brothers and sister. He knew his mom was in Columbus. Maybe he figured if he was bad enough, we would send him over to his mom just to get rid of him."

Smith then asked for their evaluation of Charlie. "I'm embarrassed to tell you everything," Uncle Charles said. "He was completely out of our control. I have a pretty severe temper. When my patience is drained for a long time, I can lose control. I was afraid I would really hurt the child. I just don't understand. Charlie was trained to obey and I found his defiance very upsetting." Uncle Charles continued, "We tried to reason with him. We tried to bribe him with ice cream and candy. Nothing worked. But the most difficult thing we had to contend with was he would defecate whenever and wherever it pleased him, including once on the living room carpet. Not in public, mind you, but here in the house."

Charles then said, "We think he is going to turn out to be a criminal, just like his dad. Forging checks and stealing, leaving his job, deserting the army." Smith responded that Charlie had been wounded enough to explain his behavior without attributing the cause to heredity.

Edna Abele interviewed Eunice and her second husband in their two-room apartment in Columbus. Abele described

Lloyd Vandelier as a, "tall, well-built man with rather large, coarse looking features. His manner and speech are brusque," she noted, "bordering on the belligerent."

When asked about the four of us, Vandelier said he wanted the four children, "because he thought a lot of their mother. Those children would much rather be with their mother than in some strange home." Abele commented that not every stepfather would assume the additional burden of four children, particularly when he now had a child of his own. When asked why he hadn't made any contribution to our care and expenses, Vandelier told Abele he could have furnished clothing for the children, but, "they were not going anywhere, anyway, and the county was taking care of them." Abele reported that Eunice said little but sat holding their new baby with a half smile of satisfaction on her face when Vandelier said, "he was not going to stand for the children being placed in another home."

So, our biological family was perfectly happy to put us in a county children's home at taxpayers' expense and forget us, but not willing to have us adopted into a family that would love, nourish, and protect us. Lloyd Vandelier's comment, "They were not going anywhere, anyway, and the county was taking care of them" rather nicely sums up the attitude of our biological family.

Once the social workers and Mrs. Norman agreed the solution for us was adoption, they got word out informally that we would probably be available. They would try to place the four of us in one family but if that proved impossible, they were prepared to place us separately. When they learned that a social worker in Athens, Ohio, thought she might have a home for Janey, Lois Smith began to draft the comprehensive memorandum that would petition the Court to commit us permanently to the Scioto Country Children's Home, "so that adoptive placements can be made. It is anticipated that the mother will oppose this adoption, but, after careful study, it seems doubtful that she can provide care and security for these children."

On September 1, a notice was sent from the Scioto County Juvenile Court to Mrs. Lloyd Vandelier in Muskegon, Michigan. The letter informed her that a court hearing would be held September 10 to make our commitment to Inez Norman of the children's home permanent. Eunice did not respond to the letter. Since this first notice was sent General Delivery, Muskegon, Michigan, the only address she had left with the children's home, and had not been sent by registered mail, a registered letter was sent on September 10. By then Lois Smith had located our mother's current address, 1178 Ransom Street in Muskegon. This second notice informed her that a hearing would be held at 10 AM on September 21. The first notice was in her personal papers years later, which suggests she received both notices. She also did not respond to the second notice before the hearing and it was held without her.

Judge Emory F. Smith signed the order to change our status to a permanent commitment to the Home's superintendent, Inez Norman, on September 21, 1943. Eunice sent a registered response to the court that arrived a day after the hearing, nearly three weeks after she received the first notice and over a week after she received the second. She wrote she was unable to make the trip to Scioto County "because of transportation difficulties." She said she did not want her children adopted and offered to send some clothing and school supplies to the county children's home. This offer to help pay for some clothing and school supplies was the first time she or anyone else in our biological family had offered to contribute to our support.

Our mother's late response seems timed to miss the hearing and yet claim forever after that her children had been "stolen," thus avoiding the truth that she had abandoned us. A similar pattern is common today. In cases in which parental rights are to be terminated, mothers will accept legal language that state their children are being taken from them but not words that suggest they have willingly given them up.

I will be forever grateful to Judge Emory F. Smith of the Juvenile Court of Scioto County for acting promptly and decisively, for bringing an end to our perilous and often unhappy first years of life. Judge Smith freed us for the possibility of a better future. I am grateful my biological mother finally acted, with intention or not, on Grandma McNelly's plea to take care of us, or give us to someone who would. Abandonment is a long adult word that does not fully capture what for a child is a stark and terrifying reality, closer to physical death than to anything else. Too often, once children are out of sight, they are out of the minds of biological parents and biological families. And yet the family's permission for adoption to a better life is often denied.

CHAPTER 5

An Angel Arrives

I N LATE JULY, 1943, Ann Minnis, the child welfare representative in Athens, Ohio, asked for and read Janey's file and then discussed her by phone with Lois Smith in New Boston. When Lois told her Janey had three older brothers, she asked for our case files too. Ann noted frequent references to the unusually strong bonds among us and the recommendation of psychologists and social workers that we be kept together if at all possible. She shook her head as she read through the files, knowing the chance that any couple would adopt four older children was slight.

Ann drove down to Wheelersburg in mid-August to meet us. She wanted to see us herself. She had one couple in mind in Athens, a popular Presbyterian minister and his wife, but they had asked only for a four-year-old girl. She also wanted to begin to prepare us to enter families whose education and values could be unlike anything we had ever known, with the exception of the summer I had lived in the family of Judge Vernon Smith. The files told her we were bright and attractive children but also that we were wounded children, especially Charlie and me. Janey's health was poor. She had nearly died a few months earlier. Ann Minnis also noted in the files that the social workers in Portsmouth and at the Home had recommended that Billy have a neurological examination. She wanted to find out what that was about. Ann worried there might be something that did not appear in the files, a pattern of behavior or some defect that would frighten off prospective adoptive parents. After meeting us, she wondered if potential parents would be dismayed by our ungrammatical speech or offended by the casual use of cuss words we had learned in the children's home. Older girls at the Home had found such words on the lips of four-year-old Janey amusing. Fortunately, Ann thought, anything Janey says will be difficult to understand. She does indeed talk like a baby, Ann said to herself.

Though Ann knew she could not remake us in a few weeks, she could put any unusual or questionable behavior in context. She thought that would reduce the chance we would be rejected. Ann also wanted us to begin to feel at ease with her and, if possible, begin to trust her. She told herself she must be careful in making promises and vowed to herself that she would keep every promise she made to us. Ann was also beginning to realize that if there were families that decided to welcome us into their homes, she would have to deal with me. If, as was likely, she would have to split us up among two or more families, she would somehow have to bring me to accept that as the best solution available, better than staying at the children's home.

To achieve all these objectives Ann hit upon the idea of taking us for rides along the Ohio River and out into Scioto County in her navy blue 1940 Plymouth coupe, a car without a back seat. Putting all four of us in Ann's coupe was only possible if two of us stood in the narrow space behind the front seat. Billy and I volunteered. Then Janey and Charlie could ride in the front seat next to Ann.

I don't remember the first time I met Ann Minnis but I can still see her dimly after all these years. Her hair was auburn, with reddish tints, and she was nice-looking, a short woman an inch or two above five feet. The tone of her conversation was professional, but she was quietly friendly and had a gentle and sympathetic voice. And, yes, I almost forgot, she smelled pretty. I liked that, that she always smelled pretty.

On one of those early rides Billy, ever the mischievous adventurer, discovered a small passage door into the trunk of the coupe on the floor behind the front seat. The opening was just big enough to squeeze through. He, followed by me, climbed into the womb-like chamber of the Plymouth's trunk which was at first totally dark. Once our eyes adjusted, we could just make out each other's form with what light leaked through the passage door. I could see Billy's face more clearly when Ann applied her brakes and the tail lights cast a red glare across the trunk. He looked weird, distorted in such light as if incomplete, and the effect was eerie. Not much later, drawn by the sounds of Billy and me happily playing, Charlie and Janey scrambled over the top of the front seat and down through the passage door to the trunk.

The four of us played in the dark, bumping into each others bodies, tickling, laughing, squealing, and seeing each others faces up close in the glare of the red tail lights when Ann pushed her foot on the brake pedal of the Plymouth coupe. We continued to play in this secure and darkened chamber of our rebirth during the weeks that Ann prepared us to begin a new life. On September 4, 1943, the four of us were given the Kahn test, used to check for syphilis. The results were negative.

After spending a day with us during the last week in August, Ann decided to call the Reverend Fred Luchs and his wife, Evelyn, to see if they were still interested in adopting a child. She learned they were away on vacation until the beginning of September. She had the highly positive foster parent study prepared on the Luchs two years before in her files. Both the Luchs were professionals with advanced degrees, hers in education, his in theology and psychology. Fred Luchs was the youngest son of six children of Swiss immigrants. Evelyn, whose maiden name was Coulter — Scotch-Irish like the McNellys — was the oldest of six children. A niece, Grace Monigold, now a student at Ohio University, lived with them as did other boarding students.

The Luchs had contacted the child welfare office in Athens in 1941, eight years after their marriage, to request a four-year-old girl. Evelyn would soon be 40 and in the 1940s, the general practice was not to accept adoption applications from women over 40. The Luchs application references included two of Evelyn's favorite professors at Ohio University, Dean Gamertsfelder, who the trustees had just named president of the university, and Dean McCracken of the university's College of Education, which at the time was one of the best education colleges in the United States.

Ann called again the first week in September and talked to the Rev. Fred Luchs and, on his suggestion, called his wife, who was attending a New York City conference as a member of the executive board of the National Council of Presbyterian Church Women. Evelyn at first was reluctant. There had been many disappointed hopes. Children they were told were available, were not. Last minute legal difficulties arose in other cases. She did not wish to go through the emotional strain of letting her hopes rise followed by yet another disappointment. Besides, their life was full of professional challenges and despite an occasional complaint — "life is just catapulting me along" — she had once written in her journal, they enjoyed each other and their busy lives. Yet something important was missing — their own child. Evelyn said she would call Ann back the following day after talking with Fred and agreed to meet with Ann when she returned to Athens. Ann said nothing to them at that time about us, our sister's older brothers.

Ann had never met the Luchs, but she knew they were prominent in Athens where he was a youthful and dynamic preacher who drew overflow crowds of students to the First Presbyterian Church. Ann thought all week about how she would handle the meeting and particularly wondered if she should just present Janey, place her first, and then hope that eventually the Luchs would be open to taking at least one of her brothers. She decided she would simply mention the older brothers and tell the Luchs how close the children were and gauge their reaction.

On the day of the meeting Ann immediately liked Evelyn Luchs, who projected warmth and caring. Ann thought at once that Evelyn was a natural mother. She began describing Janey by telling the Luchs that Janey was petite, with blond hair and blue eyes. Ann told the Luchs, "Janey is bright. The Bureau of Juvenile Research in Columbus tested her IQ twice. She had some serious health problems earlier this year, but those seemed to be cleared up. She's a spirited child and she loves to talk but, at four years, I must tell you she is not yet easy to understand. The psychologist who tested her is sure her speech will clear up when she is in a family where she hears correct speech."

Evelyn asked, "How long has she been in the children's home, Ann?"

"Let me look in the folder. Let's see. She arrived in late August 1941. So a little over two years."

"So she was two when she was placed in the Home?"

"That's right, she and her three older brothers."

"Three older brothers?!!" Fred could not hide his surprise.

Evelyn asked, "Where are they, Ann? Have they been adopted?"

"No, they're all together in the children's home. I should add that the social worker and superintendent at the Home tell me the children have an unusually close relationship."

"Tell me more about them."

Ann began, "The children are close in ages, just 15 months apart. Dick is the oldest at seven, almost eight. Bill is six and Charlie five. Like their sister they are bright and attractive children. Bill has light brown hair and blue eyes. Dick and Charles have dark brown hair. They've been through some difficult experiences, but their general health seems to be OK. They look like perfectly normal children."

"But, but," Fred stammered. "Evelyn. We agreed on one little girl. Are you seriously thinking about adopting all four of these children?"

"How many brothers and sisters do you have, Fred?"

"Five. But Evelyn!"

"And how many do I have?"

"Five. But four and all at once? Four children that we've never met?"

"Why not? We've always said we wanted a real family and if we take Janey into our home and hearts, how can we possibly separate her from her brothers?"

Ann beamed inwardly and tried to be helpful. "Well, you don't have to decide today." she said. "You'll have more questions about them and you will want to meet the children first. This is what I propose. I suggest we all meet in Columbus in a week or so. Mrs. Norman will bring the children there and you can spend a day with them. We'll take our meals together and go for walks and perhaps you could take them to the zoo to get to know them better."

Evelyn said, "Columbus is fine, Ann. We can talk dates later."

"Then Columbus it is."

As she left to return to her office, Ann thought that even if Fred and Evelyn Luchs improbably decided to take them all, it would be better to place them one by one to ease the adjustment for all concerned.

On September 27, in a letter to Home superintendent Inez Norman, Ann Minnis confirmed that the Luchs could come from Athens to Columbus to meet us on Friday, October 1. Ann told the superintendent that she had been offered the use of a "very nice hotel apartment" owned by Abbie Hawk, the supervisor of the Columbus welfare office. The children and foster parents could visit in comfort. Also, Ann wrote, "I think there is some advantage in permitting the foster family to talk with the children without either of us being present." She suggested everyone meet at 11:00 am at the Bureau of Juvenile Research, where Billy was scheduled for a neurological examination, and from that point the four children would be left in Ann's care until it was time for Mrs. Norman to drive them back to Wheelersburg.

Ann suggested that we could all go immediately to the apartment and have sandwiches and milk shakes brought up. "However, since I promised the children a meal in a restaurant, I think we should carry through with the restaurant plan." Ann told Mrs. Norman that she had been giving a lot of thought to the order of placement of the children, "should the children and foster parents want to follow through after meeting each other." She said she wanted to talk very frankly with . . . . about it. (Here the name had been completely whited out in the record and I have not been able to determine who she meant.)

Ann proposed to Mrs. Norman that on this first visit, "No definite arrangements should be made, but an opportunity be provided for the parties involved to get acquainted and then both have a period of time to think about it."

Mrs. Norman's response the following day, in her formal style, confirmed she would bring us to Columbus on Friday, October 1, and agreed it would be better for us all to meet without her being present. Then she added, "If you will permit me to make a suggestion on the matter, it would be that the children meet them in a way that their names (the Luchs) would not be brought back into the Institution. That would offer further protection to both parties which I believe we both realize is very important."

I have vivid memories of that visit to Columbus because I had never been in a hotel or visited a large, throbbing city with honking yellow taxis. Crisp fine linen table cloths and napkins and grand silver-colored table service were a novelty for us. I had never leaned back in a hotel armchair to gaze in wonder at the high ceilings full of white plaster moldings and huge golden chandeliers, nor walked on plush carpets so thick and soft I could fall on them and not be hurt at all. Nor had I ever been in an elevator. The one in the hotel was manually operated by a woman in a dark blue uniform. She held a brass handle and a brass arrow moved along a semi-circle to indicate the floor. The hotel and my dormitory at the Home had in common only the steam-heated radiators that clanged and hissed in the early morning.

I am quite sure we stayed overnight in Abby Hawk's apartment the night before the October 1 meeting with the Luchs. I had never heard sirens in the night streets before, which frightened me at first. Too excited by this new world to fall asleep early, I watched the bright lights of downtown Columbus through our windows and the patterns of flashing red and yellow neon signs against the walls of the hotel bedroom.

I was startled by the crowds on the wide sidewalks and was thrilled to see dozens of uniformed men, soldiers in khaki and sailors in blue bell bottoms and white caps, often in groups of three and four. America was at war. I particularly admired the boots of the paratroopers that I called high tops, and wondered if the servicemen knew that every morning at the Home I sang "Anchors Aweigh" and "Caissons Go Rolling Along."

The Luchs arrived in Columbus mid-morning on October 1 and we were introduced to them in the small living room of Abby Hawk's hotel apartment. Mrs. Luchs was rather short, just a little taller than Ann Minnis. She was small boned and buxom. The first thing I saw was her smile. Then I noticed her face was a perfect oval, her facial features regular and delicate, her eyes deep brown, her hair dark brown like mine and pulled back from her face. The face of Reverend Luchs was broad and square with a heavy brow above steel blue eyes. He parted his light brown hair in the middle and combed it back to the sides which covered most of the beginnings of a receding hairline.

Ann and Mrs. Luchs talked easily together. After a few minutes of conversation we all rode down in the carpeted elevator with the woman in the dark blue uniform to the hotel dining room for the restaurant meal Ann had promised us. All I remember about the lunch is the high ceilings of the dining room and the sugar bowls. These were stuffed with individually wrapped packets of sugar which we had never seen. Sugar was rationed in 1943 except, it seemed, in hotels. We asked permission and then stuffed all our pockets, front and back, full of sugar packets to take with us back to the Home.

Only Janey wasn't having a good time. She cried a lot during the lunch and Ann tried to console her. After lunch Janey continued to whimper and after ten or fifteen minutes at the zoo later that afternoon, Fred Luchs said out of our hearing to Evelyn Luchs, "The boys are OK but we're not going to take that little girl. She doesn't have all her marbles."

At the zoo we boys spent most of the afternoon running excitedly from cage to cage. Not long before we left the zoo, Evelyn, who was sitting with Janey on a green bench still comforting her, said, "Janey, why don't you go put your hand in his hand?" indicating her husband, Reverend Luchs. Without any hesitation Janey stopped crying and ran up behind him and stuck her tiny hand in his. He, surprised to find her there, closed his hand slowly around hers. "When I saw her," Evelyn would later recall, "hanging onto his hand as her blue eyes looked adoringly up into his face, I knew he was hooked." From that moment on, whatever he had said about her missing marbles, Janey became his little girl.

"Well, what do you think?" Ann asked the Luchs while she and the Luchs drove back to Athens.

Evelyn said, "Oh, Ann, they're such lovely children. We can't wait to see them again."

"Well, talk it over and let me know what you decide."

"We already have," Evelyn replied. "We want them all, Ann. Bring them back to us soon."

That night Evelyn sat for a few moments on the edge of her bed pondering the events of a busy day while her husband went down to the study to work on his sermon. As she looked up at the framed print of Fra Angelico's Annunciation she had kept next to her bed for many years, she felt a deep joy in her heart.

Ann Persuades Me

Early the next week Ann returned to Wheelersburg. The hardwoods of the southeast Ohio hills had just begun to reveal their glory. Great yellow hickory trees, red and brown oaks, red maples, covered the hillsides and giant white sycamores with yellow leaves lined the river banks. She stopped for coffee at a diner in Jackson, Ohio. There was one more hurdle she thought as she sipped her coffee, one more person she had to convince to move forward to placement and possible adoption. Dickie.

That afternoon as I returned with Dutch and Billy to our dorm from school, Mrs. McKenzie told me that Superintendent Norman wanted to see me. She didn't say Mrs. Minnis. She said Mrs. Norman. My reaction to a summons of Mrs. Norman remained an instant wave of fear based on my undying belief in the Great Electric Paddle. I conducted a quick review of my recent behavior but found nothing that might bring me to Mrs. Norman's attention. What was I forgetting? This question nagged at me as Mrs. McKenzie said:

"Go over now, Dickie."

I walked into the hall and stood along the wall outside Mrs. Norman's door. My heart thumped in the silence. Light leaked into the hallway from under the door to Mrs. Norman's office. I could hear women talking but I could not understand what they were saying. In the distance children shouted on the playground and late summer cicadas wailed.

I was counting the hall's polished brown floor boards when the door opened and Mrs. Norman, a rare broad smile on her face, came out with Mrs. Minnis. "Mrs. Minnis has some good news for you," Mrs. Norman said, and turned and walked back into her office and closed the door.

Mrs. Minnis was dressed in a blue suit and her short auburn hair, as always, was nicely combed. She still smelled pretty. I could tell she was nervous. Perhaps it was because she wanted nothing to go wrong as she closed in on what she saw as a heaven-sent opportunity. She still could not quite believe the Luchs wanted to begin the process of adoption as foster parents at once and wanted to welcome all four of us into their home.

Her voice was soft and gentle. She began by asking me if I knew what it was to be adopted and I said I did. I said I had lived one summer with Judge Smith's family and that had not worked out. Besides, I wanted all four of us to be together in the same family.

I also was nervous, my tongue sticking to the roof of my mouth. She told me the Luchs liked us a lot and wanted to be our foster parents. "There is a good chance they will adopt you, once and for always." she said.

"All of you," she smiled. "The four of you together. Isn't that wonderful?!"

Then she talked about the Luchs, their large brick house of many rooms and the pretty college town they lived in a few hours by car from Wheelersburg. She said we would be going to a good school, a university-sponsored school. She said Mrs. Luchs would make a good mother for us. She was a teacher and understood and loved children.

I told Ann I liked school and I liked my teachers.

"Well, then, would you like to go live with the Luchs?"

I was silent but she sensed immediately my reluctance to give my consent. She had been told and believed that my attachment to our biological family was so strong I would resist any placement at all. Edna Abele believed I had declined to return to spend a second summer with Judge Smith's family for that reason.

But I had given up on my mother and Grandma McNelly was dead. With Lonnie it was different. I couldn't get over Lonnie. I still believed he would come back for us. I was reluctant to give up forever the happiness I had once known with my charming father. Despite everything, deep in my heart I was still Lonnie's son, still tied to him by emotions beyond my understanding.

But also in my mind was fear of the unknown and my loss of trust in adults, their behavior and their promises. The adults in my life had let me down. After a bumpy beginning we had become survivors at the Home. Moreover, we had known far worse than the children's home in the sordid Old Gray House on Bahner Road. And in the tenement apartment in South Portsmouth in a neighborhood so bad that my aunts Mary and Martha were afraid to walk there to bring us bags of groceries. What would this new and unknown world bring? Better or worse?

The one place I knew was safe and warm was the children's home. I could count on Mrs. McKenzie and Mrs. Norman, however little time and affection they had to give me. We had learned to live in the county children's home, especially since Dutch had stepped forward to be our protector. Gray and drab and isolating and boring as it was, the Home had become our home. I had no reason to believe the Luchs would be any different from Judge Smith's family or our Uncle Charles and Aunt Elizabeth, who had so abused my brother Charlie.

Ann continued to try to persuade me for another half hour or so and I continued to deny Ann what she wanted so much to hear, a "yes" from me to go live with the Luchs in Athens.

"I'd like you to think about this tonight, Dickie. I hope you'll begin to see this is a good opportunity for all of you."

The next day Ann again drove down from Athens to Wheelersburg. She was already in the hall by 10:00 am and she smiled when she saw me come through the door from the Little Boys dorm and said,

"Well, have you thought about what I said, Dickie? Have you decided?"

"Yes," I said, meaning I had thought about what she had told me. I told her I didn't want us to go. I watched disappointment darken her face.

She said nothing for a moment or two and began rubbing her forehead with an open palm as if collecting her thoughts. When she spoke, she spoke calmly and slowly. I was looking directly at the floor in front of me but I could hear her moving towards me and then I could feel her bearing down on me. I was determined — it had now become a power struggle — to continue resisting her.

"Dickie, how can I make you understand? These are good people. They will take all four of you. You can be together with your brothers and sister in a real family. Forever, Dickie. Don't you see? Do you want to miss this chance for happiness?" I didn't say anything because I did not want to disappoint her and I didn't want to spoil anyone's chance for happiness. I was confused and, feeling upset, I began to cry. I suppose there was a part of me still clinging to the old dream of reunion with Lonnie and Eunice, despite all the neglect and abuse and the evidence since we entered the Home that our biological families did not care what happened to us. I still believed Lonnie would return for us.

Ann walked away from me again down the hall, the heels of her shoes sounding in the silence against the wooden floor. The hall seemed suddenly unfriendly to me. Ann turned and faced the wall opposite me. Again, in the stillness of the hallway, I could hear the shouts of children from the playground. My head was still down, but I could see Ann coming towards me again. I sucked in my breath and held it as she moved near me.

"Dickie, you may go now."

Late that afternoon Mrs. McKenzie told me to go again to the hall to wait for Mrs. Minnis.

Ann greeted me warmly and was, as always, gentle and kind. She had worked patiently for my consent for two days. When, once again, we reached our impasse because I refused to give in, she played her trump card.

"Dickie, I don't want to hurt you, but I believe firmly that what I am going to do is right. For you. For Billy and Charlie and Janey. For the Luchs. For everyone. Mrs. Norman and I have talked this over. We believe this is a wonderful opportunity. If you won't agree to go, then your brothers and sister will go and you will stay at the Home."

"No, No!" I burst out, "You can't do that! You can't do that!" I began to cry.

"Wait!" she said. "Wait!"

Then, while letting the threat stand, she immediately made an offer and a promise. She talked slowly, saying each word clearly.

"I will be visiting you at least once each month during the first year or so you are with the Luchs. We'll go out to dinner and talk, just the two of us. If for any reason you decide living at the Luchs is not right for you and your family, I will see that all of you are returned to the Home."

"You promise?"

She knelt down, put one of my hands in hers, moved her face close to mine and looked me straight in the eyes. She said, "I promise."

I smiled through my tears. "OK. OK."

"Thank you, Dickie, Oh, thank you!" She gave me a little hug and then I went back to the Little Boys dormitory.

I have told the above incident as truly as I can remember it and I remember it well because, even then, I knew it was a big moment in my life. I have marveled over the years at the sensitivity and the patience of Ann Minnis, the midwife of our second birth. Today I can hardly believe that she took the views of a seven-year-old — well, almost eight — so seriously and spent two full days obtaining my consent to leave the Scioto County Children's Home for a new adventure. We were headed to Athens to try living with new foster parents, Fred and Evelyn Luchs.

I said my goodbyes to the children's home over the next few days. I can see myself sitting on the steps along the old orchard, recalling the good times: the red winter sun-rises on the hill rim; the white apple blossoms in spring; watching the honey bees craw out of the apple blossoms to fly away; the little kites we made in March of twigs and wrapping paper and white kitchen string. I recalled the gray wood pile, all gone now, in which I and another boy had constructed a tiny cardboard room; the four secret bean plants I planted in a hidden corner of a flower garden. I remember licking the spoon, front and back, for every morsel of my favorite apple brown betty desserts. I recall saying my goodbyes to Mrs. McKenzie, who was kind to me, and to Mrs. Norman, for whom I was developing some affection despite her formidable demeanor and Great Electric Paddle. Dutch lifted me up on his shoulders one last time before I left. We were both shy and our goodbye was awkward, but I remember him fondly even today. I'm sure I was glad to be leaving the dull routines of the Home, the utter boredom, the sameness of days so typical — and in some respects so necessary — to institutional life. Looking back, excepting possibly Kline and Alice Dawson, I now remember thankfully the staff members of the Home, dedicated and miserably paid. Their work was physically and emotionally exhausting and had to be done within skimpy budgets. If our minds and hearts were malnourished in the children's home, at least they kept us fed, clean, and alive. Janey had her close brush with death in early 1943 but some "good angels," presumably the Portsmouth benefactors of Mercy Hospital, paid for her five weeks in an intensive medical ward and nurses and doctors had cared for her around the clock. I cannot expect the supervisors in the Home to have provided the emotional nourishment we so badly needed given the crowded conditions that then existed. But once our survival was assured, the need for love — warm, healing love — was our most basic need and the lack of it surely affected many of the children who spent most of their childhood in the Home. That is the best argument I know against re-establishing traditional children's homes.

I bear no grudge against the authorities of Scioto County, one of Ohio's poorer counties, for not being more generous in funding their children's home. The devastating flood of 1937 severely damaged the area's economy and eroded the tax base of the county after a decade during which the steel plants, then the life blood of the Ohio Valley, had been idled by the Great Depression. The State of Ohio, aided by federal funding, did somewhat better by us. It is truly remarkable that in the early 1940s we were interviewed and tested on three separate occasions by Persis Simmons and Mary R. Smith, psychologists from the Ohio Bureau of Juvenile Research.

Some children at the Home found Superintendent Inez Norman forbidding and once she retired, positive changes were made in the life of Hillcrest, the new name for the Scioto County Children's Home. But my memory of Inez Norman is good, and the children's home monthly board meetings and records show a dedicated but poorly paid professional woman doing a difficult and mostly thankless job with an untrained staff and skimpy budgets. I am grateful to her.

My last memory at the Home is packing to go, putting three or four pieces of underwear and one shirt in a brown grocery bag with my treasures: three worn marbles, a wad of white kitchen string, a few rusty nails saved from the woodpile we played in, a well used yo-yo, a photograph of my McNelly grandparents and my dearest keepsake of all, the green fountain pen my father Lonnie had given me. I was already thinking ahead to Athens and to our new foster parents, Fred and Evelyn Luchs. I wondered who they were and what living with them would be like.

One of the few photographs taken of us before we were placed in the Scioto County Children's Home. Billy (on the left) and I stand behind Charlie in the back yard of our McNelly grandparents

This is the only photograph taken of the four of us during the 26 months we lived in the Scioto County Children's Home.

This series of three photos (the third is at the top of the next page) were taken during our first weeks in the manse. We are building a dog house for Billy's new puppy, Jippy.

We are introducing my white rabbit to Jippy in the manse back yard as our new foster mother looks on

*ie on the donated tricycle he loved to ride. Such
ations came used but we were delighted to have
n because there were no tricycles or wagons or
s equipment of any kind in the children's home.*

*Billy carries Jippy during our first weeks in
Athens. Look closely and you will see that
Billy has given himself a haircut.*

Baptism Portraits

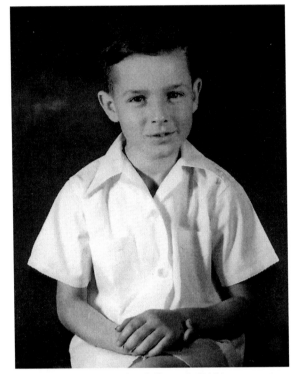

Lewis Richard (formerly Dick)

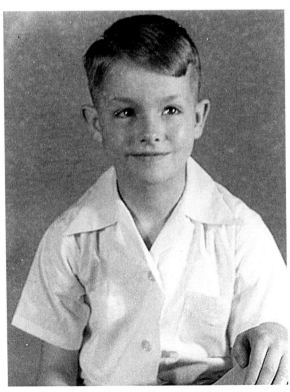

Mark William (formerly Billy)

Michael Charles (formerly Charlie)

Margaret Jane (always Janey)

Twice weekly swim lessons were part of our summer school program at the university-sponsored elementary school we attended.

We often played softball and football in the manse back yard and

The manse was full of books as the children's home was not.
We were often read to as in the above photograph

*The four of us on a wagon and a tricycle in front of the
funeral home next door to the manse.*

We were given piano lessons almost as soon as we arrived in Athens after our teachers pointed out that all four of us had good voices and loved our music classes. Janey and I continued to study piano, Michael took up the violin, and Mark began his romance with horns.

Three happy scouts.

Mom and Dad stand in the manse backyard in 1945 with the lovely home of Mrs. Lawrence in the background.

Family portrait in the manse living room, Easter Sunday, 1950

PART II

"Who makes the woman in a childless house
the joyful Mother of children"

Psalm 113, verse 8

CHAPTER 6

The Honeymoon

FRIDAY, OCTOBER 15, 1943

T HE POSED PHOTOGRAPH OF our arrival in Athens on this book's cover shows the four of us in front of the manse toting suitcases almost as big as we are. North College Street traffic glides behind us on a sunny late October afternoon as our smiling new foster parents, Fred and Evelyn Luchs, eagerly greet us — their instant family of four. We have just bathed, our freshly cut hair is combed, and we are dressed in bright new clothes — corduroys and striped jerseys for us boys, a pretty dress for Janey, and Buster Brown shoes for all. This is not quite how it happened.

For starters, we did not arrive with suitcases but carried one wrinkled brown grocery bag each for all our worldly goods. The clothing we wore the day of our arrival in Athens was faded and ill-fitting. Five-year-old Charlie stumbled around in an oversized pair of brown and white wing tip shoes. When our new foster mother telephoned the children's home to ask about the pretty blue coat Janey wore in Columbus for our first meeting with the Luchs, a Home staffer explained we had been dressed in "loaner clothes" that day, used only when children were presented to prospective adoptive parents.

Nor did the sun shine on the afternoon of our arrival. The day was rainy and chilly and the drive up from Wheelersburg long and tiring. Near Jackson, Ohio, Ann Minnis pulled over to a roadside stand selling large orange pumpkins and gallon jugs of brown apple cider to give us a break. She unsnapped her black pocket book to pay for paper cups full of cider and for a large pumpkin she encouraged us to select from a pile near the stand. She also bought masks for us when we showed interest in those. Billy selected the face of a monster that resembled Quasimodo, the hunchback of Notre Dame. Charlie pulled a rubber band over his head attached to the mask of a troll-like creature with pointed ears. Janey struggled to put on the face of a craggy witch with an ugly chin wart. Janey's mask was on upside-down until Ann helped her straighten it. I immediately liked the narrow face of the devil, red skin, small black horns, black goatee, and a devilish smirk. We pulled our false faces on and off during the rest of the trip, laughing and pushing up against the windows of Ann's blue Plymouth, trying to frighten passengers in other cars when they pulled near us.

The rain slowed as we reached the outskirts of Athens. Through the mist and drizzle I could barely make out trees in autumn colors, white frame houses and big, red brick university buildings. The town seemed to be set upon hills almost surrounded, as a castle by a moat, by a broad curve of the Hocking River. I was beginning to feel nervous and a little sick to my stomach. Billy and Charlie, who had been romping in the Plymouth's trunk, stuck their heads up over the back seat when they heard the rumble of the car's tires on the slick brick streets. Ann steered her blue Plymouth up Richland Avenue across Memorial Bridge to Court Street, and quickly found a parking spot on College Street, one block from the university.

"We've made good time," Ann said. "We're early."

She had parked her blue Plymouth in front of a large, red brick house, as large as any house I had ever seen, on a street of large, brick houses, all sheltered by great elms half-emptied of their yellow leaves. "That's the manse," Ann said, pointing to one of the red brick houses. "Fifteen North College. That's the residence of the Presbyterian minister. That's where you'll be living." I looked at the porch of the house Ann had pointed at, most of which was a semicircle supported by half a dozen white columns that made the porch resemble the entrance to a Greek temple.

Ann held a blue umbrella over the four of us while we ran up a cement walk between two of the white columns of the porch to the front door. She closed and shook her umbrella while we huddled against the chill wind. We were feeling shy and when we asked, Ann said we could put our masks on before we entered the house. Then she found and rang the doorbell.

A tall young woman with brown hair and wearing glasses with milky plastic rims slowly opened the door and peered through it.

"Oh, my! You're here already!"

"I'm Ann Minnis," Ann said. "I think we're early. Are the Luchs home?"

"Come in, come in," the young woman with the white rimmed glasses said as she opened the door wide. "Mrs. Luchs is having her hair done. I'm Grace Monigold. I'm Mrs. Luchs' niece."

"And these are the children," said Ann, looking down at us. "Dick, Bill, Charles, and Jane."

"Oh, my! What's this?" said Grace as she drew back in mock fright on seeing our masks, which pleased us.

A man suddenly bounded down the hall staircase from the second floor. His hair, thick and black, stood straight up like a shoe brush and was perfectly flat on top. He was of medium height and frame, but his voice was low and booming.

"You're here already! Oh, my goodness! Where's Mrs. Luchs?"

"She's having her hair done at Anna and Minnie's," Grace said, "pushing at the center of her glasses with a finger. "Why don't you run through the back alley, Harold, and get her?"

"Good idea, Grace," the man said. I could tell he was nervous because he blinked his large dark eyes a lot and he talked rapidly. He didn't even seem to notice our false faces.

"Yes, I'll do that," he said. "Good idea. Good idea. Yes, that's a good idea. Now don't you be worried, Grace."

He ran down the hall and out through the back door to the beauty parlor a few minutes away. Ann asked us to pull off our false faces to meet our new parents. While we stood in the middle of the hall waiting for them to arrive I looked around to inspect the house.

The ceilings of the manse were the highest of any residence I had ever seen. To my right was a room full of dark wood book cases with glass fronts and a large desk. A bay window behind the desk looked out on the brick pavement and elms of College Street. The next room on the right held a rectangular table with chairs and a sideboard with mirror, all in dark wood in what I was sure was the dining room. Directly in front of us was a long, wide staircase with a burgundy runner to the second floor down which Harold, the man with the shoe brush hair, had come. Along the staircase was a wide dark walnut banister that curved around to the left, as did the staircase at the top. Also in front of us, to the left of the staircase, was a long hall. To my immediate left, as my eyes continued to explore the downstairs, was a formal living room with floor length windows that also looked out on College Street. I turned to look behind us at the large door through which we had entered. Two-thirds of the door and the side panels were full of prism glass in geometric designs.

I looked up at the young woman who identified herself as Grace, the niece of the Luchs. She was telling Ann that she and Harold were students at the university who lived in the manse. She was a freshman while Harold — who looked much older than a university student — had just begun his senior year. There was a third student in the house, one who roomed with her, Grace was now telling Ann Minnis. Betty Lou Gregg helped Reverend Luchs as a part-time secretary. Grace spoke softly and was reserved. She wore little makeup.

Just then a much shorter woman with long, dark brown hair raced down the hall toward us from the back. At first I didn't recognize her. She was out of breath and her wet hair was hanging in strands down her back.

"Ann, how are you?" she asked, and without waiting for Ann to answer, she knelt down, gathered the four of us to her and with her arms around us, said, "Mother is so happy to see you. I am so glad you're here." And suddenly her smile, her voice and her friendly manner confirmed this was Mrs. Luchs, the woman who had walked through the zoo with us in Columbus and was our new foster mother.

"I will never forget that scene," Grace later recalled, "Because here she was with her hair down and wet and she was so tickled to see you guys. It was 'mother this' and 'mother that' right from the start. It was as if in that instant, in her mind, she became your mother and you became her children."

Then Mrs. Luchs said, "Daddy will be here soon. Now let's all go into the living room and sit down." I liked the warmth in her voice. She was still kneeling with her arms around us.

I asked her, "Can we play our game first?"

She smiled at me. "And just what game is that?"

Billy said, "You see, we put our false faces on and you try to guess who we are."

"OKaaay!" she said. "Let's play your game."

Thinking some more explanation was in order, I said, "First, we'll go hide, like hide and seek. If you find us, then we say, who am I? And you have to guess who we are. If you guess right, then...then we have to take our masks off. If you're wrong...we get to scare and chase you. Then we hide again."

"All right," she said. "You go hide and I'll come find you."

We ran excitedly all around the first floor of the house playing the game, asking "Who Am I?" then taking off our false faces when Mrs. Luchs got our names right but chasing and scaring her if she was wrong. Reverend Luchs arrived and joined in the game as our play and voices grew louder and louder until we were all running and laughing through the downstairs rooms of the big house together.

Ann later wrote to Superintendent Inez Norman, "Upon arriving at the foster home, all the children put on false faces and walked in to scare the foster parents. It was a happy idea because it broke the ice immediately."

Janey, overcome by the highly charged emotional state we were all in, suddenly began sniffling and then sobbing. Ann led her to a blue needlepoint foot stool in the living room where she sat, looking like a little thunder cloud. Ann asked her again and again, "Are you all right, Janey?" which just made Janey cry more.

We had tired of the mask game when Tom Lange and his father walked into the manse carrying a big box of toys. Tom was about my age. They had brought Lincoln Logs, an Erector Set, Tinker Toys and some board games. We ran up the burgundy carpeted stairs, down a wide hall, and into what we were told would be our new bedroom. I at once began building a log cabin with the Lincoln Logs, which were new to me. Somehow it was comforting to build a cabin, even when I knew it was too small to live in. While I fitted the logs together and watched the walls rise, I thought of the cozy cardboard lined nest I and another boy had built in the pile of old lumber at the children's home.

Our foster mother wrote of that first evening, "All four ate vigorously and all four talked at once at dinner." We were no longer constrained by the rule of silence at meals observed at the children's home and had not yet learned to wait our turn to talk, or not to talk when our mouths were full. After dinner Mrs. Luchs spread newspapers over a large oak kitchen table and Reverend Luchs put on a frilly red apron to carve the pumpkin Ann had bought for us. We watched intently as he sliced a circle at the top of the pumpkin with a butcher knife and lifted that piece out. The four of us were invited to climb up on the table and take turns reaching in to the pumpkin to dig out the squishy pulp and damp white seeds with our bare hands. The strong pumpkin odor was new to us. We had never watched a pumpkin being carved. Nor do I remember any previous observance of Halloween before we arrived in Athens that rainy autumn afternoon.

Mrs. Luchs brought a candle which Reverend Luchs placed in the pumpkin and lighted. He carried the jack-o'-lantern to the dining room window, where we watched in delight as it flickered through the eyes and mouth of the pumpkin. Later our foster mother would write of that first evening in the Manse, "Father, who always had a dream of sitting by the fire, everybody well-fed and relaxed and listening to Father read a story, discovered that the dream didn't happen. These children didn't know the joy of having stories read to them and they were far too excited to sit down, even after supper."

So, with us all still excitedly chattering, our foster father carried the jack-o'-lantern up the long set of stairs and down the wide hall to our bedroom. This room was so large it contained a full-sized bed for Janey and Michael and individual beds for Billy and me. There was plenty of room left to play and a walk-in closet where we could dress. We undressed and ran down the hall, three whooping boy Tarzans and one Jane, to the house's only full bathroom at the back of the second floor. The bathroom was long and narrow, but the claw-foot tub was so big we could all climb into it at the same time, which was exactly what we did. Once washed and toweled down, we were given new pajamas and back in our room, we watched the jack-o'-lantern flicker its orange light for a few more minutes. We climbed between the sheets and under warm comforters. The sheets were crisp and clean and smelled good. Then the Luchs blew out the candle in the pumpkin, said a prayer for us, and closed our door. We were still too excited to settle down. We threw our pillows at each other and romped happily from bed to bed. After we had been hushed three or four times, Janey and Charlie feel asleep. Billy and I talked in low voices for a few more minutes about everything in the new big house that was strange and wonderful before sleep finally overcame our great excitement.

Recently I asked Grace Monigold for her first impressions of us the day we arrived at the manse and she said:

"Janey was hard to understand. She was a strong-minded little kid after all you had been through. Charlie, he was kind of hanging back I guess. He seemed more hesitant to interact with anyone at that time. Billy was that sunny little guy. He seemed to take life in stride and enjoy the day. And you, you were serious, very sober for a seven-year-old."

October 16, Saturday

Mother began typing quick journal entries the day we arrived in Athens, a practice she had followed before we arrived. Reading through her notes I was surprised to find her record of our first ten days in the manse covered many of the places that would be central to our lives in Athens: a visit to the university laboratory school, Rufus Putnam; our first Sundays in the First Presbyterian Church; a drive out to Happy Howell's shrub and tree nursery west of the city, where we would develop a large victory garden; a stroll through the main campus of Ohio University, slightly more than one block from the manse. It was as if she, the teacher, planned our first week as an orientation to our new lives, which she probably did.

The event I remember best on our first full day in Athens, she did not record at all. We ate breakfast of freshly-squeezed orange juice, cereal, and buttered whole toast. Then the two of us went shopping for my birthday dinner, which we would celebrate on October 18, the following Monday.

"You're the birthday boy!" my new mother said as I chewed up a second piece of toast, "So you get to chose what we have for dinner next Monday. What would you like?"

"Anything I want?"

"Well, almost anything."

"Chicken! Roast chicken!"

Before Athens I had no memory of a birthday celebration. I have confirmed that birthdays were not observed in our children's home. There were, the supervisors said, just too many birthdays and, except for Christmas, there were no special meals at the children's home. So I could not imagine there was a day when I could have anything I wanted to eat. Besides, I believed only rich people could afford to buy chicken, a much more expensive meal before chickens began to be mass produced after WW II.

""Well," she said. "We're not rich but you may certainly have roast chicken on your birthday. And what else would you like?"

"Mashed potatoes and gravy?" I asked tentatively, another favorite.

"OK, she said. And what else?

"Noodles." I had grown to like the high carbohydrate diet at the children's home and I was running out of ideas.

145

"Wouldn't you like a vegetable instead of noodles, and maybe a salad?"

"Ve-ge-table?" I pronounced the word as if I had never heard it before. But I did know of one vegetable I liked. "How about butter beans?"

We were served white lima beans at the home, but the truth was I had had little experience with vegetables other than potatoes and beans. We were never served green salad. I don't think I had any idea what a salad was. My new foster mother's brown eyes looked at me quizzically, probably thinking that mashed potatoes, noodles, and butter beans would not make an ideal birthday dinner.

"How about peas?" she suggested, trying to lead me in a new direction.

"OK," I said.

"And how about a salad of apples and nuts and raisons?"

"OK," I said.

"Anything else?"

"No, I don't think so."

"Don't you want a birthday cake?!!"

It hadn't occurred to me to ask for a birthday cake. There were no birthday cakes at the children's home because there were no birthdays at the children's home and I had no memory of a birthday cake before going to the Home. By then I was feeling overwhelmed by possibilities I had never imagined, and decisions I had never had to make. But my foster mother and I completed the menu with a chocolate birthday cake with chocolate icing. Then we set out on a crisp sunny October morning to buy a chicken for my first birthday dinner in the manse.

She pulled on a blue cardigan sweater and we walked, just the two of us, under the yellow elm trees, past the funeral home next door to the manse, and then around the corner at Washington Street across from the Methodist church. The sidewalks were still damp from the previous day's rain and stray dark branches lay where they had fallen. We passed a large open garage in a red brick building where sat a handsome bright red fire engine. "That's the city hall building," she told me," and that, "indicating a square steel-gray brick building with large, glossy oak doors we were passing, "is our church, First Presbyterian." As we stood in front of the church at the corner of Washington and Court Streets waiting for a red light to change, I craned my neck back to look up at an enormous brick building across from us. There was a woman painted white near the top of the roof with a blind fold over her eyes and something in her hand. "That's the county court house," my new mother said, when she saw me looking at it. "And that's Lady Justice, blindfolded, and those are scales in her hand."

Court Street was alive. The sidewalks were full of people, many of them female students in sweaters and skirts and brown and white oxfords and a few of them male students in slacks and sweaters. Farmers walked about in blue overalls shouting friendly greetings to each other or stood in groups around the court house, talking and spitting tobacco juice into brass spittoons. They were in town on Saturday to do the week's shopping, meet friends, and get haircuts. Townspeople stood in clusters catching up on the news and gossip as they greeted friends while a constant stream of black and brown cars rumbled slowly up and down the two brick lanes of Court Street. The women shopped in Woolworth's and Scotts, the dime stores, and Zenner's Department Store. Most of the students were in and out of Gallagher's Drugs or Logan's, the college bookstore.

We walked past the First National Bank and into Bethel's, a butcher shop. "We need a good roasting chicken for this boy's birthday," my new foster mother said. Together we chose one and the sales clerk wrapped the chicken carefully in shiny pink paper and tied it with a white string from a large coil behind the counter. "You'll like this one, Mrs. Luchs. Comes from the Barnes farm near Amesville. They feed corn to their chickens."

"This is my son," my new foster mother said, introducing me. "His name is Dick." I avoided eye contact. I looked down, shy in meeting strangers.

"Well, Happy Birthday, young man," the clerk said.

Then Mrs. Luchs and I walked north on Court Street and crossed in front of Zenner's Department Store on our way to the Ohio Market. Opposite us was the front of the Buckeye Cafeteria, then the most popular eatery in Athens, and the Hotel Berry, the largest and nicest hotel in town. My new foster mother again introduced me as her son, this time to Norman Dean in the Ohio Market. Again I looked at the floor, too shy yet to look into the faces of strangers in this new town. We bought some potatoes and other groceries she needed for my birthday dinner and then walked back to the manse through the alley behind the church. Our back yard was separated from the alley and noisy Court Street by a high green board fence. It was a shortcut to the church and to Court Street I would soon be using every day.

I could hear excitement in our new foster mother's voice as she and the four of us headed off to tour Rufus Putnam, Ohio University's laboratory elementary school, the next event during our first full day in Athens. We walked past the funeral home again before which a black Cadillac hearse was parked and then she stopped to instruct us on crossing College Street at East Washington, as we looked up at the tan brick tower of the First Methodist Church in front of us.

"College is the only street you'll have to cross to go to school," she said, bending over and putting her arms around

Charlie and Janey. "This is the safest place to cross." She turned her head from side to side up and down College Street when she said," Always, always look both ways."

"Let's get a move on!" We picked up our pace to pass in front of three large white sorority houses as the central campus of the university at the south end of College Street came into view. Taken together, I thought the yellow canopy of autumn elms above the street, the blue sky of a fresh October morning, the green grounds and red brick buildings of the campus the most beautiful scene I had ever seen. We passed Howard Hall, a women's dormitory used by the army in 1943 for military training, then turned left down East Union Street past the university president's house on our left and Memorial Auditorium, the rectangular performing arts center of the university, across the street on our right.

At that point East Union Street, along which we were now walking, descended sharply. Suddenly we were peering down the longest set of concrete steps I had ever seen. We happily jumped down most of them, one hundred and ten steps, arranged in sets of two and threes. At the bottom was another red brick building trimmed in white, the façade of which was filled with unusually large and beautiful windows. This was our new school, Rufus Putnam, our new mother was now explaining.

We walked into the school office where we found Dr. Edith Beechel, the principal of Rufus Putnam, and also the university's director of student teaching. I could tell by the way they greeted each other that she liked my new foster mother. I would later learn that Beechel, like all Putnam teachers, was a graduate of Teacher's College, Columbia University, and that all were master teachers and faculty members within the College of Education, as our new mother had been. All were disciples of John Dewey, whose philosophy of education included building education programs around the interests of the child, to provide opportunities to learn by doing, and to

combine thinking and doing. Also important was encouragement of the child's initiative and helping children build self-
confidence. This last objective was much on the mind of our
new mother as she undertook the adoption of four children
with our history.

I found Dr. Beechel's white-hair and thick glasses intimi-
dating, which was the way principals were supposed to be in
the 1940s, but I did manage to blurt out a question.

"Why is the school called Rufus Putnam?" I asked her.

"Oh, yes," she sighed. "Why Rufus Putnam? Why don't
you come with me?"

She led us past the nurse's clinic, where everything was
white, and then into our new school's gymnasium to see a
large mural painting of Rufus Putnam, Revolutionary War
general, the founder of Marietta and Athens, Ohio, and a co-
founder and trustee of Ohio University. As Dr. Beechel talked about Putnam, probably best known as General George
Washington's engineer, we looked at the mural. Putnam
seemed to be about 6' 4", a handsome frontier Ulysses, rather
than the 5' 7" rather odd-looking man he was in real life. He
stood in black boots and an open shirt on top of a hillock, his
right leg cocked up on a chest that held surveying equipment.
Military officers in bright uniforms, frontiersmen in buck-
skin and coonskin caps, and one lonely Native American surrounded him. A stream of settlers from the East flowed from
the horizon, following him across the Appalachian Mountains
to what would soon become the state of Ohio.

After Dr. Beechel left we explored the 2nd and 3rd grade
classrooms where Billy and I would be sitting the following
Monday. The classrooms were spacious and bright. Each came
equipped with a kitchen and a large open area for reading and
other activities as well as a cluster of traditional desks.

"You'll go to school all year except for August," our new

mother was saying "but the summer program is only a half day. And twice each week you'll hike down to Crystal Pool to take swimming lessons. Now, won't that be fun! Your classes will be small," she continued to brief us, "under twenty. There will often be a student teacher in your classroom and sometimes more college students will visit just to observe. Any questions? No? Well, then, let's go up to the art department."

We walked up to the third floor and through the art department, which filled the space of two regular classrooms. The art teacher, Mary Leonard, was present on a Saturday morning and gave us a tour. She was small, with reddish hair cut short, and had a voice full of enthusiasm. You could tell she liked what she was doing. I most enjoyed seeing the clay room filled with large gray crocks of native Athens County clay and did not realize how quickly I would be shaping pottery and painting in oils. Another classroom, on the second floor and beneath the art department, was reserved for music instruction. "Each grade has three art and two music periods each week." our new mother was telling us. I told her there were no art or music classes at all in the Wheelersburg elementary school.

The next item in our new mother's journal notes of October 16 was "naps". The Luchs began taking daily naps during the years Reverend Luchs was recovering from tuberculosis and then, later, when he was recuperating from undulant fever. His vocation made it possible to have some control over a daily schedule which usually included frequent evening church or university activities which the Luchs hosted or were expected to attend. A one-hour nap in the middle of their long days was a rarely-missed practice. They decided midday rest would also be good for our health and their peace of mind and insisted that we "go down for naps" when not in school. We knew it was nap time when our new foster father began wrapping a blanket around the telephone. I rarely slept during nap time after the first few weeks of adjustment. We protested this enforced midday inactivity at first, but then it was agreed we could read during naps if we were quiet. Only when I learned the manse was a library full of books and magazines did I willingly take naps.

After naps on our first Saturday in the manse, the six of us piled into the Luchs 1941 green Buick coupe for our first visit to the tree nursery of Happy Howell, out beyond White's Mill on the west side of Athens. Happy and his wife Mabel built their log and stone house with their own hands. When he courted Mabel, Happy — a pixie of a man with a quick wit and a boyish sense of fun — was working for a florist. He once had flowers delivered to Mabel and every other coed in Lindley Hall, the largest women's dorm at Ohio University. He wanted to impress Mabel. Happy later became a Johnny Appleseed who did not wander about but did in his lifetime plant more trees in southern Ohio than Johnny Appleseed or anyone else since.

On that first afternoon outing to the Howell place we walked over a plot of land along a creek that we were told would be our victory garden. Our new mother talked about how next spring we would all be working in "Daddy's Garden," and we would plant the pumpkin seeds we had just saved from our first jack-o'-lantern. We also met the Howell's adopted daughter, Nancy, who at five was Charlie's age. Mother noted in her journal how we scurried to the car when Nancy yelled, "I'm going to loosen my dog on you!" "As long as we live," she wrote, "we'll never forget the sight of those four scared rabbits running for that car." We were afraid of all dogs when we first arrived in Athens. Except for my experience with Queenie, Judge Smith's gentle old collie, none of us had been around dogs, not in our biological family or at the children's home.

October 17, Sunday

When I look at our new mother's journal for Sunday, October 17, and see church services at 9 and 11, Sunday school, Sunday dinner — the most elaborate and formal meal of the week — naps, a trip to the state mental hospital grounds to feed the ducks, a Presbyterian Preference tea for new students hosted at the church, and a late afternoon wedding some forty miles from Athens — there comes back a sense of what a beehive the manse was on Sundays. Sunday was the crescendo and culmination of each week, always a busy day and often a day that included special events.

The Wedding

Of the remembered events in our first ten days in the Manse, the wedding in the village of Stockport stands alone. That memory is like a milky dream of beautiful women with pretty hair holding bouquets in two hands, their bodies erect, parading and posing for photographs in shimmering white satin and lace. The groom was a stocky man with dark hair and oddly fat chipmunk cheeks. But I paid little attention to him or to his blond bride because I could not keep my eyes off the flower girl, who was about my age and a vision of youthful beauty.

There is a less happy memory from that same afternoon. We attended the reception but not the wedding where our foster father officiated. During that event Mrs. Luchs took the four of us for a drive over a bridge that spanned the Muskingum River. Janey became car sick and our new mother could not stop the car in time before the damage was done. She pulled over at an Ohio state roadside park on a high bluff above the river to clean up Janey and the two of them disappeared into the bathroom. We three boys ran to a wooded bluff at the edge of the park, which dropped off sharply to the river. Billy, ever the daredevil, began to walk dangerously close to the edge of the bluff. I ordered him to stop, afraid he would fall into the river. Charlie began crying hysterically and pleaded with

Billy to come back from the edge of the bluff. But Billy just turned and grinned at us as if he was enjoying our discomfort and then smiled broadly as if to say, "Don't be silly. I won't fall." Only when Mrs. Luchs reappeared with Janey did Billy step off the bluff.

The journal notes that after we had been put to bed, "Daddy and mother entertained a group of the church people at an evening of music." Sing-a-longs at the manse usually meant a dozen or more students and faculty members standing around the piano, singing old favorites and the more recent Broadway show tunes that everyone then seemed to know.

OCTOBER 18, MONDAY

My eighth birthday was also my first day in the third grade class at Rufus Putnam. My new teacher, Agnes Eisen, short and dark haired with glasses and keen bright eyes, was one of our new mother's colleagues when both had been teachers at the West Side Elementary School in Athens. Miss Eisen, as we always called her, seemed strictly business in her approach to education and did not at first appear as warm a person as I later discovered her to be. Her class, with fewer than 20 students, was a mix of the sons and daughters of university faculty, kids from the neighborhood adjacent to the school, and a few children from the local children's home. Putnam's enrollment goal was a mix of students typical of the community, not an academic elite. I was anxious and felt shy and awkward during the first week or so but had little difficulty adjusting to my new school and began to thrive in a program that placed importance on writing and art and music, as well as reading, spelling, and arithmetic. The Putnam curriculum also stressed health and diet and the importance of rest and exercise, none of which was ever mentioned in my former school.

In those first days I learned that when my turn came, I would be a cook for our hot lunch program. I would help plan the menus, purchase the food, collect money from other students for the program and learn how to keep careful accounts. Miss Eisen reported to parents, "We took every opportunity to use our reading and number skills in our daily activities, learning how to count change, do our milk (at 3 1/4 cents a half pint!) bills, read recipes, and play dominos. We also wrote stories and often read these and books to each other."

Sometimes the John Dewey philosophy of learning by doing involved a maintenance project, such as improving the outdoor basketball court, about which I came to care a great deal. "Judging from his many ideas and hard work fixing the basketball court," Eisen wrote later in the year, "Dick should excel as a drainage engineer!"

I began from that first day at Rufus Putnam to learn that becoming good citizens was another theme of the Putnam program. "Growth in all these things is important for citizens in a democracy," wrote Eisen. "That is, room duties, sharing responsibility, but each child takes care of his own 'wrap', own desk, and develops independence. Over all, these activities encourage a sense of responsibility to self and to the group." In the third grade we had the responsibility, by two students in turn each school day, of raising, lowering, and folding the American flag. At Rufus Putnam, a laboratory of progressive education, one of Eisen's reports noted, "We learned a new prayer to say before lunch."

During the day, while Billy and I were in school, our foster mother wrote in her journal that she had "fixed the cake with candles and cooked the chicken with noodles and gravy and mashed potatoes." To please me she prepared noodles as well as the peas and salad she had suggested.

That evening we celebrated my eighth birthday. Rather than one, there were many gifts. The Luchs invited Margaret Hampel, in charge of teaching university students special education at Rufus Putnam, as a guest. Margaret Hampel became a favorite of ours so quickly we never addressed her as

Miss Hampel and yet, at that time, could not properly use her first name. So we simply called her Hampel. Hampel was tall, thin, elegant, and always nicely dressed. She had a warm alto voice and she read like a trained professional actress.

In addition to my favorite dinner and the first birthday cake I could remember, chocolate with chocolate icing and eight colored candles to blow out, I was given my dream, a chest of woodworking tools. I was also given a football. Ann Minnis surely told the Luchs I wanted a tool chest with saw and hammer and plane and brace and bit above everything in the world. I was just discovering the wonders of carpentry and what one could do with tools. I was about to discover the frustrations of carpentry and the difficulty of making my hands do what my mind could imagine. At eight years, I could not even master the fundamental skill of sawing a straight line. Even so, during those first weeks in the manse I happily spent every free hour sawing boards into unusual shapes and hammering them together, while bossing my brothers into holding boards for me and in other ways assisting me to become the master carpenter I then wished to be.

At first I was disappointed in the football because it was old and used. It was full- sized and looked like the survivor of some tough games, which turned out to be accurate. Reverend Luchs had managed to extract a practice ball used by Ohio University's varsity team from a coaching friend. Once he told me the history of the football, I was pleased with it. A croquet set and a pair of mittens were also among my gifts, but in those I had no interest at all.

October 19-25

Our new mother continued to make entries in her journal for the week of October 19 to 24 during our "honeymoon" with the Luchs. She walked the four of us down the long steep steps to Rufus Putnam on Tuesday the 19th, our second day of school. After Bill and I were settled in our classrooms she noted that "Charlie and Janey stayed to play on the playground" and, the following day, that "Charlie and Janey were invited to stay at school tomorrow," to join the 4 and 5-year-old kindergarten classes. Members of First Presbyterian continued to bring toys and books for us and I hurried home from school each day to resume my woodworking projects.

After watching us run "like scared rabbits" from Nancy's large dog during our visit to Happy Howell's tree farm, the Luchs decided we should have a dog and found a little tan Spitz-mix female puppy and gave her to Billy. He named her Jippy. That week I made a doghouse for Jippy, a square box with no entrance. I also made an asymmetrical file box with no drawers for our foster father. On Thursday our foster mother spent the day in Columbus at church women's meetings, and on Friday Jippy was lost but was soon found. On Friday evening after baths we gathered in our new father's study so that he could indulge his deferred dream of reading to us. Janey was cuddled up on his lap while we three boys sat on the carpet around his big easy chair. He was about to begin when, asserting my accustomed role as leader of our little pack, I reached up and took the book from his hands, saying, "I can read that." And I did. No one objected. My siblings did not object because this was the behavior they had come to expect of me. Our new foster father did not object because he was so startled by my action he was speechless.

On our second Saturday in Athens our foster mother hustled us up to Stanley's on Court Street for new shoes. I wanted paratrooper boots, which I called high tops, but when the salesman pushed the little silver colored indicator against the ball of my foot to measure width, he whistled in surprise. "Double A," he announced. Stanley's had only one shoe that could properly shod such a narrow foot, the standard Buster Brown oxford, not the most exciting shoe ever made but comfortable and healthy for growing feet. Charlie's foot was even narrower, a triple A, and soon we all were wearing new Buster Brown shoes. Then we took turns looking at each other's toe bones wiggle in the weird green light of the store's fluoroscope.

Our next stop that morning was Zenner's Department Store where our new mother purchased a modest wardrobe for each of us. When she asked for my favorite colors, I told her red and blue. Billy said he liked green and brown best. Billy and I wore the same sizes. From that day forward all my clothes — jerseys, socks, corduroy pants, and jackets — came in reds and blues, Billy's in browns and greens. That made separating the wash and getting the right clothes into the right drawers a lot easier.

Then we all burst into the barber shop across the street from First Presbyterian. A single barber, an ascetic appearing man in his 50s who wore a green eyeshade and bands around his upper arms, was trimming the hair of a bald farmer in blue overalls. Every few minutes the barber would lean over and spit tobacco juice into a brass spittoon and then continue to talk to the farmer out of one corner of his mouth as he chewed up some new stories. We three boys watched intently each time the barber spat. We were sure he would miss but he didn't. When my turn came the barber put a black leather covered board across the arms of the chair and then decided I didn't need it. Then he enfolded me in a striped sheet. Each time his hand clippers nicked the back of my neck, I flinched. "Sit still, boy!" he commanded. Everyone in the barber shop could hear him, which made my neck and face turn red as he sheared the sides of my head almost to the skin.

After naps we rode in the green Buick out to a farm to collect black walnuts and hickory nuts. The afternoon was warm and sunny and the nuts lay in abundance under the trees. The walnut husks were dark brown. Some were wet and messy but most had begun to dry. The white hickory nuts had popped out of their brown husks. Billy and I became car sick on the return trip to Athens, our second experience of the winding, hilly roads of Athens County. We recovered in time to spread the nuts across the attic floor of the manse to dry.

On the following day, Sunday, October 24, Mother noted in her journal, "To Sunday school. Dick stayed for church." I can still remember that day and my first impression of a major service at First Presbyterian. I was new enough to be an object of curiosity. If members of the congregation looked our way, my new mother would tip her head slightly towards them and beam. She did a lot of beaming that morning. I had the feeling at once that she was proud of me. I liked the hymns and choir anthems best. The choir of 20 voices, directed by a music professor from Ohio University, was the best I had ever heard. In her journal that same Sunday Mother wrote "Dick set the table for a party that evening" and "the goldfish arrived," yet another gift from a family in the church.

Mom told me years later something I had said to her during our first weeks in the manse. She was still in her bathrobe early one morning and had not yet put up her hair, which then fell down her back. In a matter of fact tone I asked her not to wear her hair down again "Because your long hair reminds me of my mother." The last comment in her brief notes of our first ten days at the manse ends with, "Charlie surely is a happy boy."

Her journal ends on October 25, possibly because she intended to jot down notes only for the first few days after we arrived, but more likely because she simply became too busy to do so. Also unrecorded is a phone call that closed our honeymoon period in the manse. I had begun to believe we were in the right place and I told our new mother how happy I was.

"Well, would you like to call the children's home and tell them?

"OK," I said. How do I do that?"

I had never made a phone call before. She dialed zero for the long distance operator, placed the call, and we were connected with Wheelersburg ten minutes later. "Yes, this is Mrs. Luchs. I'll put him right on," and she handed me the phone. I told whoever was at the other end we were happy at the Luchs and wanted to stay.

In a letter to Home superintendent Inez Norman, Ann Minnis wrote, "I know you will be pleased to learn that the Boggs children have adjusted nicely. They have already started to call their foster parents 'Mama' and 'Daddy.' I think there is no question but that this is a suitable placement. There will be rough spots, I am sure, but the first few days have gone better than I dared hope. Dickey particularly is delighted."

It was true, as Ann wrote, that we were happy at the Luchs and that our first weeks had been a honeymoon. No wonder. The four of us were together for the first time in two years. We had never been in such comfortable, spacious surroundings, eaten such good food, or slept in such pleasant rooms or beds. We had privacy for the first time I could remember, and our own closets and dresser drawers for our new clothes and new shoes. We could talk at meals in our turn and, incredibly, second helpings of food were available just for asking. We had a bathtub where, if we wished, we could bathe alone rather than having to stand in group showers as at the children's home. Our lives were suddenly full of excitement and beauty — carpentry tools, boxes of books, field trips to the country and free and noisy romps through the woods, a delightful neighborhood of people and buildings to meet and explore, a large back yard to play in, and a red-brick school on a university campus three blocks away. We were beginning to make new friends. While unending tedium filled our hours at the children's home, we were now involved in a stimulating round of activities that never seemed to end. Janey would later sum up our first years in the manse and the surrounding neighborhood with, "What an exciting place to be a child!"

But Ann Minnis was right. There would be rough spots. We were unnaturally thin, our health was poor. The Luchs had not begun to deal with our emotional wounds, nor had the four of us begun to make the adjustment to the new culture into which we had been plunged. We had not yet started the process of letting go of our past. All that was to come in the weeks and months ahead.

CHAPTER 7

Reality Sets In

A THENS SUDDENLY TURNS COLD in late October and everyone talks about the first frost of the season. Early morning fog settles in the valleys and mists drift across the meadows. As the honeymoon period drew to a close and reality began to disperse our illusions of unchallenged bliss, the Luchs introduced new programs to restore our physical and emotional health.

"Good morning, let's line up," our new mother said as we entered the spacious white manse kitchen for breakfast.

She guided me by the hand to our father who held a tablespoon in his right hand and a suspicious-looking dark brown bottle in his left. He poured some of what was in the bottle into the spoon and lowered the spoon to my mouth. "Down the hatch!" he said, "Now wash it down with your orange juice." The cod liver oil was thick and unpleasant tasting, a wintertime dose of vitamins A and D in one gulp. The memory of the foul fish oil taste lingered and caused me to shudder at the thought that this little ritual would begin all our days in our first winter in Athens.

Evelyn Luchs believed in the importance of predictable schedules and programs as one means of restoring our physical health and fostering emotional security. Apparently she was right. Many years later, when in training to become a Court Appointed Special Advocate (CASA) for children in Lane County, Oregon, I was given a copy of Twelve Guidelines for Working with Wounded Children. Guideline Number 3 is "Be predictable. These children need order and predictable adults in their lives."

Each day in the manse had its own rhythm. Monday, for example, was wash day. With her article writing to pay for the service, mother had a weekly cleaning woman. Carolyn came on Tuesdays to clean and help with the ironing.

Every day in turn, assisted by an adult with drying towel in hand, one of us would wash the dinner dishes. Also on "our" day, with some adult help at the beginning for Charlie and Janey, it was our responsibility to set and clear the table for the evening dinner, always a relatively formal occasion in the dining room. As part of our special day we began taking turns saying grace and were encouraged to use our own words rather than repeat a formula prayer. The result was often amusing. My favorite grace that first year came from Janey.

"Thank you, God, for this food and for the student girl who repaired it."

Our foster mother also believed, as a good Presbyterian, in filling time with useful activities, when possible in the service of others. We quickly learned not to complain when we had nothing to do. "Well," she would say, "In that case, I will find something for you to do," which usually meant a chore. All these predictable activities and regular schedules were not just for our physical and emotional health and the welfare of our souls. They also made it possible for the Luchs to continue their busy lives in the church and community, and include enough time to be with each other as they integrated the manifold needs of four active children into their daily round. All four of us were happily settled in our new school within a month of our arrival. This permitted our parents to spend two or three hours together each weekday morning, beginning with an eggs and bacon breakfast she cooked only for him. Then they would discuss or work on the week's sermon or an article one of them was writing.

During the week, Rufus Putnam and its programs provided the basic structure for our lives and for nearly eleven months of the year. On Sundays, we attended Sunday school, at least one church service, and a junior choir or youth fellowship program. The most elaborate meal of the week, always served on white Wedgwood china at 1 PM, gave a definite shape to our observance of the Christian Sabbath. And, to be sure, daily periods of quiet reading in bed, our substitute for a nap, were standard when we were not in school. The bedtime of 8 P.M. in summer light and winter darkness was firm. Bedtime almost always came with a bath and sometimes was followed by being read to by Margaret Hampel or our mother, or just reading to ourselves to relax and quiet down after a busy day.

Of the students who roomed in the manse, Grace Monigold — the tall young woman with glasses who greeted us the afternoon we arrived — played the largest role in our first year in the manse. Grace was soft-spoken and had a delightful if quiet sense of humor. She helped prepare meals and took turns as the adult in our evening dish washing teams. Grace helped nurse us when we were sick. She also was the only person our new mother would trust to take care of us when she had to be away for speaking engagements. Grace was a second mother for Janey.

There were other rules and routines in the manse. We stayed out of the study to not disturb our father's preparation of the weekly sermon. As a treat we were invited in on Sunday evenings to gather before the radio to listen to Jack Benny before a later-than-normal bedtime. The living room was "off limits" because it had to be ready to receive drop-in guests during the day. We had our own spacious rooms on the second floor but even those had to be in order because strangers sometimes came upstairs to meet us. There were exceptions. An event on no regular schedule was an occasional wrestling match in the living room. Our foster father had wrestled in college and refereed intramural wrestling matches at Ohio University. For our own wrestling matches, furniture was pushed to the side of the living room, all lights were turned off, and in the darkness we were free to pile on and dive under and pommel our new father to our heart's content while he tried to grab and pin us. The manse was suddenly filled with squeals and grunts and childish screams and occasional crying when the play got too rough. Our foster mother stood near the hall, issuing cautions, "Fred, be careful! Fred! Fred!" She was afraid one of us would be seriously hurt.

Grace commented years later, "Everything was so planned and structured...you did this and this and this...somebody read stories to you, they took you here and there, or did this or that. Always something was planned." I don't remember we seriously objected to such a structured life, probably because the Home's sterile environment — with no sports equipment, no music, and no books — was also structured and was much less fun than the mostly pleasant round of activities available to us in the manse. Despite all the scheduled activity, I remember free play time around the neighborhood. The period after school was free many week days and quickly became a time to play ball games, season by season — football, basketball, baseball or softball — as we developed bonds with new friends and practiced hard to develop our retarded ball handling skills.

The bigger adjustment was to the daily bustle in the manse. Encouraged by the Luchs' open and informal style, members of the church and university community felt free to drop in at almost any hour and often did. Many passed through the front door each day for meetings or for counseling or just to drop in for a cup of coffee. The manse was the scene of singing nights around the piano, lecture-discussions, get-acquainted social events for students, ice cream socials, and informal "bull sessions" for students and faculty alike.

The telephone seemed to ring constantly throughout the day. "At least 1,000 phone calls today!" an exaggeration Mom entered in her journal a year before we arrived after she had entertained some church women to tea. "We had some tea — and some of the 700 cookies I made yesterday. Several people came in and the telephone rang incessantly. And I was trying to get the curtains ironed to take back to the church. I think the women thought the manse is a madhouse."

The Interior of the Manse

As I filled in my first impressions of the manse during the weeks after we moved in, I could see the walls were papered in delicate floral patterns. The doors and window frames were a deep chestnut color and unusually tall and narrow. Every doorway had a transom, a small rectangular window on top that could be opened for ventilation on sultry summer evenings. Conversations that would normally not be heard behind closed doors were audible to an ear cocked to a transom opened at just the right angle. It was also possible for adults willing to stand on a chair to peek unnoticed at us behind a closed door.

The prism glass of the east-facing front door of the manse projected rainbows of color on the stairwell and I had already discovered the pleasure of sitting on the carpeted stairs to be warmed by the morning sun, looking out at the white columns on the porch and the grand elms beyond. At night, shadows of the dark branches of the elms were projected by moonlight in grotesque and frightening designs all along the screen of the stairwell wall. The bare branches seemed to be reaching out to grab us when the wind blew on wintry nights.

Even more frightening was the windowless, unlighted back stairwell to the kitchen — used by servants in the 19th century in the decades after the manse was built. During our first weeks I dreamed a dream often repeated during the next year. I dreamed the devil, red tail and all — who apparently had nothing else to do — was spending his nights sitting on those dark back stairs. I would awake from this nightmare sweating with fear and immediately realize I had to go to the bathroom. To get to the bathroom, I had to pass the opening to that unlighted stairwell coming and going. I streaked past the opening in both directions. When I told our mother about this nightmare she bought a small copper night light that glowed orange in the hall but did not illumine the dreaded back stairwell. I only believed in the devil when the house was dark, in the middle of the night.

One winter night some two or three years after we arrived Billy opened a door in the kitchen to head up into the same dark stairwell for his evening bath. He quickly returned. Janey had dish duty that evening and mom was helping her.

"It's scary, Mom," Billy said.

Janey marched over to Billy in her apron, put her hands on her hips, and said, "Billy, don't you know God looks out for us ALL the time? And if He's busy... Jesus takes over!"

Ancient Athens and holy Jerusalem lived on in the entrance hall of the manse. Against the right wall stood a white marble bust of a demure young woman with tiny wings. This I would learn was Psyche, whose Greek name means soul and also butterfly. Psyche was so beautiful she aroused the jealousy of Venus, won the love of Cupid, the son of Venus, and eventually emerged, like a caterpillar from her earthly chrysalis, a goddess of radiant beauty.

Halfway down the downstairs hall, on the left side, was a glass cabinet with items that our new father had collected on his trips to the Middle East, including tiny clay oil lamps from the Holy Land old enough to have been used during the lifetime of Jesus. Fascinating to me was a pint medicine bottle of clear glass filled with water from the River Jordan. I wondered if it came from the same springs as the water in which Jesus was baptized.

Most of the manse rooms had original gas fireplaces, installed well before the days of central heating. These had been plugged and covered with black metal shields. Pipe stubs stuck out from the walls, left over from the days the house was lighted with gas lights with bright mantles. There were no furnace ducts to the second floor at all. What heat reached that floor rose naturally through the open stairwell or through a single crosshatch opening in the upstairs hall. Just before we arrived the Luchs had the gas pipe in our bedroom opened and connected to a new gas room heater that stood on the floor in front of the old fireplace. I enjoyed jumping out of bed in winter, in a room dark and cold, quickly striking an Ohio match with the blue and white tip on the strip on the side of the box, and then, by simply turning a valve, lighting the gas fire! How magical that seemed after trying to coax fires and heat from the pot-bellied stove on cold winter mornings in the Old Gray House. Back in bed and cozy under a thick comforter, I would wait for the room to warm up, watching as the white ceramic cylinders, began their ever-changing fire dance of blues, yellows, oranges, and reds.

When inside the manse, we spent most of our time in the kitchen, a room large and comfortable, designed for a house with servants. The kitchen had last been remodeled about 1915. The refrigerator and range were gas-fueled and the white sink with brass plumbing fixtures was hardly larger than a dish pan. But the kitchen was always warm in winter and filled with the delightful smells of cooking food: casseroles and baking muffins and fresh rolls.

In most respects the manse had not changed at all since it was built in the early 1870s. Except for one work area with a brick surface, the basement floor was dirt. But we did not mind that as children. We loved the spaciousness and comfort of the old manse. In time I was able to explore and become familiar with the "inner sanctum" of the house, our father's study. This room was filled with book cases with glass fronts. Near the entrance was a rocking chair on the back of which had been carved a corpulent cellist, circa 1830, wearing Franz Schubert glasses perched halfway down his nose. Near the rocking chair stood an early carving that John Rood, an artist in residence at the university, made from a solid rectangular hunk of heavy dark wood about two feet tall. Rood had carved an aging black man, his face drooping, his body crouched, his head resting on one large, beautifully shaped hand. Rood titled the sculpture, "Nobody Knows the Troubles I've Seen."

But in a room filled with unusual objects, there was a portrait lithograph of Jesus that dominated everything else in our father's study. He had purchased the print in a shop on Trafalgar Square during late August 1939, just before Hitler's invasion of Poland. He always believed it was one of a kind in North America. Inscribed below the lithograph was the text: "And the Lord turned and looked upon Peter and Peter remembered..."

What was most remarkable about the portrait was the Dutch artist's treatment of the eyes of Jesus. It did not matter where we stood within sight of that portrait; the stern eyes seemed to stare directly at us. I could not avoid them. I felt their presence as soon as I entered the room even when I ran into the study only briefly looking for a paper clip or some mucilage. I would suddenly feel the cold glare of Jesus though my own eyes were fixed on the floor in order to avoid having to see the portrait at all.

At first, Janey was so afraid of it she refused to enter the study even if our father was there.

"You don't have to be afraid of Jesus," Dad assured her. "Jesus loves you. Jesus is your friend."

A month or so later our father returned from hospital visiting for a meeting with church elders in his study. Janey put on the homburg hat and leather gloves he had just deposited on a hall chair. She climbed on her tricycle, rode into the midst of the meeting, saluted the portrait, and said, "Hi, Jesus!"

BUILDING OUR HEALTH

In October of 1943, Inez Norman responded to a letter from Ann Minnis asking for our health histories. Norman wrote that we had all had whooping cough in 1941 and chicken pox in the spring of 1942. Janey also had mumps in 1942 and I had the three-day measles. In August of 1942, doing what our biological family had failed to do, the children's home gave Janey and Billy small pox and diphtheria immunizations. Charlie was then out with our Uncle Charles and I was with the Judge Smith family. The two of us were not given those vaccinations until we arrived in Athens. Charlie had pneumonia in May of 1943 and I had a tonsillectomy, about which I have written. I have also told the story of Janey's brush with death in early 1943 when she was down with scarlet fever, followed by pneumonia. This pattern of frequent illness did not change at once. During our first year with the Luchs at least one of us was in bed sick at all times and sometimes all of us were ill at the same time.

As soon as we arrived our new foster mother immediately set up short and long range programs to restore our health. We had never been to a dentist. We had never used a toothbrush before we were abandoned to the children's home. Members of our biological family typically lost their teeth before the age of 40 and our mouths were full of cavities when we arrived in Athens. The worst of these were filled during our first months in Athens, a process that began with large syringes full of novocain that suddenly emerged from hiding behind a dentist's back.

Our mother believed that good health begins with healthy food. The Department of Agriculture poster listing the seven basic food groups for good health was posted in a conspicuous place on one kitchen wall. We learned early it was important to eat from all the major food groups, with a special emphasis on fresh uncooked fruits and vegetables. In winter hot cereal was served, either oatmeal or cream of wheat. Eggs, which were not served at all at the children's home in the early 1940s, were most often weekend treats in the manse, too expensive to serve daily. The first time our mother prepared fried eggs for us, Janey, standing on a stool and looking into the frying pan asked,

"Are dose peaches, Mudder? "

Our foster mother spent a large chunk of her monthly food budget to buy as much fresh milk as we would drink, delivered daily in quart bottles to our back door, and enough oranges to have a freshly squeezed glass of orange juice every winter morning.

Her cooking was nutritious but plain. She believed, "If you can read, you can cook," a high claim for literacy that the more traditional women in her family scoffed at. But most of our food was tasty and all of it was healthy. She tended to overcook meat by today's standards, especially the beef roasts that we loved which she did in the English fashion. She also seemed to have a special talent for turning calf liver into green rubber. As vigorously as we ate and however much we appreciated whatever was put before us, we in time learned not to praise too highly. The risk was we would be served the same dish at least once a week for the next six months.

In the kitchen there was a large bowl kept full of fresh fruit, most often bananas, oranges, and apples, to which we could help ourselves at any time. No other snacks of any kind were available, except for a relish bowl of carrots, green peppers, and celery strips we could munch on before dinner. Teaching about nutrition, linked to a national program during World War II, was also a priority at Rufus Putnam. A healthy hot dish to supplement our bag lunches, prepared by the students under teacher supervision, was served each school day.

Being sick in the manse had certain advantages. Chicken soup, juices, hot chocolate, and full dinners were brought to us in bed on pretty painted wooden trays covered with colored dishes and matching cloth napkins. I could read all day in bed when sick, only stopping from time to time to gaze at the ceramic cylinders of our gas fireplace where gas flames danced through their cycle of reds and yellows and blues. I could play with Tinker Toys and toy soldiers on the soft comforter which covered my bed and lie down to snooze any time I pleased.

When sick we were regularly visited by Grace or our mother who peered at a tiny glass thermometer under the lamp on top of our bureau, looking for the thin mercury line that would tell our temperature. We could often look forward to Margaret Hampel — our dear Hampel — coming in the evenings to read to us. If our condition was contagious Hampel would pull a chair under the hall light next to the banister rail. Her well-modulated alto voice, filled with animation and crisply articulated, could reach all four bedrooms on the second floor at once.

"Now, what shall we read this evening?"

We all shouted our favorites at once, "Littlest Angel!" "Engine that Could." "Bartholomew Cubbins!"

Sometimes she would read all three just to please us. When reading dialogue Hampel changed her voice so that we knew when the King of Didd was speaking and when Bartholomew Cubbins was speaking. Hampel was an artful and entertaining reader. We loved to hear Hampel read.

When it came to our health, our new parents spared no expense. On the other hand, carbonated soft drinks were never available in the manse. When we ate out, which was rare, hamburgers and French fries were not on "our" menu. Baloney sandwiches slathered with yellow mustard — the main course of school lunches at the children's home — disappeared forever. The Luchs put baloney in the same category as carbonated drinks and hamburgers and French fries. They were unhealthy and because they were unhealthy, they were not available.

After the drab menus of starchy carbohydrates at the children's home, we did not protest our new diet, not even the absence of candy. We ate what was put before us because we had learned at the Home that those who do not eat, go hungry. The rule on new foods was that we had to try them. If we did, even one bite, then we could have dessert. Desserts were simple, often pudding and sometimes gingerbread. As a special treat, Grace Monigold, a fine baker and candy maker, would on occasion use up our World War II sugar ration stamps to make pineapple upside-down cake or chocolate fudge. Lots of casseroles were served in the manse, especially our favorite "Marzetti," which was a mixture of chili and spaghetti.

Our candy-free environment was the rule at the manse partly because of sugar rationing during the war but also because the Luchs did not think candy was good for us, especially for our now expensive teeth. We early gave up on the line "But other children can have it." I can still hear mom's firm retort, not missing a beat, "But you are NOT other children." She did not mean we were different from most other children because of our early experiences, though we certainly were. She meant we were her children and she would decide what was best for us. What she had to accept because she could not change in the larger world, she did not have to accept in the world of her family where she could make the rules. That other children could have something was the least persuasive of reasons for Evelyn Luchs. Using that line with her was wasted effort as was, "But other children do it." There were exceptions to the "no candy" rule. Halloween trick or treating normally produced a few pieces of candy, though in those days most of our neighbors gave us fruit or home-baked cookies. The Luchs gave us candy only at Christmas and Easter.

If good food was the beginning of health, it was not the end of it. Adequate rest was also important because, as Mom often said, "you children are so easily over-stimulated." That we found the manse a stimulating environment after the gray routines of the children's home is no surprise, but it's also true that we were high energy children.

Eight PM was bedtime. Without fail. Lights out. Quiet. We fudged the rules sometimes. After we were given pen lights for birthdays and at Christmas, we read under the covers. When we did not go to sleep right away, the three of us, Charlie, Billy and I, began to take turns telling each other stories. Sometimes the stories were based on something we had read, but often they were products of our imagination. Charlie had the most original mind and was also a good mimic. As long as our voices were low, the Luchs either did not hear or did not mind our story telling. Sometimes we sang ourselves to sleep. Again, our parents did not ask us to stop singing. They — who were less musical than we — loved to hear us sing, alone or together. Rufus Putnam supported our mother's health program. Agnes Eisen, our third grade teacher, wrote to parents in a Putnam progress report, "We have found children who are in bed by 7:30 or 8:00 and who rest 30 minutes at noon are doing the best work at school."

Probably because of his health history of tuberculosis and undulant fever, our new father pursued whatever new health preserving product or practice or procedure was in fashion. Over the years he had developed a moderately severe case of hypochondria. During that first year with the Luchs we were introduced to acquaintances of his known as "The

175

Experts." He often quoted "The Experts." They seemed to be his friends. Most of them apparently worked for a magazine called the *Reader's Digest*. When we asked for the source of his information about some practice we were to undertake or some product we were to be denied, he would simply say, "The Experts say so," a phrase he spoke with a hushed and reverent tone.

One night we discovered our bed pillows were gone. When we couldn't find them and raised a fuss, we learned "The Experts" had proclaimed that pillows were harmful to the postures of growing children. We would have to do without pillows. A few weeks later the nice-tasting commercial tooth powder we had been using disappeared. In its place was a small bowl of salt and baking soda. "The Experts" had spoken again! Our father had read that the best dentifrice was salt and baking soda. Healthier and less expensive. So offensive was unadulterated salt and baking soda to our mouths that we soon stopped brushing our teeth altogether. He nagged and we balked. We balked and he nagged. He did not give up easily and did not lift the ban on commercial tooth powder until it was evident that his already large dental bills were growing even larger.

One evening he lined us up for eye exercises. "The Experts" again!

"Now, watch me." He rolled his eyes around, looking at the edge of his peripheral vision. "Can you see what I'm doing?"

"Yes," we nodded.

"OK. We're going to try it all together. Roll your eyes around and look as far as you can to your sides and above and below as you do. See?"

We tried it, again and again, with minimal success.

"Not bad," he said. "Not bad. It's hard because your eye muscles are undeveloped. That's why "The Experts" recommend this exercise. Now try putting your hands in front of you with your index fingers extended and make them...no, no, that's not the index finger, Charlie."

"Oh, Fred. Let the children be!"

"But honey! They're getting it and "The Experts" say it's good for their eyes."

After another ten minutes or so we began to get the idea, but eye exercises lasted only a few weeks as experts with opinions on other subjects came to visit us from the *Reader's Digest*. The world seemed to be full of an endless procession of our foster father's friends, "The Experts." They seemed determined to make our lives less pleasant than they had been. But I never heard him complain about the large amounts of his salary going for the purchase of fresh oranges and gallons of fresh milk or our expensive dental bills and other programs and services to build our health. We began to grow rapidly, gained a pound a month, and grew in health under our new mother's regime. Except for Janey. Mother had noticed Janey was not gaining weight and was running low-grade fevers. Twice she walked her up to Dr. Goldsberry's office on Washington Street for examinations. Dr. Goldsberry could find nothing wrong, but mother worried.

JANEY'S OWN ROOM

Once, during our first weeks in the manse, we broke the quiet rule during naptime. Unknown to us, our foster mother had pulled up a chair outside our closed door, climbed up on it and peeked through the transom window. What she saw was Janey systematically emptying the goldfish bowl with handfuls of water which she then threw at her brothers. That, mother later said, was why she moved Janey into a room across the hall, going against the counsel of the children's home and social workers that during the first year we should all sleep in the same bedroom. Because Janey's new bedroom had been our mother's study, she moved her desk out into the hall to an empty space behind the entrance to her bedroom and ours. Janey was as pleased to have a bedroom all to herself as we were to turn our room into a boys dormitory with three equal beds, side by side. Now that she was separated from the Luchs by only a communicating door, four-year-old Janey could flee from night goblins to the parental bed, which she often did.

CHAPTER 10

A New Neighborhood and New Culture

YEARS LATER JANEY RECALLED our first months among the 19th century brick homes of College Street and the public buildings and commercial establishments of adjacent Washington and Court streets. "I arrived in Athens with a feeling of not belonging, of being passed around. But after a few months I felt the town was mine. We had everything. At four I believed it was all made for me."

Immediately south of the manse, at 9 North College Street, was the Dowler and Ferguson Funeral Home. A dark blue Chrysler ambulance came and went during the day and a black Cadillac hearse was sometimes parked in front of the business. On the second floor lived Davy Hughes and his wife Tillie and their two sons, Jimmy and Donnie. Davy was a friendly, cheerful man. I used to wonder how he could be so happy when he worked with cadavers most days. An occasional errand took us inside the front door of the funeral home, an eerie place because it was associated with the dark shadows of death. While we waited with a message or something we were to take home, we were sometimes able to peek unnoticed at one of the recently departed. With makeup on, they looked almost alive, though sleeping. Davey's wife Tillie was a registered nurse and wonderful help to our new mother in her program to recover our health. Mom tried not to bother Tillie but when she was concerned and did not know if a doctor was required, she consulted Tillie.

Beyond the funeral home, at the corner of North College and East Washington, was the grand James D. Brown house which in our time was divided into two large town houses. James D. Brown founded the Bank of Athens across from First Presbyterian and sponsored the church's largest stain glass window, "Christ Blessing Little Children." Our neighbor to the north at 21 North College was the handsome white brick house of Mrs. Isabelle Lawrence, an immaculately dressed banker's widow with white hair. Mrs. Lawrence had a gardener and a chauffeur with a black cap and black suit and a full-time maid, also dressed in black, with a white apron. Mrs. Lawrence was one of the few residents of College Street who could afford the living standard once common on what had earlier been Athens' most prestigious street. Her meticulously maintained green lawn was off-limits to us and we were forbidden to chase vagrant balls that landed even a foot on her side of an invisible property line. Her garden was a haven of beauty and peace in a bustling neighborhood.

Despite our central location in downtown Athens, we trapped an angry possum in our backyard our first autumn in the manse. A day later we watched it amble out of the green trap on Happy Howell's nursery farm where we released it. In our back yard we surprised toads and turtles, chased after squirrels and cottontail rabbits, and dug stage one, five feet deep, of a tunnel to China.

To the left of the high green board fence that sheltered our back yard from all that was behind it, we could see the barred windows of the city jail and the windows of the apartment of the city's fire chief and jailer, Charlie Dalton. At first I was afraid of Charlie Dalton because his face reminded me of the feared Kline Dawson of the children's home. Even his name, Dalton, sounded like Dawson to me. I believed they were related and was sure they held similar views about small boys. Charlie's wife cooked for the jail's "guests," mostly weekend inebriates, who could rarely have eaten better food than she prepared in the city jail. Mrs. Dalton put her delicious pies on a window sill to cool. They were within smelling range but too high for us to reach.

Janey and Charlie soon discovered they could climb up on top of a wrought iron fence and peer at a window of the jail. They struck up conversations with the men behind bars. They recall they had no fear at all and the men were nice to them. They would ask what the men had done, how long they would be in jail, and if Mrs. Dalton's cooking was as good as it smelled. Charlie Dalton caught them at this one day and spoke with our father, which ended the jailhouse dialogues.

The Berry Hotel, largest and grandest of Athens hotels, was built, owned, and managed for many years by Edward C. Berry, a talented African-American entrepreneur. Athens banks refused to extend Berry credit to build the hotel but two men in the community, C.L Kurtz and Charles Grosvenor, quietly advanced him money. Kurtz was the owner of our house at 15 North College Street before it became the manse and reduced the $9,000 market price of the house to $6,000 as his contribution to the church's finances. Charles Grosvenor was for many years a member of the U.S. House of Representatives.

The Hotel Berry's ballroom windows opened on our back yard. On Saturday nights we lay in bed entertained by live bands playing the fox trots and jitterbugs of the 1940s. In sum, College Street, only three blocks long, boasted two doctors, three clergymen, a university dean, three fraternity houses and as many sororities, two churches, a banker, a women's dorm, the Men's Union, and, of course, the funeral home. One could go from birth to death without ever having to leave College Street.

ETIQUETTE IN THE MANSE

Grace Monigold said of our first winter in Athens:

"I look back on it now and think how lost you must have felt there in that house, with people coming and going all the time. And then, to start having to conform. It's not that you were out of order and I'm sure there were rules and regulations in the children's home, but the kind of discipline, the expectations they had, there was no way you could meet instantly ... because you had no background to build on. You were all smart. You learned pretty fast. But it must have been quite a struggle."

I don't remember a struggle but I do remember being uncomfortable at first with the busy flow of men and women in and out of our new home and the sometimes constant jangle of the telephone. Even our bedrooms on the second floor were invaded occasionally by strangers our proud foster parents wanted us to meet. Sometimes we felt we were on display. At first we were shy with new adults. We fixed our eyes on the floor and tentatively offered — but only when prompted to do so — a limp hand to shake. We had not yet learned the two most important words on a child's lips, "please" and "thank you," or the next two most important phrases, "you are welcome" and "excuse me." When we arrived our speech was ungrammatical and spiced with words that widened eyes and created gasps, words not normally heard in the homes of the Presbyterian clergy. The Evelyn Luchs approach was to ignore all such language and also our "ain'ts" and "Billy and mes." She believed that if we no longer heard these lapses of grammar, they would drop out of our vocabularies. Janey's problem was more challenging. She talked like a four-year-old Elmer Fudd, struggling towards some understandable articulation of the English language. At first Janey could only manage to say "Mudder" for our foster mother and settled on "Fwed" for our foster father.

It turned out Mom was right. In a year or so our expletives were deleted and we were all speaking standard English. But our colorful language and mild abuse of our mother tongue did not disappear at once and sometimes caused embarrassing moments that were difficult to ignore. Not long after we arrived, mother invited the Cless Class to the manse for afternoon tea. This group of senior women named for Mrs. Cless, founder of the group, met each Sunday at the same time as the children's Sunday school for Bible study. Many of the women were gray-haired widows who wore black daily, head to toe. We could see them sitting stiffly in straight-backed chairs behind the glass doors of the church office where they gathered. They spoke in hushed tones and rarely smiled. If we were noisy as we gathered before Sunday school, they peered through the glass doors of the office to frown their disapproval. We came to see members of the Cless Class as the ultimate guardians of Presbyterian rectitude, the vicars of the Old Testament's Jehovah in his grouchier moods.

On the day the unspeakable was uttered, the women sat in their black dresses and chattered over their cups of tea in the manse. The pocket doors between our two living rooms were opened and additional card table chairs had been brought in and placed around to accommodate all of the twenty-five or so women present. Just off the back of the living room of the manse was a burgundy curtain that concealed a small walk-through closet and a half bathroom, both within earshot of those sitting in the living room. We children normally used the downstairs bathroom during the day rather than climb up the long flight of stairs to the second floor. Unless, of course, the convenient downstairs bathroom was occupied.

On this occasion, the Reverend Mr. Fred E. Luchs was seated in the lower bathroom and four-year-old Janey arrived out of breath. She had waited much too long to make the climb to the bathroom upstairs. She turned the knob and found the bathroom door locked, considered running upstairs, and decided it was too late. So she shouted,

"Let me in, Fwed! I've got to potty"

She squeezed her legs together and rocked back and forth on her feet from side to side, her situation increasingly desperate. The lively chatter of the Cless Class began to die. Some of the women held their tea cups in midair poised for the next sip, their ears now directed to whatever was going on behind the burgundy curtain. Silence settled like fog on the gathering.

"I'm in here, Janey. Go upstairs, my dear."

The Cless Class women found the dramatically articulated baritone words of their minister reassuring.

"No, Fwed! I've got to go! Now! "

Cless Class eyebrows rose slightly and the stillness in the living room became uncomfortable. One of their more anxious members rattled her cup in its saucer. "Patience, my dear. Patience," said the pastor.

Knowing smiles were exchanged around the living room. The women leaned forward in their chairs to hear more of the thoughtfully delivered counsel of their minister to his new daughter.

Thinking she was about to burst and unable to forestall the inevitable another second, Janey began to kick the bathroom door as hard as she could and shouted,

"Let me in! Let me in, Fwed, you old bastard!"

Well! Little Janey's words blew a fuse in the living room. Some of the women winced. Others gasped. Just when there seemed to be no possible Presbyterian solution to the crisis, the bathroom door opened and closed and the matter was resolved. Two of the women began to giggle.

Our foster mother blushed but did not say a word. Nor did anyone else break the silence of the living room. Moments later the incident seemed to have passed so quickly it did not seem real and the women of the Cless Class resumed chatting and sipping their tea.

Our maternal grandmother, Lottie Coulter, came to Athens for a few weeks to help out that first winter. During cold weather, when the downtown chimneys of Athens were full of soft coal smoke, it was necessary to carry baskets of laundry washed in the basement up three and a half flights of stairs to the attic, where it was pinned to rope lines to dry. Grandma Coulter was a serious Methodist but not a pious one. I had become annoyed with Charlie as we played with some neighborhood friends and wished to be rid of him. I told Charlie mom was trying to find him. He left at once for the manse, as I hoped he would, climbed all three and a half flights of stairs and, having arrived in the attic out of breath, said,

"Dick told me you were looking for me."

"He did? I wonder why he said that. I'm not looking for you."

"That bas-tard!!!" Charlie shouted.

While it was true that our grammar and speech changed naturally over time, our father — his ears aching with our abuse of English — could not let our "aint's" and other grammatical lapses go by without correction. This kept him rather busy. Perhaps he was so fastidious about English grammar because his parents were immigrants and he spoke only Swiss-German before he began school at the age of six.

In some cases learning about the new culture we had entered required more than observation and imitation. We were given lessons. I remember one morning we stood in a cluster in the front hall as father Luchs delivered instructions for greeting church members and others who came through the manse front door.

"Stick out your paw," he said. "Look 'em in the eye, smile, and say....Here's mud in your eye!"

"Oh, Fred!" Our foster mother was watering plants in the living room but could hear us.

"But darling!"

He shifted out of his tough-guy James Cagney voice back to the Reverend Mr. Fred Luchs. Now he was looking directly at me.

"Introduce yourself," he told me. "Say 'My name is Dick and I'm glad to meet you!' And smile!"

"Or say"....Now he was looking at Billy...."My name's Bill. May I help you?"

And so it went as he played the visitor coming through the front door and we stuck our hands, in turn, to shake and greet him. Greeting adults with confidence took time and practice. We were also schooled in verbal address. Friends close to the family were honored as "aunt" and "uncle," titles attached to their first names as in Uncle Harold and Aunt Dorothy. All other adults except Margaret Hampel were Miss, Mrs. or Mr.

TELEPHONE ETIQUETTE

Early on, we got a lesson in answering the manse telephone, number 417, which rang many times a day. We were instructed to pick up the phone, if we were near it, and say,

"Presbyterian Manse."

Four-year-old Janey liked the novelty of answering a telephone and ran to the phone wherever she was in the house to take as many calls as possible. She would lift the big black receiver to her tiny ear with two hands and strain to pronounce the words, syllable by syllable, as clearly as she could. "Pres — BYE — Tear — rian... manse!"

"Once the caller recovered her poise, Janey heard, "Hello. Is Reverend Luchs there, please?"

"Yes. Yes." Janey replied, and then raised her head and shouted, "Fwed! It's for youuuuu!"

Only Janey, his special girl from the start, got away with calling our father — the dignified minister in the homburg hat — Fwed or Fweddie, imitating what she heard him called by our mother.

Dad liked to drive Janey around with him from time to time to keep him company as he made afternoon calls on members of the church. Once during those first months he asked her to stand behind the green Buick as he backed it out of the narrow garage he rented down an alley on the other side of College Street. The difference between clearing the garage door and scraping the 1941 Buick's almost new finish on his blind side was a matter of about six inches. As he slowly backed out of the garage he called to Janey, "Am I coming out straight, Janey?"

"Ya do'in all wight, Fwed!" she shouted back.

We almost always ate dinner in the dining room, using crystal, china, silverware, and a linen table cloth and napkins. In the midst of such finery, manners tended to improve. But we had to learn some house rules. One rule was that we waited for our father to begin eating before we could lift a fork. When we sometimes complained about waiting for him, he would tell a story of how in his Swiss immigrant family the adults ate first. Children came to the table only after the adults had finished for what was left, a practice he must have sometimes wished he could continue.

During one of our first dinners in the dining room, our foster mother had placed in front of her four large rings, each with a different design.

"Do you know what these are?" she asked.

"They're for napkins." I said. I knew that because I had lived with Judge Smith's family.

"Good for you. Dick! We each have our own napkins and when we roll them up, we put one of these rings on them and then we know which one is ours for the next meal."

"Now, who would like to try folding a napkin? No one? OK, I'll show you how the first time."

We watched as she folded the napkin in two and then rolled it up in a cylinder and slid her napkin ring over it. We chose our own rings, and after a few tries managed to fold the napkins in a manner that looked almost as good as hers.

I noticed that our foster mother used her knife and fork one way, our foster father another way. His Swiss family followed European practice, his fork in his left hand, the knife in his right. He cut meat piece by piece against the back of his fork with his right hand and then loaded some potatoes or vegetables on the fork before putting it in his mouth. Our mother followed the American custom of cutting a piece of meat with a knife in the right hand, putting the knife down at the head of the plate, and then using the fork to pick up the meat.

At the beginning we did what we had been permitted to do at the children's home, which was to grasp our utensils in our fists. We cut up an entire piece of meat into more or less bite-sized pieces, after which we would set the knife down and go to work with the fork. Janey and Charlie got help with meat cutting at first, but soon we were all cutting meat piece by piece, and choosing for ourselves whether we wished to follow European or American practice or a mixture of the two.

Pushing peas onto forks or spoons with our fingers was frowned on, but we found stabbing peas with our forks a tedious business which didn't seem worth the effort. Wiping gravy or anything else off our plates with a piece of bread, normal in the children's home, was frowned on but we were allowed to use bread as a pusher, though we rarely did.

Harder to learn was how to take turns entering a dinner conversation without interrupting and with our mouths empty. We were not supposed to talk until our mouths were completely empty. Choosing between eating and talking was not difficult. The first ten minutes of our evening dinners were as silent as a monastery refectory, which gave our foster parents a chance to exchange the news of the afternoon. After most of my food was down and my mouth empty I found entering the conversation a question of timing, like skating onto a crowded roller rink in the middle of a number. But once in the flow, it was tempting to dominate the conversation, so we also had to learn to take turns and let others talk.

No arms or elbows were allowed on the table. Clowning behavior of any kind at meals such as flicking bits of mashed potatoes off a fork at a brother was discouraged, especially during the more formal evening meal. No spatting, no bickering, above all no arguing, or no silent paybacks such as stabbing a sibling under the table with a fork. No making faces, no teasing, no pinches. If we breached these prohibitions more than twice at one meal or were just being generally raucous or disagreeable, we were banished to our rooms for the night which meant no food at all until breakfast the following morning. No exceptions.

Arguing was particularly frowned on and not only at the table. The prohibition against arguing was one of the first Luchs rules we had to learn. In a letter to our new father at Ft. Benning two months after we arrived, our foster mother recounts an incident with Janey.

"The other morning Jane started to say something that sounded like arguing to me and I quickly said, 'Remember Jane, we don't do any arguing about things.' She answered, quick as a flash: 'Oh, Mudder. I'm not arguing. I'm just fussing.' I had an impulse to say, 'A rose by any other name...but I didn't.'"

Our new mom distinguished between happy and unhappy noise. There was no objection to the normal levels of noise made by happy children. Happy noise in most situations was OK and interrupted only when it was disturbing to those outside our family. Unhappy noise of any kind was discouraged.

OUR GUESTS

We often had guests at our evening meals. Some were invited in advance, but many guests father invited to the manse half an hour before dinner began. He always called and asked first if he could bring a guest or two for dinner and our mom always said yes. Sometimes the fare was plainer than she would have liked to serve guests, but she managed somehow to dress it up. Sometimes it wasn't possible to simply reduce the size of the servings of whatever we were eating. One evening we were having veal cutlets. One cutlet each was available for the six of us. And one was served to each of us, and one to our guest. It was as if Mom had discovered the New Testament formula for multiplying loaves and fishes. The observant would have seen that our mother's veal cutlet was in fact a piece of bread cut in the shape of a cutlet and artfully coated with batter and smothered with gravy.

I found I enjoyed the conversation of adults. While Billy, Charlie, and Janey normally asked to be excused from the table after dessert, I would linger to listen to our guests. People from many backgrounds and walks of life sat at our dinner table, though most of them had some connection to local or national church affairs or to the university. Good conversation was a practiced art for these guests. They were full of stories and humor. I particularly enjoyed those who had traveled abroad, especially missionaries to China and Japan who were home for a furlough. I could not hear enough about foreign lands and peoples.

Other than long hikes with our mother, our father's chief recreation in the fall was hunting in the rolling brown fields and brilliant autumn woods of Athens County. We ate lots of cottontail rabbit during WW II when meat at the market was either rationed or unavailable. That winter we had rabbit fried, stewed, roasted, and in hasenpfeffer. One of our distinguished guests, a charming senior missionary from China with the long German name of Lautenschlager, taught us a new dinner grace at the end of yet one more meal of wild rabbit.

It went:

"For rabbits hot, for rabbits cold,

For rabbits young, for rabbits old,

For rabbits tender, for rabbits tough,

We thank thee, Lord, we've had enough!"

Beginning a few months after we arrived, we were encouraged to invite our own adult guests to the manse dinner table. We learned to host by hosting. We made the centerpiece, did the place cards and helped Grace Monigold or our mother set the table. We greeted our guest at the door, escorted her (most of our chosen guests were our teachers or other single friends of the family) to the table, seated her by pulling out her chair, and were encouraged to take some responsibility for keeping the conversation going. We were practicing the art of hosting in which the ultimate goal was learning how to make a guest feel at ease.

The Luchs were often invited out for dinner by church members and other Athenians and we were sometimes invited to go with them. These were opportunities to use the table manners we were learning at the manse and to begin to feel confident in social situations outside our home. I remember best the more formal occasions when we dined in the homes of older members of the church including Dr. Gamertsfelder, then the president of Ohio University, and Dr. Creed, the superintendent of the state mental hospital. Dr. Creed's dining room used freshly ironed linens, china, silver table service, individual salt cellars and gave us our first experience with finger bowls.

One Sunday we were invited to the neoclassical home of Anna Pearl McVay, the Grande Dame of the Alexandria Presbyterian Church in Albany Ohio, ten miles west of Athens. Anna Pearl — there was only one Anna Pearl in all of Athens County and almost everyone knew who she was — was elected president of the Athenian Literary Society in 1897 when a contemporary described her as "easily the outstanding member of her organization." She was frail and elderly by the time I met her, but I could see in her bright eyes and hear in her voice an inner and lively spirit. We gathered in her living room after church on a sunny, bitter-cold winter day. She had a fire going in the living room and as I looked over her fine paintings and mementos, I was drawn to what I would later come to learn was a framed print of Jean-Louis David's "Death of Socrates." I asked her what the picture was about. She rose to my child's question and, marvelously animated, in beautiful words I can no longer recall, she told me the story of the trial and death of Socrates. Anna Pearl was looking at me intently — and it seemed only at me — the whole time. I was so enchanted I was hardly aware the rest of my family was there listening as she talked. That afternoon, in Albany, Ohio, Anna Pearl McVay awakened in me an interest in the philosophy of Plato and other philosophers that has nurtured me even until now.

When they arrived on the OU campus a few years later, Mom invited international students, including Nigerian and South Asian princes, to our evening meals. She made the following offer to them: I will find and purchase all the ingredients for one of your favorite dishes from your home country if you will help me prepare it. Amazingly, all of the students, male and female — including the two princes — turned out to be excellent cooks. Then we would all sit down in our dining room to enjoy what they had prepared. In time we came to feel comfortable with people from all walks of life, including those from other cultures and countries.

Photographs

Janey's efforts to collect photographs of us from our biological family produced only five pictures and only one of the four of us all together. What we lacked in a photographic record of our lives before Athens, however, was quickly made up during our first months in the manse. The wealth of the photographic record from that period and later reflected the Luchs pride in their new family and the responsibility they felt to document our childhood for us. Through his contacts at the university, Dad was able to arrange for student photographers in the journalism department to come with a Speed Graphic or Rolliflex camera to take professional quality shots of us riding on tricycles and in wagons, catching softballs, playing football or swimming at the city swimming pool.

There were indoor photo sessions as well. On one such occasion a tall student with slicked down brown hair and wearing a worn tweed sports coat with leather elbow patches set up a large format camera with a viewing screen and a black hood in our living room. We all wanted to look into the viewing screen. One by one we left our places and climbed up on a stool as the student lifted the black hood so that we could peer in. We noticed, of course, that since we were behind the camera, we no longer appeared with the rest of the family on the viewing screen. Except Janey. She climbed up on the stool, disappeared under the black hood, looked a long time at the screen and then pulled her head out and said, most unhappily, "But...where's me?!"

MY SPECIAL ROLE ENDS

Ann Minnis predicted there would be rough spots in our first year with the Luchs. My delight in our new life in the manse did not mean I understood how the Luchs would challenge my special role in the lives of my younger siblings. What the Luchs and eventually my siblings saw as bossing, I saw as faithfully discharging my responsibility as the leader of our little pack against an indifferent world. Moreover, I was truly afraid during those first months that any misbehavior on our part might cause us to be sent back to the children's home. I sometimes encouraged good behavior with the verbal threat, whispered out of the hearing of our new parents, "If you don't stop that, we'll all be sent back to the children's home." It usually worked.

I also did not understand that as the Luchs began to replace me as our parents, relations with my brothers and sister would change. We were unusually supportive of each other when we arrived in Athens, a characteristic Grace Monigold would remember many years later. "You weren't like other kids," she said. "You stuck together. You really did." Over the course of the first year in Athens, however, the special bonds that had helped sustain us through years of neglect and shared danger began to weaken. My three siblings began to move away from our mutual dependence and the close cooperation the psychologists had observed while we were at the children's home. They began to behave more as normal siblings do, at times cooperative and loving but also at times competing with each other and challenging me.

I saw this rejection of the role I had played as a rejection of me and I took it hard. The increasing refusal among my siblings to accept my parental role hurt especially in the case of

Billy. Billy and I were often taken for twins. We had not been separated since he was born except for the few months at the children's home before he joined me in the Little Boys dormitory. With Lonnie out of the picture, my closest human relationship was with Billy. We had been through much together and were so closely bonded that I sometimes felt the two of us were almost one being. Billy's new refusal to accept my direction as the Luchs began to become our mother and father hurt my feelings most of all.

So after the first honeymoon weeks, tensions developed between the Luchs and me. They were not interested in accommodating the child-adult I had become. My fierce sense of independence and strong resistance when I thought my interests or what I thought was best for my siblings was being challenged, surprised and frustrated them. They especially did not enjoy having a rival eight-year-old parent in the house. My behavior, formerly important to keeping the four of us together and even necessary for our survival, was no longer appreciated. Once they had recovered from their surprise, they decided they did not like my taking the book out of our new father's hands, announcing "I can read that," and doing so. I did not try to undermine them. I participated as enthusiastically as my siblings in the programs and activities they organized for us. But I did resist surrendering the special role I had played for as long as I could remember.

I look today in disbelief at some of the movies of us that first year. I was like a drill sergeant inspecting new recruits. Once we were in position to be photographed I would step in front of the other three, look them over, tuck in a shirt here, pull an arm down straight along the body there, and make sure everyone had their hair combed and our line was straight. Only then would I step back in place as the last in line. During our first months at Rufus Putnam we all went together to the stairwell where two women behind a table sold war bond stamps each month. I lined the other three up, counted and put the correct amount of money in their hands, and one by one as they came forward, told the war bond women how much money they had and how many 10 and 25 stamps they wished to buy. Then I showed them how to paste the stamps in the new books we had been given. No adult help was asked for or needed. In the first month in the manse my siblings found such behavior perfectly normal and the Luchs did not object. The Luchs sometimes even found my behavior amusing. But not for long. They began to see me as a difficult child. I was standing in their way. In their view I was resisting their wish to be our parents. In my view I was behaving as I always had and protecting a role that defined who I was. The tensions between us day by day were an undercurrent hardly visible to an outside observer, but I could tell when the Luchs were annoyed with me, as they could tell when I was upset with them.

The Luchs wanted me to become a dependent child again. But having enjoyed some aspects of being a parent to my brothers and sister, I could not easily surrender my role as leader and protector of our little tribe. I felt the Luchs did not understand my situation and I sometimes accused them of being unfair. Moreover, accepting them as my father and mother was not easy for me. For one thing, they would have to earn my trust, which could no longer be freely given to any adult. In the back of my mind lurked the possibility that the adoption would not work and we would be on our own again, one more time failed by adults. I also continued to feel a bond with Lonnie. There were days when I was angry with the Luchs and even periods when I thought I wanted us to go back to the children's home, though no one remembers that I ever said so out loud.

More and more the Luchs challenged what they saw as the bossy sergeant in me, mostly by sending the sergeant off to his room alone and without supper. It became a test of wills. If they denied the sergeant supper, the sergeant was determined to remain in his room until they confessed their error and begged him to return to the family table. On their knees! Pleading! If the sergeant had to go to school the next day, he went but he refused to eat breakfast and fasted all day.

Of course, the Luchs did not confess their error or beg me on their knees to come and eat at the family table or offer any special invitations to rejoin the family fold. They were as determined as I to win this contest of wills and authority and assumed I would return to the family table after 24 hours of hunger and I did. My return was a delicate matter. I avoided eye contact with everyone, ate quickly and quietly and intended to ask, as was the rule, to be excused as soon as I was no longer hungry. If anyone had made any reference to the incident for which I had been disciplined, I would have bolted from the table. After a few minutes it felt good to be back at the family table, to be included again. Usually someone, often Charlie, would say something unrelated and funny to break the tension. We would all laugh and our fellowship began to be restored. I was not the only one sent to my room, but I held the record during our first year in Athens.

CHAPTER 9

Religion in the Manse

A FTER THE LUCHS, THE manse and our school, the most important influence in our lives in Athens was First Presbyterian. Known in Athens as the "church on the corner," First Presbyterian was a sturdy Romanesque revival structure of gray pressed brick trimmed with Vermont limestone. Romanesque architecture was popular among Presbyterians when the church was built in 1903 because it was the architecture of the early Christian church with roots in ancient Rome and Byzantium. Also, Presbyterian leaders were concerned about defections to the Episcopal Church, which at that time favored Gothic architecture. The interior of First Presbyterian used the "Akron Plan," an interior design invented by Lewis Miller of Akron, Ohio, that quickly spread to almost every Protestant church built in the United States in the late 19th and early 20th centuries. In an age without microphones, sanctuaries were built shallow and wide, with pews in concentric circles to enable all members of the congregation to see and hear clearly. The Akron Plan also referred to a design for Sunday school class rooms which opened into a common space from which a Sunday school superintendent could monitor all classes at the same time. In the case of First Presbyterian, a floor to ceiling screen on the right side of the sanctuary was raised on Sundays to open up the Sunday school common area and classrooms, which were then filled with folding chairs to double the seating capacity of the church from 300 to 600.

As a child I didn't think First Presbyterian looked much like a church because it had no steeple and no belfry or bell. When First Presbyterian was built, the bell belonging to the former Presbyterian Church on the same site was sold to St. Paul's Roman Catholic Church just down the street from the manse on College Street.

First Presbyterian was located only one block from the Ohio University campus and next door to the red brick neo-classic Athens City Hall. The Security Bank building, the tallest building in Athens, was on the other side. As if that were not enough to make the church part of the established Athenian order, the church also shared the central crossing of downtown Athens with the massive Athens County Court House and the two oldest banks. Surrounded by such neighbors, our church lived daily with the corruptions of government and the temptations of Mammon.

Our father directed much of his ministry toward Ohio University's students. He enjoyed the company of young people and found them and the faculty members more receptive to his version of the Christian Gospel than had his first congregations in rural Pennsylvania. However, he was not appreciated by some in the Athens city power centers. They had successfully pressured the university to withdraw its invitation to Norman Thomas, the Socialist candidate for president, to speak on campus. When that came to my father's attention, he invited Thomas to speak in the manse backyard, an event that drew hundreds. Though these same folks were not Presbyterians and rarely heard our father's sermons, there were whispers that this young preacher, however popular with students and professors, was a radical, a self-confessed socialist and probably a Communist. Absurd as it was, the rumor that our father was a Communist continued to be whispered around Athens for years.

A national magazine profiled Father as "The Popular Pastor of Ohio U" after WW II veterans on the GI Bill arrived to more than double the university's enrollment to 7,500 students. Carol Hagen of *Coronet Magazine* described the typical Sunday morning scene at First Presbyterian at that time as follows:

"Students outnumber the regular congregation four to one. They fill the sanctuary, overflow into adjoining Sunday school rooms. Chairs are set up in the church offices where the sermon is heard over a public address system. But despite these extra accommodations, crowds often reach "standing room only" proportions a half-hour before the opening hymn."

Few of the older adults in the Athens congregation — who paid most of his salary and the church's bills — objected to our father's focus on students, probably because First Presbyterian had always had a special relationship with the university. Many of these same senior members of First Presbyterian took a benevolent interest in the four of us. Church elder Mary Connett, who was also the dean of women at the Athens High School, published a history of First Presbyterian in 1959. She wrote of our arrival in the manse:

"It was a wonderful experience ... and brought untold happiness, along with some problems which needed much wisdom, patience and love." (Mary had surely heard about the day Janey entertained the Cless Class with her command of non-Presbyterian vocabulary.) "The church members shared in the happiness these children brought into the Luchs household and the Church. With a great deal of interest and pride the members watched these children grow and develop into fine youngsters."

Coronet Magazine wrote of our father's sermons: "Occasionally, some campus issue provides material for a practical lesson in the application of religion to everyday living. But more often, Luchs talks of headline news and current affairs, showing how the wisdom of a Man who lived 2,000 years ago has vital meaning for today...Actually Luchs' sermons are the result of close personal friendships with students. Almost any day you can see this busy minister with the broad, friendly face and the keen blue eyes striding across the campus — perhaps bound for a classroom to be a guest lecturer, perhaps on his way to referee an intramural wrestling match, or perhaps, just headed for the "Grill", a favorite campus hangout, for a coke and a chat with undergraduates."

As a child I saw First Presbyterian and my father from a different perspective. It seemed strange to see the man I was with every day standing in the massive, raised oak pulpit in the center of the sanctuary, turning his head right and then left as he rubbed his left cuff link with his right hand, surveying the congregation before he began to speak. What most of the adults liked, his forceful delivery and dramatic body gestures, made me uncomfortable. Besides I had to worry he would include one of us in an anecdote to illustrate a point in his sermon. When he did, I could feel the eyes of the congregation turn towards me, which caused my face to flush crimson. I wanted to crawl under the pew and wished I could be suddenly whisked out of church by my fairy god mother. Since I sometimes did not understand or was little interested in my father's sermon, I distracted myself by counting the dozens of organ pipes behind the pulpit that rose almost to the ceiling and provided a background for the black robes and white cottas of the church's excellent choir. The organ pipes seemed to me just right for the church, but I would later learn that opposition to building an organ in First Presbyterian was so strong in 1903 that some of the congregation abandoned the Presbyterians to join the Methodists down the street. Then I would study the stained glass windows on the west wall of the sanctuary, especially the large central one in which Jesus, standing in a field of white lilies, blesses two white-robed children, under which are the words, "Suffer Little Children to Come unto Me." If the sermon was not over I would gaze up at the large oriental hanging lamps that cast their circles of light on the ceiling of the sanctuary and then inspect the hats of the women I could see in front of me. When my father's voice rose in volume, I lowered my head and stared at the black hymnals and little round roles for communion glasses on the back of the honey-blond pew in front of me, waiting for the rumbles of thunder in the pulpit to pass. At age eight I thought the time it took to finish a Presbyterian sermon a reasonable definition of eternity. But he was now praying the pastoral prayer, which was like a coda to signal the sermon had ended.

THE ART OF PREACHING

We saw and heard our father in the privacy of the manse as the congregation did not. One Sunday morning in the first month after we arrived, as Billy and I pulled on our corduroy slacks and jerseys for Sunday school, we heard a loud voice coming from the master bedroom.

"May—Mee—My—Moh—Mu."

Again a booming baritone voice repeated, "May—Mee—My—Moh—Mu," but at a higher pitch. Each vowel was emphasized and each syllable spoken slowly. "May—Mee—My—Moh—Mu" sounded again and again as the voice moved up and down the scale.

We ran out into the hallway to find out what was going on. Just then our mother came out of the master bedroom, bending down toward us with her finger on her lips indicating we were to be quiet. She whispered that our father was doing his Sunday morning warm-up exercises before he mounted the pulpit to preach.

"Can we see?" Billy asked. She opened the door a little so we could peek in to watch our father pacing back and forth in the master bedroom. He was almost fully dressed in dark striped pants with black suspenders and a white shirt to which he not yet attached a newly-starched collar.

With the initial warm-up exercises finished, he began reciting lines from Thomas Macaulay's "Armada," as our new mother quietly pulled the door shut. He spoke each word slowly and loudly at the bass end of his baritone range.

"Ho! Strike the flagstaff deep, Sir Knight;

Ho! Scatter flowers, fair maids;

Ho! Gunners, fire a loud salute;

Ho! Gallants, draw your blades."

Then he added a biblical passage or two and some Shakespeare to finish the morning's warm-up, pronounced with exaggerated articulation and carefully elongated vowels. One of his favorite recitations was "I am the God of your forefathers, the God of Abraham, the God of Isaac, the God of Jacob," from the Exodus story of Moses and the burning bush.

At age ten little Freddie Luchs, walking into the kitchen of his modest home in Ridgway, Pennsylvania, suddenly felt a strong urge to become a great orator who could sway people. "I felt—I knew — I could become that kind of speaker who could hold the attention of crowds," he later wrote.

But when he first arrived in Athens, intimidated by a university congregation of learned professors and still smarting from an experience with a rural congregation that had rejected his version of the Gospel, he froze in terror before the awesome challenge of preaching. He sought relief from the tensions of pulpit fright in early Sunday morning sessions with a chiropractor. Even so, sometimes his vocal chords were so tense his normally resonant baritone voice made him a squeaking tenor and would give out entirely before the sermon was over.

He was not nervous because he was unprepared. His laboriously prepared sermon texts were carefully crafted, typed out in full (often by our mother, an accurate speed typist) and then edited and reedited word for word and fussed with until he stood up on Sunday mornings to walk to the pulpit. By the weekend he knew his sermon thoroughly and rarely consulted his text. But not even such arduous preparation eased his fear.

Strangely, no one in the congregation sensed his horror of preaching. At his wife's suggestion, he began spending one week each year with a voice coach at Princeton Theological Seminary. Working with this coach and applying his own dogged discipline, he eventually overcame his anxiety. He developed as a speaker until he could, as he sometimes put it, "hold audiences in the palm of my hand. " He once wrote, "I've often felt the thrill of moving an audience. My physical presence helped little. But with a resonant voice and the use of gesture and colorful language, anyone can sway an audience." One year he was selected as one of the ten outstanding speakers in America and was already in *Who's Who in America* when we arrived in Athens.

As part of the program his voice coach at Princeton prescribed, our father routinely used the exercises we heard as we dressed for Sunday school each week. We soon knew most of the literary and biblical passages by heart and Charlie, our gifted mimic, would entertain us by standing in the hall outside the closed master bedroom door, quietly mouthing the passage from Macaulay's Armada as our Father proclaimed it, Charlie's left foot thrust forward, right arm held high and swinging in time to the cadence of the verse.

"Ho! Strike the flagstaff deep, Sir Knight;

Ho! Scatter flowers, fair maids;

Ho! Gunners, fire a loud salute;

Ho! Gallants, draw your blades."

After years of such exercises our father's voice, now accustomed to speaking to congregations and audiences of hundreds without any amplification at all, had grown so powerful that in warm weather, when our second floor bedroom windows were open and he was speaking into the early Sabbath quiet, neighbors up and down College Street — and some later claimed as far away as Washington and Court Streets when the wind was right — could also enjoy his Sunday morning exercises. That included the Hughes family who lived above the funeral home next door, Mrs. Lawrence, Charlie Dalton, the city fire chief and jailer, and, in an oblique line of sight from one west-facing upstairs window, whoever happened to be in the city jail. The only comment our father ever got about his vocal exercises came from Charlie Dalton. Charlie attributed a jailhouse conversion to the biblical recitations and said he thought our father would want to know about that. The man in question, awakened by a booming voice after a night of carousing, apparently rose to consciousness to hear "I am the God of Abraham, the God of Isaac, and the God of Jacob." The carouser imagined Judgment Day had surely arrived on Washington Street in downtown Athens, Ohio. Charlie said that when he went down to deliver breakfast to his prisoner, he found the man in his cell on his knees, begging for mercy. But no one else ever remarked or complained about our father's Sunday morning vocal workouts; such was the reluctance of the citizens in a small Ohio town to openly criticize the Presbyterian minister.

That is, until the first warm Sunday in the spring of 1945. The windows were open and white lace curtains in the bedrooms danced joyfully in the morning breeze. "May — Mee — My — Moh — Mu," our father began as usual and moved up and down the scale as he always did. Suddenly he stopped. That's strange, he thought to himself. Was he hearing an echo? He said "My" and stopped. But the echo didn't stop. The echo added "Moh" and then..."Mu." Wanting to be sure he was hearing a voice other than his own, our father began reciting the "Armada."

"Ho! Strike the flagstaff deep, Sir Knight;" He paused.

A sing-song voice shouted back.

"Ho! Don't care a peep, Good Night!"

He WAS hearing another voice! A voice unfamiliar with McCauley's "Armada."

He moved to the window and holding his suspenders out with his thumbs, looked towards the jail from which the voice was coming. Now suspecting he was being mocked, our father shouted at the unseen voice,

"My good man! Why are you mocking me?!!"

"Because you woke me up," the voiced shouted back. "You're disturbing the peace! Don't you know it's Sunday?"

"I most certainly do know it's Sunday!" our father shouted. "I'm the pastor of the First Presbyterian Church."

The man in jail was shouting something back as our pastor father slowly lowered the bedroom window facing the jail and after that Sabbath exchange, however hot and humid the weather, he kept his bedroom windows closed on Sunday mornings, which everyone in the neighborhood seemed to appreciate.

In an article she wrote for *Childhood Education Magazine* during our first year in Athens, Mother wrote that I, "found delight in arranging the altar in the children's room for evening prayers." I vaguely remember that little altar in our bedroom but I attach no memory of a spiritual experience to it and we discontinued prayers at that altar after a year or so.

I was not yet old enough to begin my own life-long search for meaning in the universe. What spiritual experiences came to me as a child took place in nature and did not seem to have much to do with our church. These epiphanies in nature were similar to my dawn watches of welcome to the rising sun over the orchard hill at the children's home. I did enjoy singing hymns in church, though I found the words of some of the 19th century hymns we sang did not describe anything I was feeling. Perhaps that's because I had a skeptical mind and a moderately rebellious spirit. It may be significant that given a choice of masks on the day Ann Minnis drove us to Athens, I chose that of the original rebel, the angel Satan. Over the years, however, the thousands of hours I spent in church and all the hymns and anthems we sang in the congregation and in choirs, and all the listening to Scripture and to sermons and prayers, and all the reading of the psalms did serve to focus my mind on the fundamental issues of philosophy and theology I've happily grappled with ever since.

Despite the objections of some of the older women at First Presbyterian, the Luchs bought us Old and New Testament comic books to supplement the great novels and plays in the Classic Comics series we were already reading. Classic Comics and Bible comics were the only comics allowed in the manse. We had to read Superman and Batman off the premises in the homes of friends, which we did. I devoured the Bible stories, both in children's books and in comic form, and read them repeatedly. I especially enjoyed the tales of the patriarchs and Moses and the Exodus and the histories of the kings and the kings' troublers, the prophets. I identified with Moses because he, like Superman, was a fellow adoptee and because, like me, Moses lacked confidence as a young man. He was reluctant to take on the role of liberator of his people from the Egyptian yoke. He was afraid the Israelites would not believe he had been chosen by Yahweh for the job because he was "slow and hesitant" of speech.

I identified with other Old Testament heroes. I was Joseph being sold into bondage by his older brothers and young David with a harp at whom moody King Saul threw spears. I was Jonathan, David's best friend, and the boy Samuel who rose in the night to ask Eli, the high priest, whose voice he was hearing. I imagined myself becoming Solomon the Wise reuniting a disputed infant with his mother. Through reading the Bible comics and hearing the same stories in church and in Sunday school week after week, all these figures became my contemporaries.

CHAPTER 10

The Preacher Goes to War

T HAT HE DID NOT balk at the adoption of four children is surely Fred Luchs' single most unselfish act. Few men would have offered their homes to four little strangers. Towards the end of his life he wrote that he had agreed to adopt all of us because splitting us up would have been cruel. His act of generosity was greater than it might first appear. He had spent a lifetime being the doted-on youngest son of a family of women, and then became the one and only object of his wife's great mothering love. Now he would have to share her love, time, and attention with the four of us. As a perceptive family friend once put it to my sister, "You must understand, Janey, that your father is your mother's oldest child." He gave up more than our mother did when they decided to welcome us into their home.

Mom would later say, "During the first year, it would not have mattered if I had taken in one child or ten. He was just not involved." He did not disagree. He was quoted in his fraternity magazine in 1944 as saying, "That first year I just sat and looked spellbound to see her go through the maneuvers of helping these children to feel secure and happy." In a printed penny post card they sent out to family and friends in late 1944, the Luchs wrote, "On October 15, we invited into our home Dick, Bill, Charles and Jane aged 4,5,6,and 7...The first month was a bit rough on the old folks and we presume even rougher on the children." Five weeks after we arrived, the shepherd of the First Presbyterian Church needed some still waters, some peace. Yes, as Evelyn said, the noise was mostly happy noise, but it was noise nonetheless and sometimes it didn't seem to stop. When we weren't in school his study door was closed more and more often as our first weeks in the manse passed, and then seemed never opened at all.

To find peace, the preacher went to war. He shipped out in November 1943 to Fort Benning, Georgia, for a temporary duty assignment as chaplain to hold services for and counsel paratroopers, his second such volunteer duty during World War II. He did not return until the week before Christmas. As usual, the Luchs wrote each other almost daily when they were separated. He was missed, mother reported in her first letter. "First question of the morning: Jane: 'Where's Daddy?' Dick wailed, 'When is Daddy coming home?' After I had listened to the prayers tonight Bill asked, 'Will Daddy come in to hear our prayers, too?' So all the talk about the distance to Georgia and that Daddy will be home by Christmas has been in vain."

Another letter she sent to Fort Benning described a Sunday of activities during Indian summer. "We've had a wonderful day!" it begins.

"After Sunday school and church, Margaret Hampel came home from church with us as Janey's special guest. Janey made a large snowman out of cotton with a Christmas tree as her table decoration. The boys made all kinds of derogatory remarks while she was doing it yesterday. The buttons that she put on the front of his coat weren't right, and his ears were too big, and he wasn't carrying the tree properly — but I noticed today that they were trying to talk her into letting them take it to the playhouse to put under their little tree!" She marveled at how much we continued to enjoy food, especially our favorite roasted chicken. "We had a roasted chicken. Gracious! How they enjoyed it!"

She described for her husband a woods outing Sunday afternoon with the four of us and Harold Sauer. We gathered mosses, ferns and lichen to make a terrarium. Harold carried Janey much of the way piggy back and we three boys raced up and down hills, rolled in fallen leaves, and daredevil Billy ran across the top of limestone caves.

"I held my breath...it was a long, long drop to the ground. I don't believe they'd ever been out on a trip where they could just run and climb and do whatever they wanted to do. As Bill said, 'Wasn't it fun?!'"

She was right. Outings in the woods at the children's home were strictly regimented under Kline Dawson. Running and climbing hills were punishable offenses. The day ended, she wrote, as "they talked Margaret Hampel into staying for supper and reading to them after baths."

Billy balked at going to school during our first months in Athens. Our mother told him,

"It's the law in the state of Ohio, Billy. All children have to go to school."

For Billy, school brought on headaches and an upset stomach apparently caused by approaching lessons in spelling or arithmetic. When his teacher reported a continuing pattern of tardiness, our mother talked with Billy at some length and when that didn't make any difference, she, in the only instance anyone remembers, used the ultimate sanction.

"All right," she said. "It IS the law in the state of Ohio and if you WON'T go to school in Athens, we'll have to send you back to Wheelersburg and the children's home."

That was the last anyone heard about Billy not wanting to go to school.

But Billy struggled during his first year at Rufus Putnam. His second grade teacher wrote of Billy, "He is happy and cheery. But fun is getting in the way of work." She added, "He needs special help in spelling." He did not read well, either.

Among the many new books the Luchs bought for us the first year was a beginning speller with pictures.

"D-O-G," Billy read to himself out loud from the book. "Dog!" Good, thought our mother, who was at her desk writing in the upstairs hall and could hear Billy reciting to himself. Then, "C-A-T, Cat!" "OK!" she said to herself. "He's getting it!" Then Billy spelled a third word. "A-N-T...Spider!"

The playground, not the classroom, was Billy's domain. Billy discovered football during our first months in Athens and loved best the informal games of touch and tackle we played with other boys on the Rufus Putnam playground after school hours. After sides were chosen, we voted for touch or tackle before beginning our football games. I always voted for touch. Billy always voted for tackle. He enjoyed knocking heads and crushing bodies with other boys, fearlessly throwing his solidly built frame around the field and taking with a smile bruising jolts from bigger boys. "I like to fight and get rough," he wrote in one school report letter that first year. Injury or the sight of blood did not bother stoic Billy. He didn't cry, even when hurt. He did not pick fights and had no meanness in him at all, but he enjoyed fighting and could be counted on to defend smaller or weaker boys or his brothers against playground bullies.

Billy was all "boy" in other ways. He considered soap a useless invention. He didn't understand what napkins, to which we were just being introduced, could possibly contribute to a happy life but used them as required. He loved mud and dirt. He was the one of us who, having arrived hungry at the dinner table, had to be asked to go wash up. He had a knack for finding mud puddles and would walk half a block to splash through a good one. He was the one of us who nibbled on anything green during walks to concerts and after school events and had to be sent home because he reeked of wild onions.

Billy could make a new pair of shoes look old in two weeks. His clothes aged quickly, too. Our mother used to wonder if he had a secret wear-out machine hidden in our shared walk-in closet. Billy's clothes never managed to reach the hooks provided for them. They preferred to lie in random piles crumpled on the floor. Billy's clothes were also peculiar in that they did not like being washed. When the weekly laundry had been folded and returned to our rooms, the colors green and brown did not appear. There wasn't any clean laundry for Billy. His dirty shirts and pants had to be sought out from unlikely places, under his bed or mattress, crammed into his clean clothes dresser drawers, or hiding out in remote corners of our closet.

When asked as we often were to pick up our rooms, Billy was pleasant and obliging and always said yes, he'd do that right away. Billy went right to work and quickly finished his half of our bedroom. But when he was finished, an observer might be forgiven for thinking it was hard to tell the difference between a room in chaos and the half of our room that Billy had picked up.

Billy, mischievously innocent, beamed with a shining, untroubled candor. "Sunny" and "happy" were the words adults most often used to describe him. His good nature and sweet smile won over adult hearts, which sometimes made me jealous, especially because his charm seemed so effortless. His eyes were — to be sure — blue, his hair blond, and he was the best-looking of the four of us.

Billy did learn to read. A year after we arrived, his third grade teacher wrote:

"Billy reads well to the group. He has poise and holds the attention of the group well." Billy also learned to spell and to write stories and do arithmetic and loved our music classes and his school headaches and stomach-aches disappeared.

I Ask to See the Athens County Children's Home

I continued to worry our new life with the Luchs in the manse would soon be over. Some students from the Athens County Children's Home attended Rufus Putnam and I recognized them at once during my first days at school by their plain, ill-fitting clothes and odd bowl haircuts. The haircuts made the girls appear much less attractive than they were in fact. Two of the Home kids, as they were called, had to wear nylon stocking caps for treating head lice, the ugly badge of shame I had always dreaded when I was in a children's home. I noticed the children from the Athens children's home stood apart in the first months of the school year, much as I had done in Wheelersburg. I wondered if I would someday have to join them. Having learned to prepare myself for whatever might come in life, I wanted to see where they lived. In late November I asked our foster mother to drive me out to the Athens children's home.

"And just why do you want to see the Athens County Children's Home?" she asked as her eyebrows rose.

"I want to see where we go if this adoption doesn't work."

"Is something wrong, Dick? Tell me, is something wrong?"

A part of me enjoyed ignoring her question. "I just want to see it," I said.

So on a cold and gray late afternoon, she drove me in the green Buick coupe far out on east State Street. She pulled over to the side of the road in front of a dark red brick dormitory building. A barn and other outbuildings stood close by. Much of the white trim paint on the dormitory building, now gray, had peeled off. The barn and the outbuildings looked dirty. I could see two or three of the children slogging through mud as they walked from the barn toward the dormitory. One of the children, a boy about my age, wore a nylon stocking cap.

I shuddered inside. The drab scene triggered my dread of the look and stench of poverty. This included anything that was broken or dirty or unpainted, or that smelled foul or was disordered. All these brought back to me life in the Old Gray House in Sciotoville. The Athens County children's home and outbuildings, mired in the mud and rains of November, looked even worse than the impersonal but comparatively attractive yellow brick Home I had known in Wheelersburg.

My first impression of the Athens County Children's Home was later confirmed. In an 1948 article, nationally distributed *Coronet Magazine* reported that a women's group in First Presbyterian had found eighty children crowded into quarters intended for 40. "They had not had hot bath water for a year, except what they heated on the stove. They had no place to hang their clothes, no place to keep even their meager personal belongings."

"Would you like to go inside?" my foster mother asked.

"No." My no was so soft even I could hardly hear it. "No," I repeated, louder. "Let's go back."

I had seen more than enough. My spirits were low and I was lost in my thoughts and silent as my foster mother drove the two of us back to the manse. Cold November rain began to fall and wind blew ripples of water across the wind shield as the car's windows began to fog and the wipers swept back and forth. The tips of the dark branches of street trees swayed. We rumbled up the brick surface of east State Street as the last brown and yellow leaves of autumn scurried along next to the Buick as if seeking shelter before the cold of winter arrived. I vowed to myself that if we were not adopted by the Luchs, neither I nor Billy or Charlie or Janey would ever again go to a children's home, not the dreadful one I had just seen, nor the one I knew all too well in Wheelersburg. I decided I would do everything I could to make our new life with the Luchs work, but if that failed, the four of us would somehow make it on our own. When we returned to the manse I was glad to escape a chilly and wet late autumn day to enter a home that was warm, nicely painted and furnished, with everything in its place, and clean. Just being in the friendly old manse made me feel safe and good again.

THE BOXCAR CHILDREN

A week later, in a box of used books someone in the church had given us, I discovered a dull orange copy of *The Boxcar Children*. I read the book through in one sitting, absorbed in every sentence. *The Box Car Children* seemed to be about the four of us. Other children had had experiences similar to ours. They had made it. So would we.

The Boxcar Children is about four children, two sisters and two brothers, whose parents have died. They are on the streets, alone and hungry. They persuade a reluctant baker's wife to give them some bread and to let them sleep in the bakery overnight. During the night Henry, the oldest child — who looks to be about twelve or thirteen years old in the book's illustrations — and the oldest girl, Jessica, — who may be ten — hear the baker and his wife saying they will put Benny, their baby brother, in a children's home the following day.

To avoid that fate Henry and Jessica rouse Violet and Benny to escape the bakery and walk through the night. Eventually, after two nights of walking and sleeping in haystacks during the day to avoid detection, they discover an abandoned boxcar. The next day they find some old dishes and discarded furniture in a dump nearby, and Jessica sets up house while Henry goes to town to find work mowing lawns and doing odd jobs to buy food. The children take care of each other, find a wounded pup they heal, build a dam across a stream, and enjoy a happy time as little adults with no real adult involvement in their lives at all.

I recognized immediately the cooperative relationships that develop among children who must depend on each other for the necessities of life and emotional support. I responded to a happy story of children making it on their own, however unrealistic that may be. *The Box Car Children* fit into the dream I had at the children's home that the four of us would escape together and somehow build a new life. The book ended improbably when an elderly and wealthy man for whom Henry had gardened followed Henry back to the boxcar, found the children, took them into his home and announced he was their grandfather. I read and reread *The Boxcar Children* many times during our first year in the manse, especially when I was upset with the Luchs. I read the book in remembrance of what had been, for I grieved the erosion of the mutually supportive relationships the four of us had enjoyed in adversity before we found safety in the manse. I was sorry to be losing my special role as the leader of our little tribe as the Luchs became our father and mother. Why is it that sometimes in this life we must surrender one good, in this case loving, cooperative, relationships among four children, to secure another, in this case responsible, committed and loving parents?

HAROLD SAUER

While our foster father was at Ft. Benning we got to know Harold Sauer better. He was the man with the deep voice and black shoe brush hair whose bedroom was next to ours. I have sometimes wondered if Harold minded suddenly finding himself living with four noisy, active children for he was a quiet man. At first meeting he was a shy man who said little and when he did speak, spoke quite deliberately. Like my brother Billy, Harold was the middle son of three brothers. When the boys were teenagers his youngest brother accidentally shot and killed his oldest brother in a hunting accident. Harold's parents never recovered. Not long after this tragedy the Luchs found Harold collecting tolls on a bridge over the Ohio River at Middleport, Ohio, liked him immediately, and encouraged him to go to college. They offered him a room in exchange for help maintaining the manse.

After we arrived in 1943, the door to Harold's room was often shut, I suppose for study, and even when it was open we were careful not to run in uninvited. But he would sometimes invite one of us in. Harold had magical hands. I enjoyed watching as he carved animal figures from pine or balsa wood with his pen knife. As he carved, he showed me some of the techniques he used and at once I tried to imitate him, using a paring knife from the kitchen and, at his suggestion, some soap bars. I followed his directions, employing a paper cutout he made for me as a guide. Over the next week I carved a dozen bars of soap into crude scraps before I gave up. My hands simply would not follow my eyes or intentions. I could not produce the lovely three-dimensional figures Harold carved as if that were easy.

Harold was then preparing to become a high school shop teacher, though he would eventually become an assistant dean of men at Kent State University. He was the ultimate Mr. Fixit. Harold could repair appliances. He understood plumbing and electricity. If there was a problem with the old coal furnace in the basement that required more than shoveling in coal or removing clinkers, Harold could take care of it. But he also learned much living in the manse. When he left a few years later, he wrote the Luchs, "The training I received while living in your home as a student meant more to me than the college degrees I earned...you gave me a portion of your understanding and insight into human nature and a large amount of your goodness of character...I will miss being able to come to you for advice and even, at times, for consolation."

CHARLIE, THE ST. FRANCIS OF COLLEGE STREET

Of the four of us, Charlie was the odd duckling. He had to wear a black patch for one year to correct a weakness in one eye. He hated the patch and lost it most days and Dad nagged him about it. He was the only one of us who had to wear inserts in his shoes to correct for flat feet. His ears stuck out further than ours did. Though Janey was 15 months younger, she tied Charlie's shoes for him when we arrived in Athens and later put on his roller skates, which he never did manage to do for himself. He was less coordinated but more intelligent than the rest of us. He was more vulnerable, more fearful, and more imaginative.

The men in his life had been hard on Charlie. Lonnie found him different from his other sons and rejected him. Charlie's namesake, a biological uncle, beat him repeatedly when he was barely four years old. But once Charlie was enclosed in the safety of our mother's arms, he walked around with a broad smile on his face and seemed to everyone a delightfully happy child. Perhaps it was Charlie's vulnerabilities that made him attractive to women. Not long after we arrived he captured the hearts of many of the women in the Luchs and Coulter families and some in the First Presbyterian Church. Though she never said so in our presence, we all knew Charlie was Grandma Coulter's favorite Luchs boy.

Spring on College Street was an exciting time for Charlie, who remembers arriving in Athens keenly curious to explore the new world in which he found himself. He was the first of us able to identify the chickadees and sparrows, bright red male cardinals and blue jays, starlings and flickers that came to feed on the dried corn and bread crumbs our foster mother and Grace Monigold sometimes spread on the ground beyond the back porch of the manse. He often came home with garter snakes in his hands and toads in his pockets, which he released in our back yard. Grace Monigold took Charlie by train to visit Grandma Coulter in Pennsylvania in the spring of 1944. On their return trip, Grace said, Charlie walked up and down the aisles of their coach, pulling yet another toad out of his pocket for the other passengers to admire. It was probably Charlie's history of abuse and his vulnerability to more wounding that made him so sympathetic to all living creatures, and especially to those in distress. In his boyish way Charlie was, as one neighbor called him, "the St. Francis of College Street."

One day, a year or so after we arrived in Athens, Charlie was playing alone in our back yard near the green fence. Suddenly he noticed a black bird fluttering out of the sky into the alley behind city hall. Curious, he walked into the alley where he saw a young fireman leaning against the red brick wall of the city hall with a rifle at his right shoulder. The fireman steadied the barrel of the rifle as he aimed it skyward towards the roof. The rifle popped. Another black bird careened out of the sky and landed with a muted thud a few yards from Charlie. He ran to the bird. The body was warm but the bird's gray eyelids were already closed in death. A bright red spot on the bird's breast was surrounded by multi-colored iridescent feathers and Charlie realized he was holding a dead starling. Tears began to drop on Charlie's cheeks.

He heard another pop of the young fireman's rifle and a third wounded bird fell out of the sky, fluttered down the canyon above the alley, and managed to land upright but immediately fell over.

Charlie ran to it, now crying loudly and shouting, "Stop shooting! Stop! Stop shooting the birds!"

The third starling managed to right itself with its wings, took a few feeble steps and fell over again. Harold Sauer, returning to the manse from the Buckeye Café where he took most of his meals, found Charlie crying hysterically and running from fallen bird to fallen bird. When Harold realized what was happening and saw the young fireman with the rifle, he shouted at him:

"Put that rifle away! You know it's illegal to shoot a gun in downtown Athens. "

The young fireman glared at Harold and then lowered his rifle and disappeared from the alley around the corner of the city hall building. Harold kneeled down and held Charlie in his arms to calm him.

Finally Harold said, "The birds are dead, Charlie. Let's go home now."

"But this one's still alive," Charlie protested as he put his two small hands under a wounded bird and lifted it off the bricks. "I want to take it home."

Harold sighed and said nothing for a few seconds. He just looked at Charlie's tearful face and the starling he was holding.

"OK. Let's go. I'll show you how to make a nest for him."

They walked together to the corner of the alley and through the door in the green fence that led into our backyard. Harold found some scrap wood in the basement and made a small box and rigged a bulb to keep the box warm while Charlie found an old towel to make a nest. They put some water and food in the nest but when Charlie came down a few hours later to check on his bird, the starling was dead.

Charlie frequently adopted fallen nestlings and distressed mice. Once while returning after school he noticed a commotion in an outdoor cafeteria line at Howard Hall, a university dormitory. He found a confused mouse running to and fro, frightening co-eds. Charlie caught the mouse and brought it home in his jacket pocket. The next morning the mouse bit Janey and Dad, to Charlie's distress, drowned the mouse in a laundry tub.

After Harold Sauer showed him how to rig a box with a light for the wounded starling, Charlie began making his own boxes to incubate fallen nestlings. Once he used a card board shoe box. The hot electric bulb ignited the box, incinerated the nestling and set our wood working table on fire. Mom rushed to the basement with a blanket just in time to snuff out the fire.

In the 1940s dime stores sold newly hatched baby chicks that had been dyed green, red, blue, and purple. They were popular Easter gifts at that time. Children played with them for a few days and then the chicks died. But Charlie had learned how to care for small creatures and his baby chick lived. She grew out of her colored blue feathers to become a white pullet and Charlie persuaded Harold Sauer to build a chicken coop for her. When the pullet became a full-sized white leghorn hen, Charlie called her Big Cluck, tied a string around her neck and, to the amusement of our neighbors, walked her up and down College Street for exercise.

As the months rolled by, Charlie paid less attention to Big Cluck. One evening at supper as our foster father was about to carve a roast chicken for our favorite dinner, Charlie turned to Mother and asked, looking at the roast chicken, "Is that Big Cluck?" When she said "yes," Charlie's face fell and he ran from the table. We did not enjoy our roast chicken dinner that evening.

Two or three years after we arrived in Athens we went as a family to see the movie starring Clifton Webb and Myrna Loy based on Clarence Day's book, *Life with Father*. As we left the movie we were walking behind John C. Baker, the new president of Ohio University. Suddenly, in a high pitched voice that carried far, Charlie announced to the world, "If you think that father's funny, you should see my Daddy!" Mother tried to hush Charlie too late. In case he had missed it the first time, Charlie was already repeating what he had said in easy listening range of Dr. Baker. "If you think that father's funny, you should see my Daddy!"

Like Pinocchio, Charlie was easily led astray. One afternoon he did not return home from school. After learning he had not even been in school that afternoon Mother enlisted Harold Sauer, the Athens City Police Department, and half of the residents of College Street to search for Charlie. Five hours later Harold found him walking through the mental hospital grounds after 10:00 PM. He was with Peter, the dean's son from across the street. They had played hookey and spent the afternoon with Nancy Howell at Happy Howell's nursery. Charlie and Peter had become lost trying to return to downtown Athens.

THE WHITE RABBIT

While our father was at Fort Benning there occurred an event so upsetting that I remember it today. The Luchs, observing how much I enjoyed Jippy, decided I should have a pet of my own. They gave me a large white rabbit because I had shown interest in the rabbits kept by families we visited our first month in Athens. They believed learning to take responsibility for a pet was an important step on the road to maturity.

Harold Sauer built a hutch for my white rabbit in a single afternoon. Having just spent weeks of excitement followed by days of frustration because my imperfect carpentry products did not match the dreams in my head, I watched Harold's skilled hands in wonder as he measured and sawed yellow pine boards. He could follow perfectly the lines he had marked with a pencil, and his saw never buckled in the cut as mine did. Every board he cut seemed to fit. I watched Harold draw nails out of a small brown paper bag, put a half dozen or so in his mouth, and then taking them one by one, he placed them with his forefinger and thumb and pounded them in. Not one of them bent under the blows of his hammer. Not one had to be pulled. None of his boards split. Not once did he hit his fingers with the hammer. Then Harold, whose black, shoe-brush hair and deep voice continued to fascinate me, made a droppings tray and tacked wire screen around the framework of the rabbit hutch. I watched every movement he made, hoping I could do what I had observed in my next project.

"Now feed your rabbit these pellets every day, Dick, and be sure to give him fresh water every day," Harold said in his bass voice. "Once each week change the straw and slide out the tray of droppings. Put them both in the garden over there," he said.

I was afraid of the white rabbit at first because of its enormous size. When it turned to look at me the rabbit's nose twitched and his pink eyes seemed to stare at me in cold indifference without any message I could understand. Jippy, in contrast, wiggled in joyous anticipation when she ran up to welcome us as we returned from school and turned on her back so we could tickle her pink belly. Billy's puppy easily joined our warm and familiar human world but my white rabbit did not.

On balmy indian summer days after school I took the rabbit out of the hutch and let it hop freely across the grass in our back yard and, as I lost all fear of it despite an occasional nip of my fingers, I began to carry the white rabbit about as if it were a furry baby and hand fed it carrots. I became affectionate with my rabbit and liked to pet the soft warm fur on its side and run my hand over the rabbit's long ears, right to the tips, so that I could watch them bounce back when I removed the pressure of my fingers. I even began talking to the rabbit as I had talked to old Queenie when I stayed with Judge Smith's family.

After a few weeks the thrill of having my own pet waned and as I became absorbed in our busy new lives in the manse and at school, I missed a day of feeding and watering from time to time. Thanksgiving came and passed. The first snow filtered down through the sooty gray skies of downtown Athens, and an early December cold snap froze the ground hard. Caught up in the exciting prelude to the holiday season I missed more than one day of feeding my white rabbit.

"Harold found him," my foster mother told me. "His water dish was dry as a bone and his food bowl was empty. You shouldn't have forgotten to feed and water him, Dick. Your poor rabbit died."

Her words stung me. I flushed with shame. I ran out to the hutch unable to believe my rabbit was dead. I tried to remember the exact day I had last fed and watered him. At first I was afraid to lift the hutch door to confirm that the rabbit's side, so recently soft and warm, was as cold and frozen as it looked. Then I did open the hutch and pushed against the rabbit's side. It was frozen stiff. One accusing cold pink eye stared directly at me. My rabbit was dead. My emotions were a jumble of sorrow and guilt. I wanted to blow life back into my rabbit's hard white body. My mind churned as I told myself my rabbit had not died of thirst or hunger. Surely it was the cold that had killed him, a point I pleaded with my foster mother and with Harold. But they weren't persuaded.

After the initial shock was over, I decided my rabbit would have a proper funeral. I wanted to make amends to relieve my guilt and shame. I had failed him in life, but I would not fail him in death. That night I talked with Billy and Charlie after lights were out for a long time about my wish to have a funeral for my rabbit. "I want him to go to heaven," I said. I was sorry he had died and stared into the darkness for a long time wondering where he was before I finally drifted into sleep.

The following morning, a bright cold December Saturday, Billy and I arrived at the rabbit hutch warmly dressed with two shovels we had taken from the basement. Our breathing made white air and we could smell the acrid soft coal smoke drifting down from the chimney of the Hotel Berry. Janey and Charlie ran up with Jippie dancing around them. The two of them were bundled up in winter coats and mittens and wool caps pulled down over their ears.

Janey asked, "Is the wabbit weally dead, Dickie?"

"Yes."

Charlie was the most upset when he saw my dead rabbit. He stared at the stiff white body without saying anything and then I saw a tear work its way down his cheek.

We talked it over and decided to bury the rabbit over near the border with Mrs. Lawrence's property, in front of a wood post with a wood cross piece, one of two that supported the metal clothes lines. Tiny frozen water crystals in the soil shimmered in the morning sun. Billy and I began digging the ground with shovels but could loosen only small bits of frozen earth at a time. We sent Charlie back to the basement to look for a hatchet and he found one. Billy and I took our mittens off to handle the hatchet and shovels better.

Janey, standing by, said, "The wabbit will get cold, Dickie. I will bwing him a blanket."

Charlie said, "He can't be cold when he's dead, silly."

To which Janey replied, "How do you know? You are not dead."

I said, "You two go get something to wrap him in while Billy and I finish digging this grave."

Janey and Charlie returned with an old bath towel.

"Go get a Bible. And a hymn book if you can find one."

While Janey and Charlie were off trying to find a Bible and a hymnal, Billy and I finished digging the grave, and when they returned Janey said, "We got a book from Fwed's study, Dickie."

The grave was about 15 inches deep, less than we planned, but Billy and I had broken blisters on our hands and were worn out with digging the frozen ground. The four of us gathered in front of the hutch, looking at my dead white rabbit.

I said, "When we take him out, we will walk slowly and we will not talk. We will whisper."

I whispered, "Do you understand, Janey?"

Janey nodded her head silently, yes.

"This is what we're going to do," I whispered. "Charlie and I will hold the towel in front of the hutch. Billy will lift the rabbit out of the hutch and onto the towel. Then we'll walk quietly as in church from the hutch over to the grave, Billy first, then me and Charlie with the rabbit, and then Janey. Billy, you'll carry the Bible. We'll make believe we have black robes on, like in church. Charlie and I will lower the rabbit down into the grave. Then we'll do the service. When that's over we'll fold the towel around the rabbit and bury him."

Billy whispered, "I don't want to lift the rabbit out. You lift it out. It's your rabbit."

"Then scoop it out. Will you do that? With the shovel!"

Billy raised the door, placed the shovel behind the rabbit's body and drew it towards him while Charlie and I held the towel ends up to the edge of the hutch floor.

Billy swept the frozen rabbit out of the hutch into the towel with such force that rabbit, towel, Charlie and I all crashed to the ground.

When we got up, we put my dead rabbit back on the towel and began, step by solemn step, the procession to the grave, led by Billy holding the Bible. The rabbit was too long for the grave and I felt myself becoming impatient with him because he would not fit into the hole we had dug for him. In a few minutes Billy and I were able to make the grave long enough for the rabbit to just fit.

I whispered, "OK. Now let's sing a church song."

Charlie said, "Let's sing 'Jesus Loves Me.'" That's the only church song I know."

Billy whispered, "We should sing something about rabbits."

Janey said, "Jesus knows it's about wabbits, Billy. We don't have to tell him."

So we sang a single verse of "Jesus Loves Me."

I whispered, "And now, I will lead us in prayer. Bow your head, Janey. Close your eyes, Charlie."

I said something like this: "This is my rabbit. You probably know who he is. He was a good rabbit, soft and furry. He likes to play on the grass. He likes carrots and spinach and lettuce, but not celery. I loved him and want him to go to heaven. Amen."

Janey whispered, "Fwed pways longer, Dickie. Say some more."

"I can't think of anything else. Why should I say more?"

Janey pointed at my dead white rabbit. "Because...your wabbit is still there, Dickie. He didn't go to heaven."

"Well, he can't go ALL-AT-ONCE, silly!"

Billy said, "Yeah, Janey. He goes in the middle of the night when no one is looking. That's why we cover him up so it can be secret."

Janey said, "Alwight. Let's covah him up."

So Billy and I pulled the towel over the white rabbit. We pushed the clods and bits of frozen earth into the grave until the rabbit was entirely under dirt and there was a mound of earth above the rabbit's grave, which totally disappeared by Easter the following spring.

CHAPTER 11

Progress at Home and at School

G RACE MONIGOLD REMEMBERS A few negative people who said adopting us would cost the Luchs too much or that it would never work out. "Of course your mother was determined to make it work, and the skeptics just caused her to work even harder to make sure it did." The Luchs wrote to friends and in articles that much was made of their new children. They received hundreds of congratulatory letters but they also received some negative notes. Some of those who warned the Luchs not to adopt us were psychologists aware of the greater challenge in adopting older children. But more in their network of friends around the country were supportive. Mom had been a teacher at the Horace Mann-Lincoln School sponsored by Columbia University. The principal wrote in response to her announcement of our arrival:

"Do you really mean you have taken four young children as your own? I think it is perfectly wonderful of you to do so. They look darling and I know you will enjoy them."

Locally, many in Athens were simply curious about us, which we did not mind. Of the majority who approved of the adoption, those who took the most interest in our welfare had some connection to Ohio University and were also members of First Presbyterian. This group reached out to welcome us and surrounded us with their support and even affection.

Forever after I would associate university communities and Presbyterian churches with caring people strong enough to help and include those who are somehow different. Those who were negative about our adoption in Athens were mostly those town folk who believed only blood relatives should be members of the same family. They seemed threatened by what they considered an unnatural family. They doubted our experiment in adoption would work. A handful believed we would murder the Luchs while they slept.

Playmates sometimes made hurtful comments that reflected the views of their parents. A few years after we arrived at the manse, Janey and a friend were having a disagreement. Finally the friend, whom I will call Patsy, put her hands on her hips, and in a singsong voice, declared:

"You're adopted! That means YOUR mother didn't want you!"

Then Janey put her hands on her own hips and imitating the singsong diction of Patsy, responded:

"Well, YOUR mother is divorced. That means YOUR mother and father don't like each other. So there!"

Such exchanges were not common, for whatever parents or children thought, they mostly kept their opinions to themselves. But some townspeople were more than curious. Some were nosey. One woman asked Janey where she had lived before she moved to Athens. Another wanted to know where her real daddy was. Janey tried to turn these questions aside, but each time she ran into these women, they asked her the same questions.

When Janey told our foster mother about this, she said,

"Janey, you don't have to answer personal questions. You can just ignore such questions."

But the questions continued. So she told our foster father. He said, "You just tell them you came from Pittsburgh, Janey. Pittsburgh's a big city. They'll never know one way or the other."

So the next time she got such a question Janey was ready.

"And where did you live before you came to Athens, Janey?"

"In Pittsburg, damn it!" and that was the last time that woman asked that question.

Another woman, probably having heard our biological father was in the state penitentiary, asked.

"Where's your daddy, Janey?"

"I don't know. Maybe at the church? Maybe out calling?"

"No, no. I mean your REAL daddy, Janey."

No longer flustered by such a question, Janey snapped,

"He's in Pittsburg, damn it!"

EMOTIONAL HEALTH

I know from my volunteer work as a CASA (Court Appointed Special Advocate for children) that were I a child in our welfare system today, I would have had psychological counseling. The case files I obtained in 1998 indicate counseling was never suggested, not by the social workers or by the psychologists who came from the Juvenile Research Bureau in Columbus to test and evaluate us. The Luchs were believers in the benefits of psychological testing and counseling. Our father was unusual among the clergy of his day because he required couples who came to him to be married to take a psychological test administered by the university. The intent was not to discourage marriages but for the couple to develop a deeper understanding of each other. He was proud that the failure rate of couples he married was phenomenally low, even in a time when far fewer marriages ended in divorce.

But the Luchs did not pursue psychological testing or counseling for us because whatever difficulties we had during our first years in Athens, in no case was our behavior beyond what they thought they could handle unaided. We were conventionally well-behaved children concerned to please, who measured up surprisingly quickly to their expectations. Mother sometimes said to her friends and fellow teachers, "In all my teaching experience, I have never known children who try so hard to please." Trying so hard to please is not, of course, an indicator of psychological health.

Restoring our emotional health was more difficult and required much more time than rebuilding our physical health. The wounds caused by neglect and abandonment, of our having to become adults too soon to make up for the failings of our biological family, required years to heal. The 26 months in the children's home had not helped us. With so few supervisors — none of them trained — to tend to so many children, there was too little personal attention and affection to go around. There was no one to show our school work to, no adult we could talk with about our concerns and worries, no one to pat us on the back for a new achievement. In sum, there were no adults with whom we could share our lives or count on for support. There was not even anyone to give us a hug once in awhile. The children in the Home were love-hungry kids, abnormally emotionally dependent on their siblings, when they had siblings, and were permitted to be with them. There was no way the healing of our earlier wounds could have begun at the Home.

Among her adult friends Mom sometimes spoke of Janey as "my little bird" because she was so fragile and thin. In the company of the same friends she called me "my little ramrod."

Each time she would reach down to give me a hug or put her arm around me, my body froze in resistance. I was even less receptive to our new father. He would come in some nights after lights were out and as soon as he opened our door and entered the room my body would freeze as I waited tensely in the dark while he approached. I soon could count how long it would take him to hug Charlie, who was first, and then Billy, who was second. I disliked our foster father's bewhiskered face as it scratched across mine, and the foul smell of his exhaled breath only made matters worse. I wanted him to stop trying to hug me. I pretended to be asleep when he arrived. Most of the time that ruse worked.

There was more than one reason I resisted being hugged by the Luchs. First, I considered myself grownup. I had learned to cope by myself, to take care of my own needs. Accepting hugs was an admission of dependence I was not ready to make. Then, I had lost the habits of affection. I've explained why there were no hugs available from adults at the children's home and we were rarely visited by members of our biological family during the years we lived in that sterile institution. And yet it was also true that I resisted opening my heart to the Luchs because of the loyalty I continued to feel to my first family, especially Lonnie.

But most important, I resisted accepting affection from my foster parents because I no longer trusted adults. Lonnie, my Grandmother McNelly, even my mother, Eunice — the three adults I had given my heart to and loved and trusted — had abandoned me. I feared and resisted ever making myself vulnerable again. My heart was no longer open for business. I was on occasion able to simulate a response to gestures of affection from adults but I felt little or nothing. My emotional center was empty, a void that was cold and yet was restless, as if I was seeking something I should have had but did not, or once had but had lost.

Despite all this, over the course of months I gradually began to accept hugs from our new mother, whom I was beginning to like more and more. She was the first adult since Lonnie and Grandma McNelly who seemed genuinely interested in me and wanted to offer me love. But I was not yet willing to trust her. She was not yet my mother. Why was it that I had to learn or relearn to be at ease in the presence of love, to permit a willing, caring adult to love me when love was what I most needed? If we are not given love at the beginning of our lives or our openness to love is damaged through abuse and neglect by those who should love us best and most, our hearts whither and shrivel just as neglected plants do. I didn't know that when I was a child. I didn't understand that something was missing inside of me. I didn't understand why I acted as I did. For you see, even as I pushed love away, I wanted to reach out to obtain what my heart knew I so sorely needed.

I did understand we had been abandoned, which made me angry. I had come to believe we were abandoned because we were not worth loving, which made me angrier. To protect myself, I denied that I needed love, which made it less difficult for me to accept that we had been abandoned but more difficult for anyone to reach me. At times my heart was a tiny red volcano of anger that erupted in blind rage. At times my mind was a turbulent jumble of confusions. It would take a heroic effort on someone's part to love me, someone willing to patiently put up with being pushed away, someone willing to calm my emotional storms. I needed someone who could free me from the inner hell of my emotions and confusions. Someone who could help me restore my sense of self-worth.

Evelyn Luchs became that someone. She nurtured all of us at all times, but she went to the child who needed her most. That first year in the manse, Janey's physical health and my emotional health got most of her attention. She later told me that she worked with me for one year before I would accept her hugs naturally without any resistance, and two years before I could spontaneously express my love by hugging her.

Our behavior in the manse during our first year was marked by other patterns that can be traced to our earliest years. The four of us lacked confidence, despite accumulating evidence that we were intelligent, talented, good-looking kids, and were better-than-average athletes. We were too easily frustrated, too anxious when facing new challenges, and excessively critical of our achievements.

I'm often asked how Evelyn Luchs approached the restoration of our emotional health. She tended first to our physical health, as the base for building our emotional health. Nourishing food, sound sleep, and robust outdoor activities were central to her regime. She believed the routines and schedules she had established contributed much to the recovery and maintenance of our emotional health. She made sure our lives were filled with challenging and interesting activities, at school and at home. She believed we are all happier and contributing to our mental health when we are busy, especially when we are stretching our minds or creating something, as in art or music. But she also believed that just keeping busy with simple duties and chores such as setting the table or helping to wash dishes contributed to our mental health. Inactivity, she thought, fostered depression.

She was an excellent listener. She was sympathetic, heard us out without interrupting, and then would ask us questions about what we had said. She was available at the teachable moment, dealing with challenges, hurts, confusions, and unacceptable behavior immediately as these arose. She shared with other members of her Coulter family a large measure of "gumption," which I define as common sense blended with courage.

In my case, I was used to talking with adults. That helped. I could talk with her as I had with my Grandmother McNelly about my behavior. She treated me with the respect appropriate for a slightly advanced eight-year-old, but there was never any question about who was the child and who the adult. Once we were again talking about controlling my anger. She was holding me, her stiff little ramrod. Finally unable to talk about it anymore, I dissolved in tears. She continued to hold me and I relaxed and stopped resisting. "Well," she said smiling, "I'll just have to love that anger out of you." I smiled back.

It surely helped that from the start we felt we were completely her children. She was not tentative at all. In her mind we became her children, as Grace Monigold put it, the moment we arrived at the manse. She was as proud of us as any parent could be, took joy in — and sometimes exaggerated — our achievements and sympathized with our problems. She was an optimist, and next to love she thought hope was what we most needed and what she could give. She believed strongly that we could and would heal. She didn't expect perfection, but she believed life was about always doing better. Supporting her positive and optimistic view of life was her conviction that most people are mostly good.

She did not believe the fates of children are sealed by the age of eight as does some psychological literature. She thought good parenting at any stage in a child's life, including the adolescent years, makes a great difference. She believed the teen years were as important as any other, perhaps more so, because in that perilous, passage everything good achieved until then can be undone. She later turned down an honor that would have involved extensive time and travel as we entered the perilous passage of adolescence, saying, "My children are now teenagers and need me more than ever."

She thought of each of us as special. "Each child is unique," begins the paragraph of an article she wrote about us during our first years at the manse. She made us feel special as individuals but did not promote a view of divine election in which some individuals or groups are special because they are God's chosen, and others are not. We were special because we, as all human beings, were the children of God.

She came down rather hard on complaining or whining as she did on arguing. She nipped in the bud occasional bouts of feeling sorry for ourselves because she believed indulging self-pity would only make our lives more difficult. If she ever felt any pity for us, she hid it well. She did so much that was right.

Progress at Rufus Putnam

Next to the manse, school was the most important arena of our activity, and in the Rufus Putnam Laboratory School, our mother knew she had strong allies in her campaign to restore our physical and emotional health. She had worked as a colleague with most of our teachers, and counted two of them as personal friends.

Putnam teachers were observant witnesses of our behavior and development, a sort of second opinion to our mother's own of how we were doing. Putnam reports, issued every two months, comprised three brief essays: the student's report of his or her activities and progress; the teacher's report of the student's progress, and a general teacher essay on the activities of the class during the grading period. These reports could be graphic. For example, under the activities of the class section, my third grade teacher, Agnes Eisen, wrote, "We are trying to control our unfair habits such as hitting and jumping on people."

In these reports the four of us are described as "easily over-stimulated," even after we had made the initial adjustment to life in the manse. There are references to our needing to learn to lower our voices. At one time or another that first year, the reports describe all of us as "tense".

"Billy is unable to lie still during midday rest periods. He plays with his hands and feet." And of Janey, "She is gradually overcoming the tenseness she shows in all her work." Our teachers note that we were all abnormally self-critical, and that I especially found failure difficult to accept.

"He is likely to be discouraged when things do not work out the first time. He needs to learn patience," Miss Eisen wrote of me. A year later, now Billy's teacher, Eisen wrote of him, "Billy needs to develop more patience. He is so anxious in beginning anything that is new to him that he does not think as well as he can." High levels of anxiety as we undertook new tasks or projects were common to the four of us.

We had other traits in common that were documented during our first year at Rufus Putnam. Janey was the most difficult to understand, but we all had some speech problems. I wrote in the student's section of a Putnam report, "I am trying to talk so people can understand me better." Our ball handling skills were mediocre because of the lack of any sports equipment at the Scioto County Children's Home. One playground supervisor at Putnam wrote of Billy, "He needs training in catching and pitching, and lacks coordination."

But these patterns of behavior did not keep us from making friends or having good relations with other children. In the first report after I arrived in Athens, Agnes Eisen wrote, "Dick plays with the other children very well." Two months later Eisen wrote, "The children feel Dick is a nice person to play with. He gets funny but not silly." Perhaps that's because I felt fully accepted at Rufus Putnam and my confidence grew as the evidence accumulated that I was one of the brighter students in my class. I think my emotional storms were played out mostly within the solid brick walls of the manse.

We immediately responded to the emphasis at Rufus Putnam on the creative arts, none of which were given any attention at our Wheelersburg school or at the children's home. "I like to write stories," I wrote in my section of the first report.

In her essay, Eisen commented, "Dick has written many good humorous stories. The children enjoyed them very much... He seems to be full of ideas for stories." We all responded to music in Miss Morley's twice weekly music classes after no music classes in Wheelersburg. "Janey is very musical," Miss Morley wrote. "Her dance interpretations are beautiful, graceful." "Dick is a good singer. He is much interested in all music activities." "Billy works so hard in music and he is very musical."

Of our fine Putnam teachers, my personal favorite was the art teacher, Mary Leonard, and her class my greatest delight. At that time I seemed to have more talent for art than anything else. Mary believed all children are natural creators, which is true, and that all children have artistic talent, which may be true.

Leonard exemplified a major John Dewey principle, building educational programs on the interests of the student. Because she believed artistic creativity in the young was innate, it followed that the role of a good teacher, like that of a good coach, was to be an encourager and to create the conditions in which the student's inherent talents could emerge. I believe Mary Leonard was one of the truly great elementary teachers of America and all of our Putnam teachers were talented educators.

Some parents of students in Athens city schools made disparaging comments about the academic program at Rufus Putnam, usually complaining there was too little emphasis on the three Rs rather than saying there was too much emphasis on literature, music, and art. But Esther Dunham, the associate professor who taught the sixth grade, made sure Putnam students were solidly grounded in math and everything else they would need at the Athens Junior High School. Putnam students did well in the city system when they arrived there, but I — and surely others — missed the small classes, the environment of encouragement, the permission to integrate my personal interests into the program, the emphasis on creativity and the arts, the study of foreign countries and cultures, and our endless games of kickball that defined the program at Rufus Putnam. Mother would sum up my Putnam experience in an article she wrote in 1946. "It is in encouraging his particular talents and special interests that the university and experimental school have been a strong environmental influence." And — I would add — a continuing source of joy all my life.

CHAPTER 12

Our First Christmas
in the Manse

I REMEMBER HOW WE made Christmas cookies, for ourselves and to send to members of the family, using the pretty Finnish tin cookie cutters our mom had brought back from Europe. But the letters she wrote to our father at Ft. Benning add forgotten details of our Christmas preparations, including one of me as the officious older brother.

"Yesterday they baked cookies to send to grandmothers. Dick wrapped them. He also took them to the post office and sent them. He cracked a full cup of hickory nuts. He put all the names on the boxes even if Charles and Bill wouldn't help pick out the nut meats. He said the grandmothers would feel bad, he knew they would, if they knew how lazy Bill and Charlie were!"

A new cousin, army nurse Gretchen Amacher, sent us our first Christmas stockings. "There was a stocking from Gretchen for each child. Boy, were they thrilled! We hung them by the fire place in the living room. They just stand in front of them and look at them and talk about everything in them. There are suckers, life-savers, chewing gum, pencils and no one knows how much else in each stocking." She also mentions how pleased I was to get two pieces of mail, the first I had ever received, one of them a letter from Grandmother Luchs. The letters were addressed to "Master Richard Luchs," the common practice at that time. Christmas mail was a major part of a Luchs Christmas. They sent out a Christmas letter each year to their large and growing circle of friends and acquaintances. Eventually their mailing list would exceed 500 addresses and they would receive over 700 cards and letters each holiday season.

A few days later Evelyn wrote to Fred, still at Fort Benning, "Christmas is looking most prosperous around here. They counted and there are at least seven boxes under the mantle for each. They spend much time trying to think what might possibly be in each box." We bought gifts for each other from a local dime store with our allowance money. This, our first experience of buying gifts, resulted in some confusion. Billy bought Janey a yo-yo, which he wanted, and she bought him doll clothes pins, which she wanted. Our foster mother wrote she thought there would be a useful exchange on Christmas Day and that we had all gone with Grace Monigold to see the enormous Christmas tree at Boyd Hall, a women's dorm on the Ohio University campus. She reported that the Whitehouse family had loaned us a lovely crèche. And she sent along a letter she had typed following Janey's dictation.

"Come back home Christmas and don't miss your bus. I want you to know about the Christmas presents. Bill bought me a snake, I think. He said it was an egg, but it felt like a yo-yo when I pinched it...Come back on Christmas. Dear Daddy, please go out in the city. Dear Daddy, go in the store and buy a doll baby. Charlie would like to have a doll baby for Christmas. Buy a doll for you too, if you would want a doll. If you go down the street, you will see the Salvation Army lady. I am Daddy's sweetheart. Janey." Janey wanted a doll—her first—for Christmas, but she did not ask for it directly.

All four of us still believed in Santa Claus. We were put to bed on Christmas Eve after our foster father, now home from the chaplaincy at Fort Benning, realized his dream of reading to us and chose *The Night before Christmas*. We didn't know it was the Luchs and not Santa who went to work preparing the music room for our first Christmas morning. After we were asleep, they brought in a 9-foot white pine tree, decorated it, and placed their gifts for us under the tree.

I woke early on Christmas morning in a cold bedroom, excited and waiting for the best day of the year to begin. As I rose to light the gas heater I discovered a stocking at the end of my bed. I quickly struck a match, lighted the heater and jumped back into bed under my warm comforter. I pulled the stocking under the comforter with me and began to explore it as the room heated up.

Billy stirred.

"Billy, Charlie," I whispered.

"Yeah."

"Look down at the foot of your beds."

They sat up to find their stockings and in a few minutes were inspecting the contents they had dumped on their beds. They found kaleidoscopes, decks of Old Maid and authors' cards, small diaries, pen lights and of course, candy bars and the hard Christmas candy we loved.

Once the Luchs were up and after they had lighted the tree and done the finishing touches of the preparations made the night before, we were permitted to come down into the front living room. When we had gathered and were now bursting with suspense and excitement, our new mother pushed back the double pocket doors to the music room to reveal a wondrous display of a lighted nine-foot tall white pine tree above heaps of colorful boxes and bows of all shapes and sizes and a few large unwrapped gifts. We were dazzled with delight.

We were allowed to look under the tree, discovering which presents were for us. Janey squealed. In the midst of the heap of presents was a doll, which could only be for her. She picked it up and at once cradled it in her arms. The doll was a pink-cheeked, porcelain-faced antique with dark brown hair, an 19th century treasure given by a woman in the church.

When Charlie discovered that many of the presents under the tree were for him, he danced around the lighted tree in his striped pajamas shouting with joy, "I was a good boy! I was a good boy!" It was a few minutes later before our mother realized that seeing so many presents with his name on them was proof to Charlie that Santa, whose verdict was the one that counted, thought he was good boy. Our Uncle Charles McNelly had so convinced little Charlie he was a bad boy that Charlie didn't think he would get any presents.

Then Father sat down next to the tree and called out the name on each package, one by one. We would take the package from him and put it in our pile. Once all the presents were distributed, we began opening them, youngest first, in rotation. In the midst of so much abundance, I remember one big disappointment. We were as eager to learn how to tell time as our new mother was to teach us to tell time. We had watches on our wish list for Santa and asked specifically for the Mickey Mouse watches then promoted on radio programs and among our new friends at school. The Luchs were aware of the importance Billy and I attached to having these then popular watches and discussed the issue between them at some length. They decided Mickey Mouse watches were a marketing fad they did not want to support. A small matter, perhaps, but I can still remember the disappointment I felt when I tore the paper from a package I was sure was a Mickey Mouse watch to find a wrist watch with a rectangular gold colored case and a brown leather band. I felt like crying but didn't. How difficult it is as a parent to decide, in a child's best interest, when to accede to marketing fads and when to resist them! While we gleefully opened our presents our foster mother sat in a chair beside the tree, yellow pencil cocked and ready, recording each gift and giver on a white pad for the thank you notes we would be asked to write in the days ahead.

We were about to go to the kitchen for a special bacon and pancake breakfast when Janey announced, "My side hurts, Mommy." Janey was still cradling her doll in her arms. Mom pulled Janey aside and reached inside her red bath robe and lifted her night gown. On her left side, along the rib cage, was a purplish protrusion the size of a small grapefruit. Mother gasped. The growth looked grotesque on Janey's tiny body.

In November she had taken Janey to the family doctor because she thought Janey was not well. Old Dr. Goldsberry told her, "Evelyn, you may be a new mother, but you're still an old maid school teacher. Now stop fussing about her health. With her pink cheeks she could not be ill."

But she was seriously ill, never having fully recovered from her long illness in February of 1943 while we were still at the children's home. Davy Hughes lifted Janey into the ambulance from the funeral home next door and rushed her to Sheltering Arms Hospital. The diagnosis was advanced empyema, or the accumulation of pus in the chest cavity from a serious infection in her left lung.

A surgeon operated on her Christmas Day afternoon, removing parts of her ribs and half of one diseased lung in a procedure that had just been developed in military hospitals during WW II. Without that procedure Janey would have died, her second close brush with death in 1943. Once her chest cavity was open, the surgeon drained a pint of pus from it.

This time Janey was in the hospital for a month. Women from the church brought her caramel custard and other treats. Margaret Hampel and others went to the hospital to read to her. When she came home, a drainage tube from her side to a bottle on the floor beneath her bed drained her chest cavity. She had to stay in bed, flat on her back, could not turn over or even turn right or left in the bed. She had to use bed pans brought by Mom and Grace Monigold and Betty Lou Gregg. The pus drainage bottle had to be changed every few hours. A few times the tube was ripped out while she slept and the drainage leaked all over her bed covers and once, she remembers, the red bathrobe she loved and her sheets were soaked with draining pus.

After one month in the hospital and four months at home in bed, the chest cavity healed. Dr. Goldsberry arrived at the manse one morning as promised, after a call on a patient at Sheltering Arms Hospital. He trotted up the long front stairs of the manse with his black bag to Janey's room, our foster mom in tow. He was puffing a little by the time they reached the top step.

"Evelyn," he said, looking at her directly as they paused on the landing out of Janey's hearing, "Removing this tube will be unpleasant for a minute or so. I want you to go downstairs, make yourself a big pot of strong coffee, and do not," he emphasized *do not*, "come upstairs no matter what you hear." Then he disappeared alone into Janey's bedroom.

Mom went down to make the coffee and was about to pour her first cup from the percolator when she heard a loud scream. Then there was some crying and then silence and she knew the dreaded tube extraction had been done. After the operation Janey's weight, only 28 pounds when she arrived at the manse, fell to 22 pounds. Our foster mom began a diet and exercise program to rebuild her strength. Janey did gain weight and health quickly and returned to school shortly after the drainage tube was removed.

How Evelyn Luchs Became My Mother

Years later, when I asked Janey if she remembered when she first thought of Evelyn Luchs as her mother, she said, "From the moment she took me and held me in her arms, I belonged to her. She was my mother, my real and only mother." I believe that. Mom had an unusually large dose of that primal force that makes most women want to be mothers. When she gathered us within her arms in the manse entrance hall that first day she began at once to call herself "Mother" and her husband "Daddy," and seemed to expect us to do the same and mostly we did. I think she also became Charlie's "real and only mother" quickly. But Janey was only four years old and Charlie five when we arrived at the manse. After 26 months in the Scioto Country Children's Home they had no memories or attachments to our biological family. Billy, who was six and like me did have a few memories of our biological family, began to think of Evelyn Luchs as his real mother later in our first year at the manse.

My experience was different. I had enduring memories of my birth family and was still emotionally bonded to my biological father. Moreover, Janey and Charlie and even Billy were too young to be consulted or to play any role in choosing our new parents. So was I, perhaps, but I had been consulted, and as a result of the agreement Ann Minnis and I had made, I believed I had been given at least a veto power over who our parents would be. If I decided the four of us should not stay with the Luchs, we would leave. In my mind the Luchs would become our parents only when they had earned that privilege by proving to me they were responsible adults who truly loved us. So, despite the phone call our foster mother had me make to the children's home at the end of the honeymoon period, the issue of whether or not we would stay was not yet settled for me. Despite my delight at suddenly finding us in such improved circumstances, I did not yet think of Fred and Evelyn Luchs as my father and mother. They were the man and woman who took care of us, rather like teachers or nannies, or what in fact they were legally at that time, our foster parents.

Yet I had begun to like Evelyn Luchs. She was winning me over. I suppose it helped that we resembled each other physically. I could see she liked the fact that people who did not know I was adopted would comment on how much I looked like her. Some of our dinner guests who had just been told we were adopted would say,

"Really? I had already figured out which one of them most resembles one of you."

Much more important than our physical resemblance, however, our foster mother was proving, in sickness and in health, that she was a responsible adult and that she loved us. Evelyn Luchs was knocking on the door of my closed heart. Looking back, I suppose that while I could open my door a crack or two — and eventually much wider — I do not think I could have returned to the wide open trust of an innocent child again. Like a few other "irreversibles" in this life, once that's gone, it's gone. In any case, during our first year in the manse, I was still holding back. I could not be open enough to permit her to become, as she did for Janey and Charlie almost immediately, my "real and only mother."

I remember once when I was singing in the choir of a cathedral as a young man, not yet a father myself, watching a boy of four or so walk hand in hand to the communion rail with his father for a blessing. The boy's face was radiant. His expression was one of perfect innocence and perfect trust. How utterly beautiful! I said to myself. The two of them together, father and son, and the trust on that boy's face! I don't know if the trust was in his father or in what his father had told him about Jesus. It didn't matter. I watched the luminous expression on that little boy's face and a few seconds later I found myself in tears. I realized in that moment that I had lost too soon and forever that boy's trusting innocence. Perhaps that is what happens to all of us, sooner or later. Perhaps that is what we call "growing up." So, much as I was coming to admire and like Evelyn Luchs, I reserved a part of me deep inside that no one entered. The risk of letting go altogether was just too great.

I can remember a specific incident when I began to realize that Evelyn Luchs was becoming my mother, a moment when I accepted her authority — that is, her right to claim my obedience and expect me to follow her rules, as well as be more open to her love. I think both are important.

I have read that children adopted when they are older are more likely than children raised in their birth families to lie and to steal. Despite our biological origins in the light-fingered Harry Boggs clan, our petty thefts (pocket change from suit coats and drawers) seem normal to me, and these petty thefts were only committed at home. The one exception I can remember is when Charlie and the dean's son from across the street were caught taking toys from a bin at Scott's Five and Dime.

So, while I can doubt our petty thefts were different from those of children with more normal childhoods, it is true we had learned at the children's home to do or say anything to avoid being caught and punished. There were no rewards at the children's home for coming clean, no appreciation for honest admission of having done something wrong. We had learned to conceal and, if accused, to deny. The less we told the supervisors, the less likely we were to get into trouble. I now see this as a survival technique. I still don't know why I parted from that policy in the case of plaster broken from the wall of the bathroom, and I imagine most of my dormitory mates thought I was being stupid, especially since I honestly didn't think I alone was responsible for the fallen plaster.

We were given allowances shortly after we arrived at the manse, but those sometimes seemed inadequate. Our mother kept a black wallet in a drawer in the kitchen to pay the milkman and other vendors. From it I would occasionally augment my allowance by extracting a nickel or dime for a candy bar or two or even double my weekly allowance with a quarter. I knew that a nickel would buy me the golden crunchiness of a Butterfinger candy bar or the icy fizzle of a forbidden Coca-Cola.

Once, when I was alone in the kitchen and could hear no one walking down the hall or the back stairway to the kitchen, I slowly pulled open the door beneath the counter, pried open the snap on the change pouch of the wallet, and slid my thumb and forefinger into the pouch to feel the cool, hard, metal coins. I quickly found a quarter, took it out, carefully re-snapped the coin pouch on the wallet, and closed the drawer. Such theft generally went unnoticed.

After a few weeks of snitching a quarter from time to time, I became bold and pulled three quarters out of the change pouch and my foster mother noticed the loss.

"Now one of you did take money from my pocketbook, which means that one of you is lying. Now, come on, which one of you is it?"

She had gathered us in a semicircle in the kitchen next to the scene of the crime. Her stance was firm with legs planted solidly apart, the muscles of her face had tensed, her deep-brown eyes were afire and her hands were on her hips. A surge of emotion passed through my body. I was afraid, I was upset. I lowered my eyes in the manner of the guilty. I knew I was about to be elevated to the role of chief suspect.

When she came to the conclusion I was probably the culprit, she dismissed the others from the kitchen and stood there, working on me alone. She was relentless in her questioning, her voice now sharp and firm. She was closing in like a police interrogator trying to extract a confession from a clever and hardened felon. Her words came faster as she began to badger me. But I was not about to surrender. This was just one more adult treating me unfairly in an unequal contest. I was beginning to like her and now she was treating me badly. The unfairness in this unequal contest between a child and an adult angered me and I defended myself by simply denying I had taken any money, again and again and again, each time with more force and more emotion. We must have gone on like that for fifteen minutes or more. Then I broke all at once. I threw myself at her and she folded her arms around me and I burst into tears. She hugged me against her warm body and held me tight. I could smell her hair. Confession and forgiveness bond the forgiven to the forgiver. Confession meant I was accepting the justice of the Luchs, their standards and their authority to impose their moral order. When I finally peeked up at her as she held me, I could see that she too had tears in her eyes. That was one of the moments when I could see that she cared about me, and it was part of the process of accepting her as my mother.

The incident was discussed briefly for its learning value and never mentioned again. Concealing and denying was a pattern all of us had learned except Billy. The pattern had to be broken. It was broken by praising and rewarding honesty. Consistently. We learned that transgressions honestly admitted were not punished or only punished lightly in the manse. We no longer feared to tell the truth. This is probably why Billy didn't have the problem. He seemed to fear nothing, and certainly not physical danger, which he appeared to seek, nor did he fear physical punishment. Moreover, Billy had an innocent candor. He even looked like a little angel, though a smudged one. Agnes Eisen, our third grade teacher, looking at a photograph of Billy, said, "That boy may look like an angel but I can tell you he's not!"

At the time, I thought our mother was making too much of the theft of three quarters and did not understand how concealing and denying had become a shield to protect us from the rough and often arbitrary justice of the children's home. But I came to understand she was not concerned about the money but about lying. I can also understand that she would find threatening any of our behaviors that might seem to be a repetition of Boggs family patterns. I found many years later, however, that the Luchs had been told little about our felonious father or his family.

In time my relationship with Evelyn Luchs led to a sort of imprinting of my new mother's image and her very being upon me. I found myself imitating her gestures, using her words and speech intonations, absorbing her views and opinions, and sometimes even anticipating her thoughts as if our life rhythms had come together, and we were in step with each other. I was a child who had lost the rhythm for the dance of life. Evelyn Luchs taught me to dance again, to recover what I had forgotten or, perhaps, had never known.

MUSIC IN THE MANSE

When Miss Morley, the music teacher at Rufus Putnam, reported the four of us had fine singing voices and were doing well in our music classes, the Luchs added to our other routines and programs four daily 30-minute piano practice sessions before and after school. Those began with me at 7:00 AM on cold December mornings as the coal furnace in the basement struggled to warm up the first floor of the old manse. Betty Lou Gregg or Grace Monigold and I began our days huddled in heavy bathrobes in front of the brown upright piano as I worked my way from red cover to red cover of the John Thompson series. A year or so later I was sent to Mrs. Robinson, the wife of a professor of music at Ohio University, for weekly piano lessons in addition to 30 minutes of supervised practice each day.

While reading through Mother's papers and journals for this book I was surprised to find this entry from 1942, the year before we arrived:

"We all went to hear the pianist Rachlin in the evening. I honestly enjoyed him ...the first pianist I ever enjoyed." (!)

I have to wonder why, if she didn't like piano music, she was so eager to have us take lessons since it could not have been pleasant to hear the sounds of forty fumbling fingers engaged in daily two-hour struggles with John Thompson's "Teaching Little Fingers to Play."

But the sounds we made improved as we progressed through the Thompson red book series and eventually moved on to Bach, Chopin, Czerny, Schumann, and Beethoven. We were never encouraged to believe our talents would lead us to performing in concert halls, but there were other rewards for the hours we spent in piano study each week. One immediate benefit was we could use our developing ability to read music in school and church choirs. Another was that piano lessons created a foundation for the study of other instruments. Charlie moved quickly from the piano to the violin. Janey played a variety of musical instruments through her school years, and while Billy continued to study piano with me, he also began a lifelong romance with horns. After two years or so I discovered the therapeutic value of piano playing, a safe and harmless means of venting my anger and other emotions. Piano playing also helped me to deal with the small crises in my life, including grief following the death of beloved people and pets. I remember how as a ten-year-old I played a mournful little piece by Tchaikovsky again and again for months as a memorial when Clifford Coulter, my new grandfather, died.

Our manse recitals for teachers and other friends of the family began in April of 1944, only six months after we arrived. Sometimes these were spontaneous affairs for whomever was at our dinner table. Sometimes they were more formal occasions, with programs our mother typed on colored paper folded into four-page booklets. The title page of the first of these concerts announced that "Dick Luchs assisted by Grace Monigold will present a recital Sunday, April 30, 1944, at the Presbyterian Manse." My solo offerings included an elementary arrangement of a theme from Haydn's "Surprise Symphony," "Good King Wenceslas," and "Blue Bells of Scotland," all from the first John Thompson book since I was only in my fourth month of piano study. We took turns being the master of ceremonies of these concerts for friends of the family. When Janey's first turn came, she stood up, smiled sweetly and said, "Today is my turn to renounce this concert," a thought which surely occurred to other members of our captive audiences.

The other half of our education in music was choral music. We began singing in music class at Rufus Putnam and then got lots of practice singing in junior choir at church and during church services. We three brothers would sing, eventually in parts as a trio, before going to sleep, an after-lights-out activity the Luchs permitted. Singing was something we all enjoyed. The four of us shared a talent for music the Luchs did not that probably came from our biological family. The Luchs also began taking us to the community concert series at Ohio University's Memorial Auditorium. At first, the only attraction for us in such concerts was staying up past our bedtime. Eventually we began to enjoy the classical music we were hearing.

CHAPTER 13

The Real Fred Luchs
Appears

B Y EARLY 1944 WE were beginning to be familiar with the daily rituals of our new parents. Because the manse was spacious and they did not want to shout at each other, our father would whistle three notes as he entered the front door: two of the same length and pitch and then a single note, up a third and held. Mom was supposed to respond with the same trio of notes in reply but was a poor whistler and would just come to the front hall to greet him. When he was out calling and invited on the spur of the moment to stay for dinner in a fraternity or sorority house, he would telephone and say, "Madam Otis Regrets" from the Cole Porter song about the lady who had to miss a luncheon engagement because she was about to be hanged. For years we thought he was saying "Madamodus Regrets" and wondered who Madamodus was.

They took morning breaks for coffee or iced tea, depending on the season, sometimes with friends or parishioners who had just dropped in, and all their life managed to work in at least one brisk walk together every day. She loved her coffee and drank six or more cups of regular coffee every day. For him she mixed a special drink that was 1/4 coffee, 3/4 piping hot water. He always asked that his drink be served boiling hot and would often request she get up from the kitchen table to reheat the drink she had prepared if it was not hot enough to suit him. Then he would ask her to get up from the table once again to bring him an ice cube or two to cool it down!

Our Father and Dale Carnegie

By the spring of 1944 our new father began to be a real presence in our lives. We were getting to know him. We already knew about his admiration for his friends "the Experts," named or anonymous. His deference to experts was part of his highly respectful view of titles and status, including his own title and status as a clergyman. This probably reflected his background in a Swiss immigrant community in which public officials and the clergy were ascribed a higher status than is common in the United States.

Although some of our foster father's expert friends seemed to spend most of their time at the *Reader's Digest*, we were learning there were others in other magazines and books: communications experts, management experts, public relations experts. But the greatest expert of all, excepting Jesus of course, was Dale Carnegie. Next to the Bible, our father considered *How to Win Friends and Influence People* the wisest, most useful, most important book of all time. Carnegie had unlocked the secrets of human hearts. Carnegie knew how to get along and get ahead in the world. What is more important than knowing how to influence people on this journey through life, our father sometimes asked? What achievement can be compared with winning friends? Friends are useful and to be used. Otherwise, why have them? It all worked together nicely. Dale Carnegie's principles enabled him to influence people and to make good use of his friends, not in any manner harmful to them, of course, but simply to get them to do what he wanted them to do. He believed what he wanted was in their own best interest, though sometimes our father admitted he did have to help them discover their own best interest. Ah, the Dale Carnegie principles were all so reasonable, made such excellent sense and what possibilities they brought forth! Our father believed he had developed skill in applying the principles of how to win friends and influence people. Just thinking about his own acute understanding of Dale Carnegie's insights made our father feel good.

You may remember that the first of Dale Carnegie's principles for winning friends and influencing people was "BE LAVISH IN YOUR PRAISE." Our father praised in person, but we rarely were privy to those conversations. What we did sometimes overhear as children in the manse was his praise by telephone. Next to the penny post card, which we will come to a bit later, our father considered the telephone — this was in the early 1940s — America's great under-used bargain. He once wrote an article for a clergy publication on how to use the telephone effectively in the parish ministry. The article was so popular it was republished repeatedly by the telephone company.

Our father praised both men and women, though I recall most easily the conversations with women, most of whom were members of First Presbyterian. The following are examples I remember overhearing as a child, though of course I could only hear our father's end of the conversation.

"Good morning, my dear," our father would begin and then he delivered one of his favorite pieces of praise. "You have such a beautiful voice! Where did you train for the opera? (Pause) You didn't train for the opera? Really? I can't believe it, your voice is so lovely!" A variation went: "What a beautiful voice you have, my dear! Have you ever considered having your own radio show?"

Father liked to do birthday greetings by telephone. To women in the congregation, he would begin, "Happy birthday! I can't believe you're 65! When I saw you in church last week you didn't look a day over 35!"

Or this one, which we heard more than once. "I bet you've won every beauty contest you ever entered. (Pause) You haven't entered any beauty contests? Well, you should!"

Occasionally he confused names and sent the right message to the wrong woman. "Did I detect a tiny change when you walked out of church last week?" he asked one woman in a telephone conversation. "Is there going to be a little event in your life in a few months?" (Pause) "I see...that's no longer possible...because you're 86 years old. Yes, yes, I understand."

But mostly things worked as Dale Carnegie said they would. Even those who realized their pastor's words were not 100 percent sincere let his lavish praise give a lift to their day.

Our father also had high regard for the US Postal Service and considered the penny post card one of America's great bargains. He liked to point out that since 1928 the cost of a cream colored one cent post card with a printed green Jefferson profile stamp had never varied. Father so loved what he could do with the penny post card that he bought them in boxes, 1,000 at a time for only ten dollars. The man who earned a modest salary and had to watch his dimes and nickels was a spendthrift when it came to spending money on postage. A brand new box full of 1,000 penny post cards made him tingle with a delightful sense of well-being and anticipation of new adventures in persuasion.

When in his study at the manse, Father banged out the brief texts of his post cards on a 1924 black Remington typewriter. The old Remington was incapable, at least beneath his fingers, of typing in straight lines or without multiple cross outs, which as often as not missed the targeted word entirely. The line of his typed text rose up and down in fits and starts across the card as if the old Remington was tipsy or had loose screws. When away from home without the Remington, our father scribbled his cryptic notes in script with pencil or pen. He used a special abbreviated phonetic post card vocabulary. "U" for you and "Tks" for thanks, of course, but also "Ur" for your, "nite" and "thru" for night and through, "enuf" for enough, "lotsa" for lots of, "tho'gt" for thought, and "ch" for church and "ss" for Sunday school. He used special post card salutations and closings. For example, for women who were friends he would begin with "Beautiful" for the plainer ones and "Gorgeous" for those on whom nature had smiled. For men he often began with "U Rascal." Since all of his cards asked the addressees to do something for him, a frequent closing was "Gobs of gratitude, Fritz the Friar."

No one within the reach of the US Postal Service was beyond father's power. He could extract a favor, cajole or remind at will. He often wondered out loud why none of the management "experts" had discovered the secret of the penny postcard. "With the penny post card," he would say, "it's possible to manage the world." No one in the United States was beyond the reach of his great persuasive postal power. Or so he believed.

Ignoring his post cards did not work. He had an abundant supply of the cream-colored cards, and any addressee who could provide him a favor or free service could expect to receive a card each month, or each week, or even each day if they continued to ignore his cards. He would not relent until he received a reply, even a negative one. He considered that no response was worse than a negative response because a negative response could be changed to a positive response with a modest investment of additional one penny post cards. He was aided in his persuasive endeavors by a peculiar visual "defect" that made it impossible for him to read the word "No." or even "No!" He couldn't even see "No!!!!!!!" In all cases he simply ignored responses he did not want, and continued to send the same addressee more of his post cards. He continued to hope he could persuade him or her to change his or her mind, or at least wear his or her resistance down. Oddly, with his visual "defect" he combined an astounding memory that far exceeded the capacities of normal human beings. He never forgot offers of assistance made in unguarded moments, or "yeses" muttered in times of weakness after having been worn down by our father's repeated, persistent barrage of post cards.

Our father did not seem to mind in the least that his penny

post card campaigns annoyed people, even Very Important People. The cards often angered addressees who swore oaths as they tossed yet another one into the waste basket. The worst of all fates for our father was not, as for most of us, to be disliked. The worst fate he could imagine was to be ignored. In any case, single-handedly he turned the penny post card into a powerful direct mail mechanism and management tool.

When he was out of town on speaking tours he always took two or three dozen postal cards with him. This enabled him to remind his Athens correspondents, including his four children, that he was still present, if physically absent. He was checking up to be sure we were doing all the chores on the "to do" lists he had left as he departed. It was as if he had uncovered the divine secret of being everywhere at the same time.

As a young man our father had scored high on tests of management ability. He took great pride in this and believed this native ability justified his wish to direct the lives and activities of others. In their best interest, of course. When he was at home, however, our father did not direct us by post cards. Instead he used torn scraps of used paper on which he wrote brief instructions. These he placed on our beds two or three times a week, circling or underlining the key words with a red pencil. We learned the art of procrastination, because chores quickly accomplished were just as quickly replaced with new tasks.

MUNCIE, INDIANA

In April 1944, our father drove me and my brothers to Muncie, Indiana, to spend a few days with the Reverend Lewis Gishler, a college and seminary friend. Our father was happy because this was our first trip together, a father with his three new sons. He had promised us a movie in Dayton. I had not seen a feature film since I went with Lonnie to watch westerns. While at the children's home we saw only documentaries, and watched those only at school, most of them made to build support for the war on the home front. On the brightly lighted marquee as we entered a theater in Dayton for the matinee I read "My Friend Flicka," which I would guess was on everyone's list that year of good movies for children. We arrived during the black and white newsreel. A thin young man with blond slicked down hair shined a circle of light on the carpet that led us into a row of seats on the aisle of the center section of the theater. Once my eyes adjusted I could see the theater was less than half full.

Roddy McDowell, who is the boy Ken in "My Friend Flicka," was a little older than I but resembled me. He often yanked the end of his belt, a mannerism I shared. His father looked like Lonnie, but sported a pencil moustache which Lonnie did not have. I was Ken immediately. I walked into another world, a screen world that was bigger and brighter and seemed even more real and exciting than our walk in the streets of Dayton, Ohio. I felt Ken's shame when he fell down a hillside and stampeded his father's horses. I cried with him when the mother of Flicka was sold and was horrified when she jumped in fear of a truck and crashed against the entrance gate to his father's ranch and died. My heart nearly stopped later as Ken watched his dear Flicka dying from a barbed wire wound. She grew worse, her fever rose, she would not eat.

Ken (and I) heard the adults around us saying, "She's going to die. Put her out of her misery."

Then Ken's father ordered a ranch hand to shoot Flicka. I couldn't take it any longer. I ran towards the exit at the back of the theater, covering my ears. Charlie also left and joined me. A few minutes later our father came out to ask why we had left our seats. When we explained our reaction to the film, he bought some pop corn for us and went back to take his seat with Billy to see the rest of the movie. Even today, I find it difficult to sit through a movie in which the life of a cherished pet or a child seems to be in mortal danger.

During the drive from Dayton to Muncie our father began talking about changing our names, a subject the Luchs had not raised before. He said he was going to name us for his college and seminary friends. He wanted to rename me Lewis after Lewis Gishler, the Presbyterian minister we were about to meet. Lewis would be my first name; Richard, my given first name, would become my middle name. Billy would become Mark, after Mark Lefevre, also a Franklin and Marshall graduate, a fraternity brother of our father, and a juvenile judge in Philadelphia. Billy's middle name would be William. Charlie would become Michael, after another of our new father's friends. He would keep Charles as his middle name. Our new father proposed to name Janey after his mother. She would become Margaret Jane Luchs.

When we arrived in Muncie I met the Rev. Mr. Lewis Gishler. I first saw him in a red Buick coupe, a convertible with the top down. He was as handsome as Hollywood's best with dark wavy hair and his voice was mellifluous like the lower range of a cello. He smiled, he laughed, he charmed. Beside him sat a beautiful brunette. Her voice was as sweet as his was mellow, and she was even more charming than he was. On the spot I decided becoming Lewis might not be such a bad idea. I hoped the name might help me someday become as handsome as Lewis Gishler. I could even dream of imitating his life, especially the red convertible and having a beautiful and sophisticated woman seated beside me. I am often asked about our reaction to the announcement our given names would be changed. We did not object. Perhaps that was because the change was not imposed suddenly but made gradually over two or three years. We had begun a new life with new parents. Acquiring new names seemed at the time to be a natural part of that process.

What the Luchs and I did not know until many years later was that my middle name at birth was Lewis. The renaming simply reversed my first and second given names. Nor did we know that Mark's original name was Lonnie, after our father, and not William or Bill or Billy. How Mark came to be called Billy while we were in the children's home remains a mystery.

CHAPTER 14

Daddy's Garden

WHEN THE SPRING OF 1944 reached full bloom, Mother bought us blue overalls and Father drove us out to Happy Howell's farm to begin the planting of Daddy's Garden. Daddy's Garden, one of our modest contributions to the World War II effort, was where we were going to plant the pumpkin seeds from the Jack-o'-lantern we carved the first evening we arrived in Athens.

Happy Howell had set aside for us a "parson's patch" along a pretty little creek not far from his house for which he did not ask a penny. I was surprised by the size of the plot Happy had prepared the week before we showed up. We brought hoes and rakes with us. Happy invited us to use the tools he kept in a shed, including a hand cultivator mounted on two metal wheels that we found so much fun to use we competed to push it. Happy told us all that remained to be done before planting the garden was to rake the area we wanted to seed. Billy and I worked to see how much raking we could do quickly. While we raked, our father retired to a shady spot along the creek to memorize Sunday's sermon. He told us he also wanted to commune with the spirit of the Old Testament prophet Amos, whose message from Yahweh on economic justice was the theme of the week's sermon. Janey and Charlie meanwhile headed down to the creek to play with Nancy, the Howell's adopted daughter.

Once we had finished raking perhaps a quarter of Daddy's Garden, Father interrupted his conversation with the spirit of

Amos and walked towards us with a fistful of seed packets. It was about 10:30 AM and Billy and I were already perspiring. Father then asked if I knew anything about planting seeds. I told him that, except for a few bean seeds at the children's home, I had never planted anything at all. At first I thought he was about to give me some lessons in seed planting. But no, he seemed to be asking *me* how to plant seeds.

Trying to be helpful, I said there seemed to be instructions on the back of the packet. I looked at one. "Yes, you see, for these peas it says, 'Sow in a sunny location, one to two inches deep.'" "According to this next packet," I said, "Bean seeds should be two inches apart and the spacing between rows one and 1/2 feet." It seemed to me we could read the back of all the packets and find out how deep the furrow should be and how far apart the seeds and rows should be.

"Now that's using your noggin!" Father said. "Yes, of course, read the back of the packets. Now why didn't I think of that?"

"Well, gentlemen," he continued. "Which seeds should we begin with?"

I knew that radishes came up quickly so I suggested we begin with radishes.

"Atta boy," he said. "Let's begin with radishes."

I waited for him to begin. But he didn't begin.

"Would you read out loud what's on the back of the seed packet for radishes?" he asked me. So I read out loud from the packet. "Sow radishes 1/4" deep, 1/2 to one inch apart with rows 6-12 inches apart."

I began to wonder if he was putting us on, as Tom Sawyer had tricked his boyhood friends into white-washing Aunt Polly's fence. Was it possible he really didn't know the first thing about planting radishes? After I read the packet I made a couple of furrows with a stick along a white string on stakes we had taken from Happy Howell's shed to guide us, ripped the corner of the seed packet off, shook some of the tiny black seeds into my hand, and handed the package to him so he could take some. Again, I waited for him to begin but he didn't, so I fell to my knees to begin planting the tiny black seeds, trying my best to place them about 1/2 inch apart. A few seconds later I looked up to see my father struggling, still trying to get some seeds out of the packet onto his open palm.

"How far apart did the packet say the seeds should be?" he asked.

"One half to one inch," I said.

A few minutes later I looked up again, this time to see him bending over slightly from a standing position, straddling the tiny radish planting furrow at the other end, dropping seeds in two and threes or sixes from between his thumb and forefinger at a height of about 18 inches. His aim — and whose aim is good enough to place radish seeds from 18 inches? — was entirely undone by a morning breeze. The tiny seeds fell everywhere and as much as a foot or two from the 1/4 inch furrow I had made with the stick. I was beginning to suspect our new father truly didn't know anything about planting vegetable seeds. Billy and I finished planting the radishes while the father-manager of Daddy's Garden returned to the shaded spot by the creek for more work on his sermon.

And so it went. I read the seed packets. Billy and I followed the instructions to plant the seeds. That worked for the lettuce and radishes and peas and beans and even the corn, but once we got to the bell pepper and tomato seedlings we had purchased at a feed store on North Court Street, we had a problem. There were no seed packets and therefore no instructions. The same was true of the pumpkin seeds we had brought along to plant. So we interrupted our father's sermon work and told him of our dilemma.

"I see," he said. "No seed packets to read. Hmmmmmmmm. You want to know how you plant the tomatoes and green peppers."

"And the pumpkin seeds," Billy added.

"Yes, of course. The pumpkin seeds."

Something clicked in his mind because his frown turned into a smile, so we thought he probably had a solution. Off he went and returned a few minutes later with Happy Howell who walked with his body tilted to one side because Happy was toting a big, full watering can. Happy showed us how to transplant tomato and bell pepper seedlings and supervised Billy and me while we planted two or three of each and explained how to do the pumpkin seeds. Having solved our problem like a good manager should, our father was already back in his spot of shade beside the creek.

The day grew hotter. Perspiration was running down Billy's face and mine as we worked as a team, one of us taking turns hauling water out of the creek with the watering can while the other planted the tomatoes and green peppers. Again, like a good manager, our father rose from his sermon labors an hour or so later to check on our progress. The sun was high now and getting hotter all the time. Perspiration flowed down our noses and dripped onto our naked upper bodies. Father watched us for a few minutes, praised our progress as a good manager should, and then again returned to his shade tree.

Father continued to drive us out to Daddy's Garden on weekends that spring, but he was always the supervisor, the manager who worked with his brain and liked to keep a respectful distance between himself and physical labor. He sometimes quoted one of the rules of another of his "Experts," a management specialist at *Reader's Digest*: "Never ask another person to do anything you wouldn't do yourself." This was a favorite maxim of his. When I hinted there might be some contradiction between the maxim and his approach to vegetable gardening, he said, "Now boy, the rule does not say I have to work along with you. The clear meaning of the rule is that, if necessary, I would be willing to do what I have asked you to do. Since you are so competent, that isn't necessary."

So that spring and into the summer, once he saw we were hard at work in Daddy's Garden, he would retire to his favorite shady spot under the tree along the creek to memorize the main points of his next sermon or go parish calling or visit ill church members in the hospital, and then return in the afternoon to drive us home. If we needed guidance, Happy Howell was usually available and pleased to help us. Once we had bikes we rode out to Daddy's Garden on our own and our father conducted his management of the garden from the manse, usually with cryptic instructions scribbled on small scraps of waste paper left on our beds. "Weed corn this week" or "Rotenone beans ASAP" or "Water tomatoes and peppers!!!" He was guessing. Only sometimes did the assigned task have much to do with what needed to be done in the garden. When he was out of town on speaking tours or at conferences, he managed Daddy's Garden the way he did much else when he was away, with penny post cards.

Our father's post card instructions or the reminders he scribbled on scrap paper and left on our beds were cryptic prompters. If he read in the newspaper wherever he happened to be that rainfall had been sparse that week, we would get a card with the message, "Drought!!! Water, Water!" even though we had had two days of thunderstorms in Athens. Sometimes his text was a single word such as "Onions!" You can see that his flawless management of Daddy's Garden got to the point he didn't even have to bother to specify if the onions were to be weeded, watered, or harvested. He thought it was probably about time to do something to the onions and apparently was confident we could figure out what that would be. Managing Daddy's Garden from hundreds of miles away suited our father perfectly and served to confirm his unusual talents in the art of good management.

We learned later that our new father was an urban boy who had never spent even 15 minutes actually working in a vegetable garden in his life. He had considerable difficulty developing any relationship at all with Mother Earth. For one thing, he didn't enjoy getting close to her. A Luchs aunt told us he was never seen settling down on his knees with a trowel in his hands to place and water and push the soil around a tomato seedling. Instead, he tried to plant tomato seedlings by bending over from a standing position, which made the task all but impossible. It was the same posture he used for planting radish seeds. It wasn't that he couldn't have worked down on his knees, our aunt told us. He just didn't. Gardening was difficult for him also because he was all thumbs, a description he often used of himself. Not one of them was green. He envied those with even a modicum of manual dexterity and went through life telling everyone with normal hands and fingers they ought to be dentists.

Charlie Delivers the Mail

Among our father's chief uses of the postal service he so admired was to send out publicity for himself as a speaker for high school commencements and service clubs. These mail-outs included his speech topics, his puffed-up biography, a separate list of his accomplishments and honors, and quotes from letters of appreciation from school superintendents, school principals, and officers in Kiwanis and Lions and Rotary. He promoted himself to high schools and colleges in four states as a commencement and baccalaureate speaker. He promoted himself to service clubs and civic organizations within a two day's drive from Athens.

Because First Presbyterian could not afford to pay a full-time secretary, and his speaking programs were, strictly speaking, not the church's business, he was always looking for volunteers to do typing, cut stencils, transcribe Dictaphone cylinders, and address and stuff envelopes. Some of the volunteers were the women from the church with the lovely voices he thought had trained for the opera or should be on radio. Sometimes student boarders at the manse came with secretarial skills. Betty Lou Gregg, who also sat with us through piano practice that first winter, had as her first priority duty secretarial tasks for our father. When volunteers were not available our mother typed his sermons and speeches, and sometimes cut blue stencils for the bulletin and other handouts at the church. The four of us were also pulled in during busy times, such as when preparing mail-outs to high schools and colleges. We learned how to form an assembly line to fold, staple, stuff, seal and stamp hundreds of envelopes at one sitting. He had a rubber stamp made with his return address and bought a purple ink pad which made the printing of the return address much easier. We learned how to use all kinds of office equipment from mimeograph machines to sponges in glass jars to moisten stamps and wet the seal on envelopes when our tongues became sore. Then we walked down to the post office with boxes of envelopes that we handed to a postal clerk or stuffed through a slot in the wall, carefully dividing the envelopes between local and out of town delivery.

Only once did our father think the US Postal Service had let him down. We had prepared a commencement promotional mailing for about 150 schools. Usually Billy or I carted the mail-outs down to the post office but we were busy. Charlie was given the assignment.

When — a few weeks later — there was no response to the mailing, not a single request for our father to speak at a commencement or baccalaureate, he called a high school principal he knew in West Virginia.

"Well, Fred, I don't think we've received anything from you, but I'll check around and call you back."

So the principal checked with his secretary, and she checked with the secretary of the superintendent of schools to whom the mailing had also been sent. They had no record of having received anything from the Reverend Fred E. Luchs. "Odd!" our father said to himself. "How can that be?"

So he spent some time running down the phone number of another principal on his mailing list, this one in western Pennsylvania. The principal's secretary had no memory of any mailing from a Reverend Luchs. Nothing from Athens, Ohio at all. "Even stranger!" our father said to himself.

So he called the Athens postmaster.

"Over 150 envelopes in a single batch? Well, no, Reverend Luchs, I didn't see any such mailing from you, and your boys usually bring those to the window in a box. But let me check with Roy and Bill to see if it came in while I was away.

A few minutes later the postmaster called back. "Sorry, Reverend Luchs. No one remembers such a mailing here. No, there isn't much chance we could lose 150 envelopes down here. One or two is unlikely. 150? I think that'd be impossible."

So he called me into the study. And then Billy. We reminded him he had given that batch of envelopes to Charlie to mail. So Charlie was called into our father's study.

"Charlie, my boy! Do you remember the box of envelopes I asked you to take to the post office a few weeks ago?"

Charlie thought for a minute or so and then said, "Yes."

"You did take them to the post office, didn't you?"

Charlie thought for another minute or so. "No."

"You didn't?!!!" What did you do with them, Charlie?"

"Well, I was late for school, so I decided the best thing was to put them somewhere they would be safe and I would mail them after school."

"And where was that, Charlie?"

"I put them in a hole along College Street. In front of Howard Hall."

"A hole? Do you mean the storm drain? You put my box of 150 stamped envelopes down the storm drain, Charlie?"

"Is that what it's called?

"Yes, that's what it's called. And why did you put the envelopes there, Charlie?"

"Well, I was going to go back and get them after school. And then take them to the post office. But I forgot."

Father made some frantic calls to the city public works office, where he was reminded we had had two heavy rains in the past week. There was no chance, a man told our father, the envelopes were not soiled, and they were probably blocking the pipes down to the river, which made the man at the public works department quite angry. So we had to do that mail-out again. Charlie did a lot of the work this time, and Father himself walked the envelopes down to the post office, happy his faith in the US Postal Service had been restored.

PHOTO AND GREEN PEN LOST

That first year in the manse I kept the photograph of my McNelly grandparents and the green fountain pen Lonnie had given me in the top drawer of my dresser. They were near the back, hidden beneath my blue socks and white underwear. From time to time I would take out the photo and spend a few minutes looking at my grandmother, now dead, and fondle the pen, remembering the day Lonnie gave it to me. It was the last time I had seen my father.

Late in May, I opened the drawer, moved the clothing away and...they weren't there! I searched with my hand under all my clothes in the top drawer. The pen and photograph weren't there. I pulled all the clothes out of the drawer and still couldn't find either one. Thinking I might have put them in another drawer by mistake, I searched all four drawers of my dresser and took out every piece of clothing. They weren't there! I thought about where else I could have put them and drew a blank. I was always so careful to put them in that special place.

I ran to our foster mother, upset.

"My father's green pen and the picture of my grandmother have disappeared. Do you know where they are? "

"No," she said, "I don't."

When he came home, I asked my foster father. He had not seen the photo or the green pen, he said.

Was it possible that one of them had taken the pen and photo because they wanted me to let go of the past, and had not told the other? But it made no sense that they, who attached so much importance to telling the truth, would lie about something they knew was so important to me. But I couldn't imagine who else might have taken them.

Would Billy have taken them? When I asked him, he said, "No. I never open your dresser drawer." That was true. He never did, and something about his manner told me he was telling the truth. I asked Charlie and Janey and they said they hadn't seen the photo or the pen, about which I knew they didn't care. They had no memories of Lonnie or our grandparents.

What about Harold Sauer, I wondered, whose bedroom was next to ours? Would he take them, thinking he was doing the Luchs a favor by removing all I had left of my biological family? But that made no sense. Grace Monigold? Even less likely. But I asked them anyway and they said, no, they would never take anything from my dresser and I believed them. Carol, the cleaning woman? She had never taken anything else from the manse, so why would she take my photo and pen?

I fretted about the pen and photo for a month or so and then dropped the subject. While still in the process of letting go of my past that first year, the last material links to my birth family, symbolic and sentimental, had mysteriously vanished. I never did learn what happened to the photo or the pen. They were never found. In time, I didn't think much about them anymore. But I continued to think of Lonnie from time to time, especially when I woke at night to hear the sound of the lonely steam whistle of the New York Central on its way to Parkersburg, West Virginia and eventually, to New York City.

ADOPTION AND BAPTISM

On June 21, 1944, Ann Minnis wrote Inez Norman to announce that court proceedings for us had taken place that day. "Soon I will send you a complete dictation of my supervision of these children in their foster home," she wrote, "as I should like you to have it for your records." She asked Norman to send a letter to Judge Francis D. White of the Probate Court in Athens to waive the six month probationary period before the final adoption decree. Ann told Norman that she would probably not have the time "to get the case dictated" before leaving on vacation. This is the last letter from Ann Minnis in the case files and if she completed the dictation and sent it to Mrs. Norman, it was either lost or never included in our files.

In the final paragraph of her letter Ann wrote that the Luchs "are very thrilled to feel that the children are really theirs now. I have lots more interesting anecdotes to tell you and Miss Kirk about them." In her usual stilted style Norman acknowledged Ann's letter on June 26 and sent a copy to Ann of a letter to Judge White of the Probate Court "since the foster parents are so eager to have the matter finally completed."

We were baptized on Sunday, June 25, four days after our legal adoption. For the occasion we were dressed in our Easter whites and our father shot a 16 mm film of us walking out of the shadows around the manse front door into the sunlight of a fresh early summer morning. Again I stepped in front of the other three to inspect them, made sure shirts were tucked in and hair combed, and then stepped back in place. The sergeant was still "on duty," nine months after our arrival.

We were baptized during the major service at First Presbyterian. The special scripture reading chosen for that day was the story of the disciples turning away parents who brought young children for Jesus to touch in blessing. Displeased by the action of his disciples, Jesus said: "Suffer the little children to come unto me, and forbid them not, for of such is the kingdom of God. Verily I say unto you, whosoever shall not receive the kingdom of God as a little child, he shall not enter therein. And he took them up his arms, put his hands upon them, and blessed them."

After the scripture reading, the four of us were arranged around the white marble baptismal font at the front of the sanctuary next to our new mother. Across from us stood two black robed clergymen, our father of course, and the kindly Walter Gamertsfelder, the much admired professor of philosophy and president of Ohio University. To our left was the church's dominant window, "Christ Blessing the Little Children," brightly illuminated by the late morning sunlight and in the baptismal font was the water our father had brought back from the River Jordan.

One by one Dad presented us for the ancient baptismal rite, beginning with me. We were about to be born a second time, to be given new names and to become, in Christian teaching, new beings.

"Name this child," said Dr. Gamertsfelder, peering through his rimless glasses at me.

"Lewis Richard Luchs," Father replied in the first formal use of my new name.

As Father gently bent my head over the font Dr. Gamertsfelder poured water on me three times as he said, "Lewis Richard Luchs, I baptize you in the name of the Father, and of the Son, and of the Holy Ghost." Then my Father wiped my head with a towel.

Again gray-haired Dr. Gamertsfelder said, "Name this child,"

"Mark William Luchs."

Mark William Luchs, I baptize thee..." And so it went:

"Michael Charles Luchs. Margaret Jane Luchs. I baptize thee in the name of the Father and of the Son and of the Holy Ghost."

And then, speaking to our new father and mother and the assembled congregation, Dr. Gamertsfelder read, "We receive these children into the congregation of Christ's flock. As God has made us all his children by adoption and grace, may you receive these children as your own sons and daughter. Amen."

OUR NEW FAMILY THREATENED

I was not alone in my earlier worry that our days in the manse were numbered. There were moments during our first year together when I was angry with the Luchs, moments when I thought I wanted to leave, but those passed. Most of the time I was happy in our new home. I did not know until years later that the Luchs, delighted with their new family, were worried that we might be taken from them. They were afraid some complication would arise that would make it impossible for them to adopt us. Perhaps there would be a legal wrinkle no one had considered. Mom had discussed this with Ann Minnis, who reassured her, explaining that parental rights had been terminated in a court of law. To help relieve the anxiety of the Luchs, Ann told them Mrs. Norman could petition the judge to waive the six month probationary period before the final adoption decree. Judge White did waive the probationary period, which is why it was possible for the Luchs to legally adopt us only eight months after we arrived in Athens.

The Luchs also worried someone in our birth family would try to halt the adoption and reclaim us. Or worse, they feared that Lonnie, who was not consulted about our disposition at any stage, might try to kidnap one or more of us. At the time we knew nothing of these concerns. I do remember wondering occasionally what it would be like to walk alone down Court Street and suddenly run into Lonnie. As much as I had loved him, I was ambivalent about seeing my biological father again after years of separation. Sometimes, when I walked downtown alone, I would see a man in the distance who I thought was Lonnie. My heart would skip a beat or two and I would prepare myself to run back to the manse. Then, as the man drew closer, I realized he was not Lonnie at all. What the Luchs did not learn until after we had been adopted was their fear that our birth family might try to recover us was justified.

There is one more letter from Mrs. Norman in the case file. On December 30, 1944, she wrote to the Luchs to warn that, "the relatives of your children, both in Columbus and in this community, are endeavoring to locate the children and threaten to take legal steps to secure control of them." While Norman told the Luchs she doubted such an effort would reverse the adoption, "they could succeed in interfering with the happiness and security of your family life." Norman strongly recommended relocating so that, "you and your children may enjoy your lives together without interference."

Norman had begun her letter saying she had been informed that, "you contemplate a change in location. The writer wishes to state that she considers this opportunity providential, believing it to be in the best interest of you and your family." The contemplated change was an invitation to become the pastor of a Presbyterian Church in Pomona, California. In their annual Christmas letter of 1945, Mom explained to friends, "It was a beautiful church, delightful town, and splendid people — but the pull of a little old church packed with university students each Sunday morning was stronger than all the salary, sun, and other satisfactions that California could offer." So we remained in Athens. If our birth families did locate us, we were never aware of any steps they took "to secure control of us." We and our new father and mother were free to continue our secure and happy lives together.

THE SOUND OF A DOOR THAT IS OPENED

We sometimes appeared in my mother's writings, which we did not mind, and sometimes in our father's sermons, which did make us uncomfortable if we were sitting in the congregation. Mother wrote an article entitled "The Sound of a Door That is Opened," for *Childhood Education* in October 1946, less than three years after we arrived, that included profiles of each of us and our aspirations at that time. By then our new first names, Michael (Charlie), Mark (Billy), and Lewis (Dick) were in general use at home and in school. Except for Margaret Jane. Margaret did not "take." Janey remained Janey.

"Margaret (Janey) is interested in clothes and music," our mother wrote, "and hopes to be the conductor of an orchestra. She loves to dance."

"Michael (Charlie) is the scientist." After citing some examples of Michael's fascination with small creatures and plants and rocks, Mom concluded, "Luckily, Michael goes to an experimental school where the teachers are convinced, as he is, that it is more important to observe how a bird builds a nest that it is to be on time for school on a certain morning." She gave an example of how Rufus Putnam used resources at the university. "While he was making a collection of moths, his teacher encouraged him to go to a university professor for help."

"Mark (Billy) is 'all boy,'" She wrote, concluding that because of his good nature and helpful spirit, he might end up in public relations, though she had never heard him express interest in any particular career.

"Lewis (Dick) is the artist," she writes of me. "His dreams of career swing from artist, to architect, to interior decorator. One of his oil paintings hanged in Daddy's study until it was borrowed for the living room of an artist friend." After carpentry and piano study and writing stories and poems, she wrote, "the sustained interest has been in creating with color and clay."

Above the piano in my living room today is an oil painting by John Rood, a regional artist better known for his sculptures. The same John Rood oil painting watched over our piano practice sessions in the manse. I'm not sure why Rood, then the university artist in residence, invited me to go painting with him, but it was not because I was Putnam's most talented young artist. True, John did borrow two of my early efforts to use in his classrooms as examples, but I never learned as examples of what. He probably invited me to paint with him as a favor to the Luchs, who at that time believed my destiny was to be an artist. But it's also possible my art teacher, Mary Leonard, suggested the outing, another example of how Putnam teachers used university resources to enrich the learning opportunities of their students. However it happened, it was an unforgettable experience for a child. In the week before the outing I packed up my black tin painting box and the rickety easel Mother had found for me, and the modest collection of oil paint tubes I had purchased with my allowance money. My favorite tube was a brown named Burnt Sienna. It wasn't the color I liked as much as the name of the color, which I enjoyed saying.

There was some doubt about the weather but the chosen day for our excursion in early May was bright and beautiful, with white clipper-ship clouds moving across a blue sea sky. Mom packed a lunch for me and sent me off wearing enough layers of clothing to spend the day in a snowstorm. With John were two women, both graduate students in the OU art department. The three of them chose a sunny hillside from which we looked across a valley at a typical Southeastern Ohio scene: a white farm house with a red tin roof, an unpainted gray barn, some gray outbuildings including a corn crib made of wood slats, and surrounding woods and fields.

I was self-conscious painting in the presence of adult artists and choose to paint the white house and only the white house, because that would be the simplest composition. John and one of the graduate students painted the entire scene, house, barn and outbuildings but in different styles. The young woman's canvas was more detailed and quite realistic. The forms on John Rood's canvas were easily recognizable but more abstract. He painted bold blocks with strong colors and thick brush strokes, rather like a sculptor might paint a landscape. The second student, another young woman, a bit heavy-set with brown hair, set up her easel behind the three of us. Only towards the end of the day would she let us see that she had painted the three of us painting.

I did not become an artist. My brother Michael did. I became a diplomat. I was surprised when re-reading my Putnam progress letters for this book to see how much emphasis the Putnam curriculum gave to international relations. The international theme of the year for my 5th grade class was the Soviet Union, of the 6th grade, pre-communist China. I choose Switzerland, the Luchs country of origin, for my major individual report in the 6th grade.

Once again, Rufus Putnam teachers called on the resources of Ohio University to enrich our curriculum. In her section on class activities Esther Dunham reported that Dr. Wilfred Smith, probably an OU faculty member, spoke to us about the United Nations. "We invited foreign students to talk about their countries: Miss Hong about Korea, Miss Rowe about Jamaica, Miss Bos about the Netherlands. John Selkus, a high school exchange student, talked about his country, Greece. Miss Harry, an exchange teacher from England, talked about England and the British Empire. At convocation we heard a discussion of Palestine."

In commenting on my progress Dunham wrote: "In the study of other countries, Lewis seems to feel the interdependence of various groups and the importance of nations working together." Did the emphasis on international studies at Rufus Putnam contribute to my eventual choice of a career in public diplomacy? Possibly. Seeds are sometimes planted in elementary school that grow quietly and unnoticed through the years after we have forgotten that the seeds were planted at all. Whatever the case, "Lewis seems to feel the interdependence of various groups and the importance of nations working together" defined my life's work and my views to this day.

Mothers and Fathers: A Postscript

Eunice Reappears

In 1964, twenty years after we were legally adopted, our biological mother sent a letter to the Luchs asking for information about us. She added an invitation to the four of us to meet with her. In part her letter reads, "I visited her final resting place (this refers to Nola Mae, our older sister who died) this summer at South Webster, Ohio, but not without remembering four more children that I put in the Home because I was no longer able to care for them... I felt that the church had failed me in a time when I needed it most. I am now 46 years old and I cannot bring myself to be active in any church. I think I am still blaming myself for all that has happened. If you are the adopted parents of the children, I don't wish to intrude in your life or that of the children, but I would appreciate knowing about them...I would like for them to have my name and address if they should ever wish to see me. I well appreciate that they may never wish to see me."

Our mother replied:

"Dear Eunice Vandelier,

"Yesterday my husband came in from the front porch with tears in his eyes saying, 'The letter I have anticipated for 21 years came today.' Over the years our hearts have ached for you. You gave birth to four beautiful, talented, wonderful children. We know. They have lived with us since 1943."

"When we had them christened as members of our family, each child kept a name and chose a new name." She then listed us by name and with some of the exaggeration not uncommon to proud and loving parents, she described our lives and achievements to that point. We did not, by the way, "choose" a new name. The Luchs gave us our new first names. Occasionally Mother's exaggerations were more than exaggerations.

None of us chose to respond to our biological mother's 1964 letter. In 1978, fourteen years later, while my brother Michael (formerly Charlie) was working as an artist in the Cass Corridor in Detroit and struggling with alcoholism, his psychotherapist urged him to have a reunion with his biological mother. The therapist believed such a meeting would challenge Michael's fantasies about his birth family and lead to the resolution of some internal conflicts. Michael ignored the therapist's advice for some months and then, as his urging became more insistent, Michael called Janey, who was living nearby in Ann Arbor, Michigan. He told Janey what his "shrink," as Michael liked to call him, wanted him to do. Michael said he could not face such an encounter by himself. He asked Janey to go with him. At that time I was overseas.

Janey recalled, "I wasn't looking for roots. I was frightened to go. I really didn't want to go." But because Michael's psychotherapist thought it was important for Michael's mental health, she agreed to go with him. "I was trying to help a brother," she said. Janey decided to ask her daughter, Julie, also living in Ann Arbor, to go with her for moral support. Michael's support, in addition to Janey, was his wife, Kathy.

Since Eunice was still living in Muskegon, Michigan, they decided the best plan would be to invite her to come for lunch to a farm house in Holly, Michigan, the residence of Michael's mother-in-law, Evelyn Raskin. Evelyn supported the idea of a reunion enthusiastically and was pleased to provide the setting for what she was certain would be a dramatic, heart-warming encounter after thirty-six years of separation. She had seen such reunions discussed on television programs and thought they were, "So wonderful! How do you know who you are until you meet your birth mother?" she asked. Evelyn Raskin began to plan a menu and looked forward to hosting the event.

Michael, with his wife Kathy, and Janey, with her daughter Julie, arrived early and positioned themselves, all a little nervous, in the living room of the farm house. Janey was wearing bib overalls in burgundy, then fashionable. Michael was in jeans with a blue dress shirt, the sleeves of which were rolled up his forearms. Eunice arrived a few minutes later, accompanied by her husband, Lloyd Vandelier. Evelyn Raskin went to the door to escort them into the living room. Kathy said Eunice looked tiny and was crying softly as she came in. "Her husband, Lloyd, was a large man, maybe 6' 3' and wide. His voice was gruff but he seemed to be a kind man."

"You must be Janey," Eunice said, as she entered the room and then gave Janey what Janey later described as a,"little hug without any warmth." "And you're Michael," Eunice continued, turning towards Michael to hug him. Her voice quavered as she backed away and looked into Michael's eyes. "Can you forgive me? Can you ever forgive me?" Lloyd stepped to Eunice's side to support her.

Michael was silent.

"After so many years," Janey told me, "I wasn't there to judge her for abandoning us. I didn't have any resentment. I just wanted to get to know her as the human being who gave me birth. Also, I wanted to learn something about the years I was too young to remember." Eunice had brought a green book of McNelly family pictures and history as an ice breaker.

Janey later recalled. "She was wearing an aqua pantsuit with a checked top. She wasn't smiling." Janey found Eunice attractive at age 60, with short white hair, nicely done. "Her mouth was turned down. It was as if she had a perpetually unhappy expression stamped on her face," Janey said. After they all spent a few minutes looking together through the green family book, Eunice and Lloyd seated themselves as far as they could away from Janey and Michael in the living room before everyone went in for lunch.

"The first time I saw her I had absolutely no feeling for her. It was as if a stranger had walked into the room," Janey later recalled. "I watched her with great care. I tried desperately to find something in her I could relate to. I found nothing." As soon as they sat down to lunch, Janey later recalled, Eunice began a diatribe against Lonnie. Lonnie had beaten her, he was always drunk. He didn't help with the children. He couldn't earn any money. She had to do everything. "I couldn't believe that was almost the first thing out of her mouth," Janey later said. "That after so many years she found it necessary to talk about Lonnie that way." Janey found Eunice articulate. Her command of English was grammatical and precise, more refined than one might expect of a woman who had not finished the 10th grade.

Trying to steer the discussion away from Lonnie, Janey began asking questions about her own childhood and about the years before she had any memories. Eunice turned such questions aside. "From the get-go," Janey later said, "she talked about nothing but how bad Lonnie was and tried to explain or rationalize why she had left us. She was so negative. On the one hand, she continued to try to build a case to justify why she had abandoned us. And then from time to time, out would come 'Can you ever forgive me? Can you forgive me?' like the chorus of a song."

Janey and Michael had also brought some photographs of their families, including their children. When these were mentioned, Eunice did not ask to see them. Not once did Eunice ask about Janey's life or her son, Chuckie, and daughter, Julie. "I wanted her to ask about our lives," Janey later remembered. "After all, for so many years she didn't have any information about us at all. She didn't seem to have the mother instincts that I think women normally have. She was so negative that I thought, what kind of human being is this? I couldn't believe she could act like that. She seemed to have no parental interest in us at all. It was all me, me, me, me, — and very defensive." Janey concluded, "She spent a lot of time validating herself, talking about what she had done in her life, and the achievements of her daughters."

Before dessert was served Janey looked across the table and saw that Michael had quietly and suddenly disappeared. After a few minutes, "deeply depressed," she left too, and walked around on the lawn to get some fresh air. "Eunice had," Janey concluded, "literally driven us out of the house." Janey wondered where Michael had gone. She heard a noise in the barn and was surprised, when she walked into the open gate of the barn, to find Michael there smoking a cigarette.

"What are you doing here?" she asked.

"I couldn't take it any longer."

"I couldn't either. I'm so depressed."

"So am I," Michael muttered.

Michael's mother-in-law, who seemed not to understand what had happened, insisted on pictures for such a dramatic and auspicious occasion. So pictures were taken, perfunctory good-byes said, and superficial hugs given. On the drive back to Ann Arbor Janey and Julie talked little about the reunion. Julie was also depressed. "She showed no interest in your life at all, Mother," Julie finally said.

When I interviewed Michael for this book, we talked about the reunion with Eunice. "What was your basic reaction to her?" I asked.

"I WANT TO GET OUT OF HERE!" he said, emphasizing each word. My first thought after meeting her was, "God, how long do I have to stay in this room?" And then Michael said, "After I met my biological mother my dilemma was: do I really want to try to explain to myself how come this woman is my biological mother?" He laughed nervously. "And I said, I cannot explain this, man. I wanted her to be interesting and there was no way I could make her interesting."

Janey said, when I later talked with her, "I have no feelings about Eunice. I know we are supposed to have feelings for our birth mother, but I have no feelings about Eunice." Since hearing Janey and Michael's accounts of that reunion, I have wondered about the reasoning of Michael's psychotherapist, who obviously did not share psychologist Erik Erikson's view on the useful role of fantasy in our lives.

I chose not to have a reunion with my biological mother. Janey and Michael were two and three years old when Eunice pleaded with state authorities to take us into the children's home. They had no memories of Eunice or Lonnie at all. They did not remember the neglect or the violence or the hunger or the rats. Janey thinks she remembers being terribly cold. Yet I wondered why I didn't care if I ever saw our biological mother again but would have, despite everything, welcomed a reunion with Lonnie. My questions were answered by the case file I obtained in 1998 where it became clear that Lonnie wished to re-establish our family and Eunice did not. Also, my long-standing disinterest in a meeting with my biological mother was reinforced by Janey's and Michael's accounts of their reunion with her. I had come to see Eunice McNelly as the woman who happened to be the instrument of my birth, God's curious means of giving me the glorious gift of life. I took comfort from Kahil Gibran's words that children come through their parents but not from them, and do not belong to them.

GOODBYE TO LONNIE

I did not know the emotional reunion in front of the Old Gray House on the afternoon he gave me the green fountain pen was the last time I would ever see my biological father. Lonnie soon remarried and raised another family of four. Prison had tamed the young wolf. From all accounts he was a loving and responsible father who held down steady jobs. When the responsibility for his family or the boredom of his work weighed too heavily, however, Lonnie continued to hop freight trains and ride the rails. He also fell off the wagon from time to time after long dry spells, usually when there was some crisis he could not face. In 1959 the sheriff of Scioto County threw Lonnie in jail for disorderly conduct the night before the funeral of his father, the reclusive Bible-reading, school-teaching, whiskey-making Republican, Harry Henderson Boggs. Lonnie thus managed to avoid attending his own father's funeral.

One year later, in August of 1960, now 50 years old, Lonnie leaped up into an Illinois Central freight car in his home town of Fort Wayne, Indiana and headed west. Night had fallen as he jumped or stumbled or was pushed out the door of the freight car in which he was riding. He was immediately pulled under the wheels of a second train he may not have seen or heard. His body was so torn to pieces by the wheels of the oncoming train that he could only be identified by the thumb prints in his prison records.

I Have But One Mother

It is common in discussions of adopted children today to say they have two mothers, a biological mother and an adoptive mother. My experience is that I have but one mother, Evelyn Luchs, my real mother in the only sense I can make of the word mother. Evelyn Luchs is my mother because she raised me and truly loved me. It is as simple as that. She nursed me when I was sick, counseled me when I was confused or upset, and was always there for me when I most needed her. She loved me when I was being unlovable. She made it possible for me to begin to trust and love and laugh again. She helped dampen down the fiery core of rage within me created by serious neglect and abandonment. She never gave up on me. My true mother encouraged my love of the beauty in life and filled me with a hopeful sense of my own life's possibilities. She helped me to believe I could make good use of the life I had been given, to contribute to my own happiness and to that of others.

Mom modified but did not erase the cold-eyed realism I had learned from my early experiences. At times I thought she was being naïve, but I came to agree with her view that it is better to live trusting and occasionally be disappointed, than to go through life suspicious of the motives of others. She let me know by her actions as well as her words that I was worthy, loved, and valued. My mother believed my story would end well. In that she turned out to be right.

As much as Mom and Dad got right, my own four sons have informed me that no parents are perfect. We have learned much since the 1940s about children who must assume adult responsibilities too soon. The Luchs had no sympathy for the difficulty I had accepting the end of my role as the child-parent of my younger siblings. During our first year together, they could have considered me, an eight year old, less a rival and more a child having difficulty adjusting to his changed role. They might have acknowledged and even expressed appreciation for the responsibility I had carried as protector and leader of my younger siblings. I am quite sure that had the discussion of "parentified" children (an unattractive label) been in the adoption literature of the 1940s, Mom and I would have had some good talks to help me understand what I was going through.

Nor did Mom and Dad realize that my occasional bouts of grouchiness as a child were a part of grieving the loss of my biological family attachments, not a permanent characteristic of my personality. Again, research and discussions of the typical behavior patterns of a child grieving the loss of biological family attachments did not appear until more recently.

The Luchs could not ease our sense of being different from other children because of our background and experiences. Instead they reinforced the sense of difference we felt as adopted children of prominent personalities in the community. Anyone whose father is a preacher will understand why. The expectations of congregations and the exemplary role clergy families are expected to play in their communities assure that such children will feel different. Much of this was unavoidable and none of it did us any lasting harm. In fact, I think being thrown into the public role we shared because our father was a clergyman was good for us, built our self-confidence, and gave us social skills that have served us well.

But these are minor issues when weighed against what they, especially Evelyn Luchs, got right in helping us recover our physical and emotional health. They didn't think they were being generous in adopting us. In an article in his national fraternity magazine, our father is quoted as saying, "It was quite a selfish venture," we thought, "but the letters that have poured in from friends seem to indicate that it was an altruistic venture. We hadn't thought of it much in that light." All their articles and their correspondence, much of which I read before and while writing this book, indicates they believed they received more than they gave. I do not remember that they ever, not even in the heat of arguments during our adolescent years, suggested that we owned them anything because they had adopted us.

WHO IS MY FATHER?

This leads to the question I've avoided until now. Why didn't the man I learned to call Father and Dad become my only and forever father years ago in the same way that Evelyn Luchs became my only and forever mother? She quickly replaced whatever bonds I still had with my biological mother. I have only one mother. But do I have two fathers?

Some years ago a psychologist pointed out that Lonnie was still my psychological as well as my biological father. I think boys and even men need a father and when I couldn't find a new one fully acceptable to me, I suppose I remained the son of the one I once had. I think that has changed. Researching and writing this book has made me more realistic about Lonnie Boggs and more appreciative of Fred Luchs. I've let go of my idealized portrait of Lonnie, so psychologically useful to me through the years.

Did I not bond in the same way with Fred Luchs as I did with Evelyn Luchs because of loyalty to Lonnie? Perhaps. But I'm quite sure a different man such as Ken Coulter, my mother Evelyn's brother, could have totally replaced Lonnie Boggs in my affections. Moreover, Fred Luchs did not become my brother Mark's father in the fullest sense of that word either. Mark told me more than once as we were growing up he did not have memories of Lonnie and felt no conscious attachment to him. So, for whatever reasons, my brother Mark and I were closer to our adoptive mother than to our adoptive father. That was not the case of my sister Janey. Dad became her father from the first day they met, completely and without any reservations. He was her hero when she was a child, a fact that would later turn bitter-sweet. He was Michael's father, too, even if Michael, like his older brothers, was also always closer to Mom than to Dad.

There's a quote in Dad's dairy of 1960 about Mark who was then 23 years old and a graduate student in music at the University of Michigan. Mark was building an apartment in the basement of our home in Ann Arbor for himself and another graduate student of music, the girl he planned to marry.

"I marvel at his aptness in handling tools and his knowledge of building. What a marvelous girl he is marrying! For a brief moment tonight I felt he was drawing close. Maybe if we had worked on projects together more during the years we would be closer.

Sadly, he and Mark never did draw close. Nor did I.

As an older man Dad sometimes asked me, "Lewis, why weren't you and I close, as you are with your sons?" It was a most uncomfortable question. I usually managed to awkwardly change the subject. I thought I knew some of the reasons why, but was sure talking about them could only hurt him, and I didn't want to hurt him. I was long past the age when we become old enough to appreciate our fathers. I was thankful he kept the four of us together and provided a safe and comfortable home. I appreciated all the opportunities he and Mom gave us to experience some of the finest achievements of human culture, and for the environment they created in which the brains and talents we had could flourish. I grew to be like him in many respects. I also have a curious mind and I share his love of reading and his avid interest in politics and social issues.

I am grateful Dad paid whatever was necessary to restore our bodies to health when we first joined the Luchs household. He had some remarkable talents and a steely old country discipline I much admired. Occasionally, in a crisis Mom would buckle while he remained steady. I admired him for that. More than all the above, I did care about him. My dancing around the subject of why we were not closer was not helpful and surely did hurt him. I think he asked the question so that I would tell him that what he feared was true, was not true. We were not, in the fullest sense father and son, whatever that may mean in today's America.

THE GIFT OF THE LUCHS

Perhaps Michael's psychotherapist was right. The case files I obtained in 1998 did destroy my fantasies about Lonnie. Perhaps by obtaining our case files I had unwittingly done what I cautioned Janey not to do, opened doors to the past that could not be closed. This past now had to be integrated into my sense of who I am. But I found my identity did not change as I absorbed this new information. There's something about the truth, even unpleasant truth, that frees us. Knowing always seems better to me than not knowing. I came to see I did not have to fear joining — or fear that my sons and grandchildren would join — the nightmarish world of the Boggs. Nor did we have to belong to the cramped little world of the McNellys. Through adoption and most of a lifetime living as a Luchs, I and Mark and Michael and Janey had become different human beings, nurtured in another culture of values different from those of our biological families. Not one of us has ever been arrested. Not one of us has spent a day in jail while our biological father and his brother and sister spent years in Ohio penal institutions. None of our children or grandchildren has ever been in a children's home or foster care. If genes are so powerful, why not? The social workers and psychologists who worked with us feared we, the damaged offspring of eastern Kentucky mountain people — the Boggs half of our biological family — would be overwhelmed in the Luchs environment. But we flourished. Genes are givens we cannot change or which mutate slowly over many generations. Shifts in human cultures can change human beings within a single generation or two. Look at what happens to immigrants who come to America. Changes in our human cultures and our consciousness, not our biology, are our grounds for hope in the future.

OUR GIFT TO THE LUCHS

Mom wrote a yearend letter to members of the Coulter and Luchs families in 1944, "Well," it began, "we come to the end of the happiest year of our lives! We never realized how much we were missing until we had the children!" She related how the two of us were talking as we washed the dishes, and I burst out with "You are such a very good Mommy!" "I don't think I ever bothered to say anything like that to Dad or Mother," she wrote, "but it sure is music to a parent's ears." A year later our father was quoted as saying, "We have been very happy in our work here, but the children have brought even greater happiness." In a card they sent to friends at Christmas in 1944, "Six months ago they became legally ours. We've been very happy and would not want to go back to the old way." And in 1945, in a letter that summed up the war years for friends and relatives, Mom wrote, "1943. The coming of the children. The biggest event of our lives." I recently found a letter she sent to me in Singapore in 1973, in which she wrote, "Thirty years ago you made up your mind to make your home with us. What a wonderful day for us!" From the beginning and all through the years they told us again and again how much fun, excitement, fulfillment and joy we brought them and how we in our adult lives exceeded their hopes for us.

ANN MINNIS KEEPS HER WORD

Even though she had kept track of our progress through regular visits to the manse, Ann Minnis did honor her promise to take me out to dinner to discuss my final verdict on the Luchs. She arrived on a warm afternoon in late May 1944, a month before our legal adoption and baptism. The College Street elms were bright green and elegant in their new leaves. Ann talked first with Mom and then I was called. I had bathed and put on the pair of dark blue corduroys and the jersey with the red, white and blue horizontal stripes that I liked. When I came down the stairs to the hall, Mom adjusted my outfit a bit and combed my hair.

Ann and I walked around the block to the Buckeye Cafeteria, my choice, and then the most popular eatery in Athens. I could hardly believe the display of food of every color and type as we went through the cafeteria line. She asked me a lot of questions about how my brothers and sister were doing and how things were going. Then, because I had told her how we had begun to study the stars at Rufus Putnam, she drove me out to North Hill to see the Big Dipper and Orion. A lovely night breeze flowed through the open windows of Ann's familiar blue Plymouth and I was full and happy. She pointed out the Big Dipper and the three-starred belt of Orion to me and then asked what I had decided about staying with the Luchs. "I want to stay. I want us all to stay." I said. "I think our new mom is a very good mother." That's the last time I remember seeing Ann Minnis, the gifted midwife of our second birth.

In addition to Ann Minnis, three social workers in New Boston and Wheelersburg were involved in our case. Helen Middleton administered the then young ADC program in Scioto County. Helen did the original family history and case notes used later by Edna Abele and Lois Smith. I have also made use of Edna Abele's children's home journals in this book. I believe keeping records of the lives of children during their dependent years is one of the most important responsibilities of child welfare agencies and institutions. In that regard, I think it is remarkable that in the 1940s the Ohio Bureau of Juvenile Research funded a field program to provide psychologists Persis Simmons and Mary Smith to test us and make recommendations for our future.

I drew many facts and insights from the family interviews and reports of L.A. Smith, who worked in the state of Ohio child welfare office in New Boston, next door to Sciotoville. Since I could find only her bureaucratic initials, LAS or LASmith, in the case records, I decided to give her the fully human if fictive name of Lois Ann Smith.

But it is for Ann Minnis of Athens that I have retained a special affection all through the years. I have used her letters and my mother's memories of her for the year that began in August of 1943. Ann kept her promises as most of the adults in our first years of life did not, small promises like the restaurant meal in Columbus and the work bench and tool kit I was given on my eighth birthday, and the big promise that I would have to agree before the four us would be placed permanently with the Luchs. My most vivid memory of Ann today is of the two full days she spent persuading me to go to Athens in the first place. But her greatest achievement may have been the manner in which she presented us to Fred and Evelyn Luchs. That surely increased the odds they would take all four of us.

Thank you, Ann, Helen, Edna, and Lois, for protecting us when we could not look after ourselves, and for making possible a new beginning. Rare are the social workers privileged to know how much difference they have made in the lives of the children they serve. Even rarer is the appreciation of the society whose children these professionals are entrusted to protect.